Racing Toward Armageddon

RACING
TOWARD
ARMAGEDDON

*The Three Great Religions
and the Plot to End the World*

| | |

MICHAEL BAIGENT

HarperOne
An Imprint of HarperCollins*Publishers*

HarperOne

RACING TOWARD ARMAGEDDON: *The Three Great Religions and the Plot to End the World.* Copyright © 2009 by **Michael Baigent**. All rights reserved. Printed in the United States of America. No part of this book may be used or reproduced in any manner whatsoever without written permission except in the case of brief quotations embodied in critical articles and reviews. For information, address HarperCollins Publishers, 10 East 53rd Street, New York, NY 10022.

HarperCollins books may be purchased for educational, business, or sales promotional use. For information, please write: Special Markets Department, HarperCollins Publishers, 10 East 53rd Street, New York, NY 10022.

HarperCollins Web site: http//www.harpercollins.com
HarperCollins® ■® and HarperOne™ are trademarks of HarperCollins Publishers.

Scripture quotations are taken from either the Jerusalem Bible, © 1966 by Darton, Longman and Todd, London, or the Authorized King James Version.

FIRST EDITION

Interior design by Laura Lind Design

Library of Congress Cataloging-in-Publication Data is available upon request.

ISBN: 978-0-06-136318-4

09 10 11 12 RRD(H) 10 9 8 7 6 5 4 3 2 1

Contents

ACKNOWLEDGMENTS

This book explores the power of ideas to both create and change the beliefs that define people and nations. Bad ideas lead to bad outcomes. And as bad outcomes go, the belief in Armageddon is one of the worst.

I am grateful for the constant support and encouragement of my wife, Jane, and my family, as they know only too well the dangers of those who act with the certainty of god burning in their eyes. I am grateful, too, for all the encouragement from my longtime friend and literary agent Ann Evans of Jonathan Clowes Ltd., London.

I owe a huge debt to my editor, Hope Innelli, vice president and associate publisher, HarperPaperbacks, New York, and guest editor for HarperOne, San Francisco. Most important, she had the intuitive ability to sense where things deeper and darker lay.

I should also like to thank Mark Tauber, senior vice president and publisher; Michael Maudlin, vice president and editorial director; and Gideon Weil, executive editor, all at HarperOne, for their interest in exploring what is a controversial and treacherous region littered with vested interests. I am particularly grateful to Michael Maudlin for suggestions as to the focus of my research.

Writing any book like this is useless unless it is put into a position where it can communicate, where its ideas can be mixed into popular culture, which, in a kind of modern alchemy, is endlessly transmuting itself. For this I am grateful to Claudia Riemer Boutote, vice president and associate publisher at HarperOne.

Finally, during the writing of this book, I was fortunate enough to have a liver transplant. I found myself overwhelmed with gratitude for the skill of the surgeons, doctors, and nurses and, above all, for the gift from my anonymous donor.

I have some extra years; I intend to do my best with them.

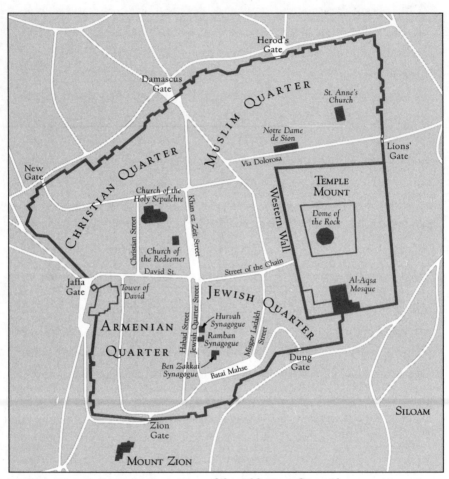

Contemporary Map of the Old City of Jerusalem

NEAR TO THE SOUTHERN ITALIAN TOWN of Terranova da Sibari are the ruins of the ancient Greek city of Thurii where the historian Herodotus lived out his final years. The site held some burial mounds, and upon excavating them, archaeologist Francisco Cavallari discovered a stone tomb.

On Sunday, March 23, 1879, before a large audience, he ceremoniously opened the tomb and found a male skeleton with a tightly folded thin gold plate lying near to his head. When this was opened, it was found to contain instructions for those passing across the frontier of death so that they might not get lost in the other world. Since then thirty-one such plates have been found, most dating from the third or fourth centuries B.C.

One plate, probably from Thessaly, and now in the J. Paul Getty Museum, Malibu, California, gives the following advice to the traveler: a question which will be asked and the reply which must be given.

> "Who are you? Where are you from?"
> "I am a child of Earth and of starry heaven,
> but my race is of Heaven (alone)."[1]

Timeline:
Racing Toward Armageddon

ISRAEL AND MIDDLE EAST TO THE END OF THE CRUSADES

4ᵗʰ MILLENNIUM B.C. —— Era of the garden of Eden with Adam and Eve according to biblical chronology.

1479 B.C. —————— Egyptian pharaoh Thutmosis III fights the Canaanites at Megiddo and captures the city.

722–628 B.C. ————— Assyrian rule of Israel.

597 B.C. —————— Jewish king Jehoiachin, besieged in Jerusalem by the Babylonians, surrenders to Nebuchadnezzar and is taken, along with leading citizens, to Babylon. Babylonians crown Zedekiah king of Judah; he was to be the last.

586 B.C. —————— King Zedekiah rebels against the Babylonians who captured and destroyed Jerusalem and its Temple. Nebuchadnezzar has Zedekiah blinded and his sons executed. Zedekiah and many Jews taken in exile to Babylon—the "Babylonian Captivity."

538 B.C. —————— Edict of Cyrus, return of Jews from exile.

537 B.C. —————— Foundation of the Second Temple.

520–515 B.C. ————— Building of the Second Temple.

333 B.C. —————— Alexander the Great conquers Syria.

319–197 B.C. ————— Judaea ruled by the Ptolemaic pharaohs of Egypt.

197–142 B.C. ————— Judaea ruled by Syrian Seleucid kings.

167 B.C. —————— Massacres in Jerusalem; Syrian king sets up an altar to Zeus in the Holy of Holies in the Temple.

166 B.C. —————— Judas Maccabaeus emerges as the leader of a revolt against the Syrians and their supporters.

63 B.C. —————— Judaea placed under Roman rule.

37 B.C.–A.D. 4 ———————— Rule of King Herod.

27 B.C. ———————— Roman emperor Octavian (Augustus) declared divine. Sacrifices offered to him—and subsequent emperors—in temples throughout the Empire, including that of Jerusalem.

A.D. 6 ———————— Birth of Jesus according to information in Luke 2:1–7. Census of Quirinius, governor of Syria.

A.D. 27–28 ———————— Traditional date of the baptism of Jesus by John the Baptist (Luke 3:1–23); beginning of Jesus' ministry.

A.D. 34–35 ———————— Execution of John the Baptist following the marriage of Herod Antipas and Herodias—according to evidence in Josephus; Jesus is still alive at this point.

A.D. 36 ———————— Crucifixion of Jesus at Passover—according to Matthew's timetable.

A.D. 50–51 ———————— Paul, resident in Corinth, writes his letter to the Christians of Thessalonika.

A.D. 61 ———————— Paul in Rome under house arrest.

A.D. 62 ———————— Roman army defeated on the banks of the Euphrates River by the Parthians.

A.D. 64 ———————— Fire of Rome and persecution of Christians by Nero.

A.D. 66–74 ———————— The Jewish War against the Romans and their Herodian supporters; destruction of Jerusalem and the Temple in A.D. 70. Fall of Masada in A.D. 74.

A.D. 68 ———————— Suicide of Nero followed by political chaos.

A.D. 79 ———————— Eruption of Vesuvius and destruction of Pompeii.

A.D. 81–96 ———————— Reign of Roman emperor Domitian; Book of Revelation written by a Christian convert, John, on the island of Patmos toward the end of this reign.

A.D. 92 ———————— Significant shortage of grain in the Roman Empire.

A.D. 115 ———————— Wealthy and influential Jewish community in Alexandria rises in revolt against the Romans and is destroyed.

A.D. 132–135 ——————— Second revolt against the Romans in Judaea under the leadership of Simon bar Kochba; Temple brought back into use; ends with final destruction of Jewish resistance.

A.D. 391 ——————— Emperor Theodosius bans pagan religions in the Empire.

A.D. 397 ——————— Council of Carthage; final agreement on books to be in the New Testament.

A.D. 632 ——————— Death of Mohammed.

A.D. 638 ——————— Muslim caliph Omar ibn al-Khattab takes Jerusalem from the Byzantine Christians.

A.D. 691 ——————— Dome of the Rock built on the Temple Mount by Muslim caliph `Abd al-Malik ibn Marwan. He or his son built the first al-Aqsa Mosque early in the eighth century.

A.D. 874 ——————— Disappearance of the Twelfth Imam whom Shiites believe will return as the *Mahdi*, the prophesied redeemer of Islam.

A.D. 1009 ——————— Destruction of the Church of the Holy Sepulchre in Jerusalem by Caliph al-Hakim.

A.D. 1099 ——————— The Crusaders take Jerusalem from the Muslims.

A.D. 1187 ——————— Destruction of the Crusader army by Saladin at the battle of Hattin near Tiberius, Jerusalem lost to the Muslims soon afterward.

A.D. 1258 ——————— Invading Mongol army led by Nestorian Christian general, Kitbuqa, destroys Baghdad and executes the caliph; end of the Islamic caliphate.

A.D. 1260 ——————— Mongol army crosses Euphrates and captures Aleppo and Damascus, then crosses the Jordan to the Jezreel Valley near Megiddo, opposed by an Islamic army from Egypt, which decisively beats the Mongols.

A.D. 1291 ——————— Fall of Acre (now Akko), last Christian city and port in the Holy Land. End of the Crusader kingdom.

MIDDLE EAST AND ISRAEL, 1917 TO THE PRESENT

1917 —————————— British army led by General Allenby takes Jeru-
salem from the Islamic Ottoman Turkish rulers;
Balfour Declaration giving British support for a
Jewish homeland in Palestine.

1918 —————————— Turkey surrenders, end of the Ottoman Empire.

1920 —————————— Council of San Remo. Former Middle Eastern
Ottoman territories divided between British and
French. British Mandate over Palestine.

1921 —————————— *Protocols of the Elders of Zion* proved to be a forgery.

1924 —————————— Ottoman Caliphate abolished by Turkish leader
Atatürk.

1948 —————————— Modern state of Israel declared. War with the
surrounding Islamic states.

1952 —————————— Foundation of Islamic party *Hizb ut-Tahrir* (Party
of Liberation) dedicated to forming a worldwide
Islamic caliphate.

1960 —————————— Excavation begins at Ubeidiya, Israel, just south
of the Sea of Galilee. Fossil remains and stone
tools 1.4–1.3 million years old found.

1967 —————————— Six-Day War begins with Israel destroying Egyptian, Jordanian, and Syrian air forces. The Old
City of Jerusalem with the Temple Mount and
the West Bank taken by Israeli forces.

1970 —————————— Publication of Hal Lindsey's *The Late Great Planet
Earth*.

1973 —————————— Yom Kippur War.

1977–1983 —————————— Right-wing Likud party with Menachem Begin
as prime minister of Israel. During his leadership
links founded between U.S. Christian fundamentalists and Israeli administration.

1978 ———————————— Menachem Begin invites fundamentalist Christian preacher Jerry Falwell on an official visit to Israel.

1979 ———————————— Jerry Falwell forms the organization Moral Majority.

1980–1988 ———————— War between Iraq and Iran.

1987–1993 ———————— First intifada against Israel throughout Palestinian territory occupied since the Six-Day War.

1991 ———————————— First Gulf War.

1991 ———————————— The red-heifer breeding program first started in the United States with the agreement between Jewish and Christian fundamentalists.

1995 ———————————— Publication of *Left Behind* by Tim LaHaye and Jerry B. Jenkins.

1996 ———————————— Red heifer "Melody" born in Israel but proves imperfect.

1996–1999 ———————— Likud party leader, Benjamin Netanyahu, elected prime minister of Israel. Increase in links between U.S. Christian fundamentalists and Israeli administration.

1998 ———————————— Temple Mount Faithful consecrates a cornerstone for the planned Third Temple.

2000–2004 ———————— Second intifada.

2003 ———————————— Second Gulf War begins.

2004 ———————————— New Sanhedrin convened in Tiberius, Israel, then moved to Jerusalem.

2006 ———————————— Fundamentalist preacher John Hagee founds Christians United for Israel.

Preface

The race toward Armageddon is the stumbling toward self-destruction.

Armageddon! The great battle against the Antichrist; when the red mist of a vast firestorm is to descend from above to envelope all living creatures in its deceptive embrace, leaving the god of war to spit out the pips.

According to the tricky and treacherous text of the final book in the New Testament, the book of Revelation, when the end time of the world dawns, a scroll with seven seals will be opened. With each seal a new horror will be unleashed against humanity. First, a great dragon will appear; this is later identified with Satan. Next will emerge a monstrous beast ominously rearing its seven heads and ten horns. Finally, a servant of this beast will arrive on the stage, a "false prophet" (16:13)—the Antichrist—who will lead his international satanic army against the forces of God. All these satanic forces will be gathered together "at the place called in Hebrew, Armageddon" (16:16).

Abruptly, a white horse bearing a divine warrior will appear from heaven, a warrior described as "The Word of God" (19:13), whom many interpret to be Christ; he will lead the "armies of heaven" (19:14) in a vast and bloodthirsty battle that will erupt against a background of terrestrial plagues and earthquakes. The three satanic allies will be defeated: the beast and the false prophet will be thrown alive into burning sulfur; their followers will all be put to the sword by the heavenly rider. According to the book of Revelation, God will take no prisoners—except, strangely, for Satan, who will be quickly locked up in a bottomless pit. Then the calm following this mayhem will usher in a thousand years of peace.

But in a curious and unexplained twist, at the end of the thousand years of peace, Satan will be released from his prison for a short time. This act of apparent mercy will immediately lead to a second great war.

It does seem a very cruel trick for God to play upon the newly peaceful inhabitants of the world. God appears to be toying with Satan like a cat toys with a mouse, because this new satanic army will also be rapidly destroyed, permitting a shiny new Jerusalem to descend from the clouds—a new Jerusalem from which Jesus will rule forever over a world where death is no more.

Personally, I have always wondered why, if Jesus is destined to be victorious, he and God should put themselves to so much trouble first. It seems to me that by delaying the inevitable, they are actually colluding with the beast, the false prophet, and Satan. It is all so pointless, and the collateral damage so extensive.

But it does not seem pointless to approximately 59 percent of Americans who, according to pollsters, say they believe in the coming battle of Armageddon.[2] And this is in addition to the millions of fundamentalist Christians worldwide who hold the same belief. Indeed, fundamentalist preaching has been pushing this kind of material out for years, material that does not allow for any doubt in the literal interpretation of Revelation. John Hagee, a prominent Texas fundamentalist preacher and author, clearly has none: "Armageddon is an actual battle, and the Antichrist is a living, breathing person."[3]

It is evident from statements such as these that fundamentalist preaching operates in the service of fear—fear of the big battle to come and fear of not belonging to the side of Jesus so as to benefit from the thousand years of peace.

Fear is all to these people, and every opportunity to spread it is taken. In January 2007 fundamentalist evangelist and former presidential contender Pat Robertson told his television audience that millions of people would die that year in a huge terrorist attack on the United States. He claimed that God had personally told him this but added, rather as an afterthought, "I'm not saying necessarily nuclear, the Lord didn't say nuclear."[4] Which is, of course, reassuring.

Such an attitude is not so far away from that of the Islamic suicide bombers who are sure that upon their deaths they will go straight to paradise to enjoy the favors of seventy-two young girls, favors they have missed out on in life due to their restrictive beliefs.

This battle of Armageddon and the return of Christ is, according to thousands of Christian fundamentalist preachers, coming soon. In fact many are convinced that our modern military involvement in the Middle East is linked to this fiery end. In the book of Revelation, Babylon is the source of all evil and is ultimately overthrown; Babylon, of course, is in Iraq, which has presently fallen to U.S. forces and their allies. To Christian fundamentalists, the connection, and the importance, is obvious.

But the Christian fundamentalists are not the only ones to believe in a final battle. Muslims, too, with increasing urgency speak about the coming of *their* messiah, the *Mahdi*, who—with the aid of Jesus— will fight against the demonic forces of the *Dajjal*, the Islamic anti-christ figure. Especially important is the belief held by many Muslims that the Mahdi will rule from Jerusalem, which the Muslims claim as their own. Muslims who follow these beliefs expect the final battle to come very soon, and this is affecting their politics, which, in turn, is affecting all of our lives.

Jewish fundamentalists, by contrast, do not think of a battle to come, but it is hard to see how their end times can appear without one. For they hold that when the Messiah comes, he will rebuild the Temple, referring to Solomon's Temple, the very first temple, according to the Bible, to serve the ancient religion of the Israelites in Jerusalem, a temple that was pillaged and destroyed by the Babylonians in 586 B.C. And with the Messiah's coming, they hold that Jerusalem will be wholly Jewish. There will be no room on the Temple Mount for any

Islamic structures, nor will there be room for the Islamic population within Jerusalem, indeed within all of Israel—which they define as stretching as far as western Iraq. They believe that the signs of the coming of the Messiah have already appeared; it will not be long now. The thousands of years of waiting are about to end. Of course, there are those who wish to hurry the time along and remove the mosques from the Temple Mount in advance of the Messiah's arrival. The anti-Islamic position of these groups is inflexible and runs very deeply. Their true relationship with Christianity is prickly and kept rather close, for they all depend upon the constant flow of funds donated to them by Christian supporters, but the tensions are there to see. For them, there is no need for compromise or tolerance; God gave Israel to the Jewish people, and that is all that needs to be said.

At its heart fundamentalism is a relentless progression deeper and deeper into intolerance and ignorance, which, unless opposed, will by default achieve its aims. Judged and measured against their own pro-nouncements, we must conclude that the fundamentalist religions of all denominations are opposing the free will and vibrancy of human life—they are, paradoxically, performing the very task they attribute to the feared Antichrist: they are attempting to convert a distorted view of reality into such a skillfully packaged shape that it might be taken as truth.

Fundamentalist religions are humanity's greatest enemy. Blunt speaking, certainly, but time is short, and I see no reason not to call it as I see it. The fact we all have to face is that the fundamentalist religions leave no room for human frailty, for compassion, for forgive-ness, or for creative freedom of thought. They are trying to return us to that time of darkness we thought was left far behind, where blind belief was considered more important than farsighted discovery, where the dogmatic was more valued than the tolerant and the false was more important than the true.

We simply cannot permit that future to occur; we must oppose that future with all the strength at our disposal. If, like those countless victims of the Nazi Holocaust, we are ever again asked to step into a cattle wagon for a trip to the Promised Land, we must remember that the correct response is always, emphatically, "No! Never again!"

But we need to move quickly for the fundamentalists are on the march; step by step they are encroaching upon the peaceful and toler-ant high ground with their perverted idea of a heavenly realm filled with comfortable seats from which those who have been "saved" can eat their popcorn and watch the slaughter below. It all sounds like some deranged fantasy based on a dim memory of the Roman arena, for there is much blood in the message and so very little mercy.

Again Christian fundamentalist preacher John Hagee does not mince his words on this issue:

> The first time He came to earth, Jesus was the Lamb of God, led in silence to the slaughter. The next time He comes, He will be the Lion of Judah who will trample His enemies until their blood stains His garments.[5]

It seems difficult to avoid the conclusion that, like those who once packed the Roman Colosseum to watch Christians or Jews thrown to the wild animals, Hagee cannot wait to take his seat before the carnage.

Hagee's position closely resembles that of Islamic fundamentalist commentators for whom, of course, Jesus is an Islamic prophet. the Egyptian Sa'id Ayyub, writing in 1987, insisted that in the final days,

> All of the books will be burnt at the end of the road. Those who sucked at deceit, spying, and hypocrisy will be burnt beneath the feet of the prophet of God, Jesus, and the army of Islam—[Jews and Christians] . . . will be trampled under after the dawn."[6]

We have good cause to be deeply worried about these people and those who read and believe their words. We must never let them near to the seats of power, else we will wake up one morning in a world where madness is called sanity and true sanity is viewed as a heresy to be ruthlessly destroyed. But, ominously, we can see this world creeping closer and closer.

The apocalyptic view of Middle East events held by recent U.S. administrations, most evidently with President George W. Bush, really began with President Ronald Reagan in the early 1980s. Famously, in 1981, Ronald Reagan revealed that he believed, "For the first time ever, everything is in place for the battle of Armageddon and the Second Coming of Christ."[7] He later echoed this belief, stating, "I turn back to the ancient prophets in the Old Testament and the signs foretelling Armageddon, and I find myself wondering if—if we're the generation that is going to see that come about."[8]

Two decades later, President Bush contented himself with advice from God. In 2003 he explained to the Palestinian prime minister, "God told me to strike at al-Qaeda and I struck them, and then he instructed me to strike at Saddam."[9]

He seems to speak like Moses or Joshua; perhaps he really *did* believe that he was leading us to the Promised Land.

| | |

We can laugh at the simplistic worldview of the fundamentalists, and we can take, like many commentators, the cynical view that they are irrelevant to the scientific and secular basis of modern Western culture, which is, in the main, a product of the Renaissance and Enlightenment rather than the dogmatic Christianity of medieval times. But we cannot so easily ignore them, for fundamentalists of all religions are setting much of the world's political agenda. And that affects each and every one of us dangerously. Fundamentalists of all religions are belligerent; they wish their opponents dead, and they claim divine sanction for this mayhem. Certainly the Old Testament, regarded as sacred not only by Judaism and Christianity but by Islam as well, is stacked with piles of bodies. If it was God's will then, why not now? they reason.

As these views encroach upon our world, and as their distortions and half truths demand our belief, we can only journey forward, resisting those who call upon us all to march to the same drumbeat and believe without question or curiosity. For it is only by continuing to seek, continuing to question, and continuing to demand answers that we will find our way out of the maze of mirrors they put before us—a maze of mirrors that has in its sights a view of Jerusalem as the capital of a new and exclusive world languishing in a thousand years of peaceful idleness.

Sadly, Jerusalem has seen it all before. History makes us only too aware of how easy it is to proclaim a rule of peace over silent piles of the dead.

Yet Jerusalem is central to this story. It is a city claimed by three great faiths and exists today within an uneasy and volatile political compromise.

As such, it is the place where we shall begin our exploration into the world of fundamentalist thinking. Before we set off, however, you should be warned: this journey quickly confronts the weird. Throughout, you will encounter a wide range of radical people and agendas whose very real threat you may doubt at first, either because of their sheer madness or their sheer charisma. Unlikely alliances will throw you as well. But you must take care to be vigilant en route to a better understanding of how this lunacy began and how it is being perpetuated today to everyone's detriment. In fact, it is best now for all of us to reach down and let a handful of the earth upon which we are standing run through our fingers—just to remind ourselves of where we are, lest we become lost in the maze of extremist rhetoric they have laid out to confuse us.

We must go now; this is not a time for delay or for trying to view the world through rose-tinted glasses; it is time to make our move to see what of their thoughts and plans can be uncovered.

RACING TOWARD ARMAGEDDON

ONE

Taking the Temple

Perhaps there is something about the summer's heat in the Judean hills that drives men crazy: when the Crusaders from Europe first poured over the walls of Jerusalem on July 15, 1099, around the middle of the day when the sun is at its most relentless, they quickly slipped out of control. They were not a happy band of singing pilgrims; many had begun their trip with a massacre of Jews in southern Germany and since then had fought bitter battles and sieges as they walked, overland, from Europe, on a dangerous and difficult journey taking three years. They were tired, they were desperate, and, above all, they were angry.

The Crusader army had actually reached Jerusalem earlier in June of that year, but the serious assault with tall wooden siege towers pushing slowly toward the walls began during the night of July 13. The fighting from that point on was relentless. It took two nights and a day of combat without respite before they first breached the strong Muslim defenses. By then the red mist had long descended, and a berserker madness ruled. Released like a mad pack of foaming pit bulls, the victorious Crusaders burst into the Temple and the narrow streets of the Old City. For all that afternoon and the next night they killed everyone they could find—Muslims and Jews, women and children. One eyewitness later recorded that when visiting the Temple area, he had to "pick his way through corpses and blood that reached up to his knees."[1]

"Everywhere lay fragments of human bodies" reported William, archbishop of Tyre, in his great chronicle of the times. "It was not alone the spectacle of headless bodies and mutilated limbs strewn in all directions" that caused the most horror—even terror—among the eyewitnesses, but it was the sight of the victorious Crusaders "dripping with blood from head to foot."[2]

Afterward, when this orgy of killing and looting had ended, the Crusaders, we are told, cleaned themselves and walked "in humility and contrition" to all the sacred sites where "with tearful sighs and heartfelt emotion they pressed kisses upon these revered spots" while others in passionate self-punishment "went about to the venerable places on their bare knees and with sobs of deep emotion bedewed everything with their tears."[3]

They threw themselves upon the altars and cried! They felt that God had been on their side and had led them to a glorious victory, allowing them to reclaim Jerusalem from the Muslims, and—in a dark and sinister echo of the Roman massacres a thousand years earlier—they had reclaimed it from the Jews as well! We cannot avoid seeing something very ancient and very pagan about dripping the blood of sacrifices and spilling tears onto the altars of a dying and resurrected god.

For those in Jerusalem at the time, victors and victims alike, it must have seemed as though Armageddon had come early.

After the shock of the massacres, the Muslims, who were previously prepared to enter into alliances with the Christian leaders and were happy to accept their presence since not all enjoyed life under their Egyptian or Turkish overlords, became implacably opposed to the Christian presence in their land. They swore to drive the Christians away, and eighty-nine years later Saladin did just that, forcing them from Jerusalem. Within a hundred more years the Christians were driven from the Holy Land itself. The Jewish inhabitants of Palestine were happy to fight side by side with the Muslims, knowing that the Crusaders could not be expected to show them any mercy. That Jesus was Jewish seemed long forgotten by these Christian forces.

The memory of that Crusader massacre in Jerusalem was not forgotten; the Crusades' destructive fanaticism had made a farce of the faith that claimed to be founded upon the love, forgiveness, and compassion of its founder. And it rekindled a similar destructive fanaticism in Islam, one which has never quite died.

Make no mistake, there is a madness afoot today too—New York's Twin Towers, the Pentagon, London's Underground and buses, the carnage on a commuter train in Madrid, the bombing of Israeli buses, nightclubs, cafes, and crowded streets; the assault on tourists in the market places, hotels, and ancient sites of Beirut, Saudi Arabia, and Egypt; and the violence in Bali, Jordan, Algeria, Morocco, and Kenya. And I do not even wish to explore the chaotic and murderous events in Iraq and Afghanistan.

All of these events are connected. Those who have caused them are hell-bent—like demonic midwives—on helping birth a future that would normally be chosen only by the supremely ignorant, the foolhardy, or the insane. Truly it is a future that is no future.

Yet, astonishingly, there are those who gain in stature, influence, and wealth by promoting this violent path, whether directly or indirectly, warning of its imminent arrival, "Believe in God, and you will be saved."

But saved by which God? Jehovah, Jesus, or Allah? Since the three figures seem to be forced further and further apart, we can be forgiven some confusion. If they are all God, are they not one and the same? Jewish, Christian, and Islamic fundamentalists are all at it; so who is correct? For each of them, it appears as if the more horrors that can be promised to fall upon those who do not share their views, the more influence they can have over the vulnerable. However—and we must be clear on this point—the Jewish and Christian fundamentalists do not go about blowing themselves up and taking away innocents who, by the teachings of all three religions, deserve much better than that. Islamic fundamentalists, at the moment, seem to be the only ones condoning this particular perversity condemned by the other two.

It is difficult to know where to start unraveling the complexities of the madness spreading across these three religions, each of which found its origins in the highlands of Palestine and the deserts of Arabia. To begin an exploration at what seems to be the beginning and progress methodically toward what seems to be the end is, somehow, all too neat and orderly for the events at play. It would bear little relationship to the reality of what is happening. While each party is acting on its own accord, events seem to be converging at a rapid pace. It seems to me that the only way we can hold so many facts and so many parallels in our minds while we explore is to simply immerse ourselves in it.

Imagine for a moment that fundamentalism, across the three religions, is like a curved lake, once a bend in a great river but now isolated, as the river, surging across its banks, has cut it off. Water no longer flows through this lake. It is still and stagnant; it is slowly dying, choking with its weeds and mud that clutch and stifle that which was once free. Yet those still living in the lake believe it to be all that exists. And they fear the river with its sparkling waters and diverse life darting and tumbling about. They think of the river as a breeding ground for evil and so distrust the freedom it allows.

Fundamentalist religious leaders want us to believe that their ways are the only ways and that we are free—but free only to swim in the turbid lake water where long ago the spirit of life was cut off.

We can no longer afford to be so indulgent toward their demands and their distorted visions. Time is short. Perhaps it has almost run out.

We have only two possibilities available to us: drain the lake and fill it with earth, or dig a channel and reconnect it with the great river so that the fresh and living water can once again flow, flushing the lake's darkness out to the sea where it can dissolve and ultimately be renewed.

But enough of playing with images; we must now seek more fully to understand what we are dealing with. And a good place to start is in the Old Testament during the time that the Israelites were heading for the Promised Land and had their desert camp surrounding the tabernacle within which was the ark of the covenant. They were the chosen people of a single God, they believed—a belief that has now spawned three religions, each considering itself the chosen representative of a single God. Truly, such a belief was always bound to cause trouble. People who have only one god are always inclined to argue that theirs is best.

Of the many enigmatic stories in the Old Testament, there are few stranger than a story related in Numbers 19:1–22 .

In this story, God appeared to Moses and Aaron, delivering divine instructions that allowed for absolutely no variation or dispute: these instructions concerned the sacrifice of a special animal, "a red heifer without fault or blemish, one that has never borne the yoke." (v. 2) Instructions oddly enough echoed in the Koran.[4] The New Testament does not ignore these instructions entirely, but it does deny their usefulness (Hebrews 9:13).

The instructions dictated that this animal be used to make possible the most important technique of ritual purity known to ancient Judaism. Only this technique could remove the most feared impurity, impurity resulting from exposure or proximity to death and most particularly, the handling of a dead body.

What exactly was the problem with proximity to death? The text doesn't shed any direct light on this; however, rabbis in later years explained that while life is infused with the divine presence, a corpse is believed to be only a shell from which all divine quality has been withdrawn. For such a reason a person who had touched a corpse was considered separated from God and thus to be in a state of ritual impurity. This belief was, of course, a very serious disability for a priest or for anyone else who served the tabernacle, which was the literal and spiritual center of the Jewish settlement.

When required to restore this ritual purity, this state of spiritual balance, the chosen red heifer was first taken beyond the settlement and then given over to a priest in whose presence it had to be slaughtered.

The priest would then dip his fingers into the blood of the slaughtered animal and sprinkle it seven times toward the entrance to the sacred enclosure. Then the red heifer would be burned on a fire fueled by cedar wood and hyssop together with "scarlet" (Numbers 19:6).

In later times, after the Temple was built, the red heifer was slaughtered on a special site on the Mount of Olives, beyond the walls of Jerusalem, but directly across from the East Gate, which, it was said, led into the Temple and the inner sanctuary.

Once consumed by the fire, the ashes of the red heifer would be gathered and kept outside the "camp" in a ritually clean location. These ashes, the text explains, were the prime substance for atonement, the "purification for sin." Indeed, the sacrifice itself was considered "a sacrifice for sin" (v. 17). But what sin might they have had in mind?

In Judaism, the worst sin is that of failing to observe the ordinances of God. And, according to Isaiah, sin was symbolized by scarlet or crimson in contrast to the white of purity (Isaiah 1:18). Could the sin be that of worshipping the golden calf?

According to the biblical report, while Moses was at the summit of Mount Sinai receiving the two divinely inscribed stone tablets of the law, his people below became restless. They wished to make a god to worship, so, gathering together all their gold jewelry, they melted it down and cast a great golden calf, exclaiming "Here is your God, Israel"

(Exodus 32:1–4). When Moses descended the mountain, he was infuriated to see the Hebrews chanting and dancing about the golden calf, and so he angrily threw the tablets of the law down from the mountain, shattering them on the rocks below. He then burned the golden calf, ground up the gold, mixed it with water and forced all to drink it. He then ordered the Levites to sacrifice around three thousand of their fellow Jews as punishment for this sin. It was because of this action that the Levites were made the priestly caste of the Jews (Exodus 32:28–29).

Or, given the link between the red heifer and the impurity of death, could it possibly refer back to the sin that saw Adam and Eve expelled from the garden of Eden into a world where error and death could never be avoided?

Opinion has remained divided over the millennia. Even the learned rabbis say that they cannot truly understand this sacrifice; it is considered a *hukkah*, that is, a demand for which there is no obvious justification, a demand that cannot be questioned, only followed.

When needed, the ashes would first be mixed with running water—spring water—then the priest would dip a hyssop branch into the mixture and sprinkle it upon all the vessels to be used in ritual or upon an individual who had become ritually unclean by touching a bone, a dead person, or a grave. It was further believed that this uncleanliness was contagious: "Anything that an unclean person touches shall be unclean, and anyone who touches it shall be unclean until evening" (Numbers 19:22).

This instruction may seem ancient and arcane, irrelevant to modern life and the concern only of those particular rabbis who immersed themselves in the subtleties of Jewish law. But there is indeed a modern relevance: someone who is unclean should never be permitted to step upon a supremely holy place, such as the true site of the Temple of Solomon on the Temple Mount and, in particular, the ancient site of the inner sanctum, the Holy of Holies.

On the 7th of June 1967 the future of the Middle East changed
dramatically. The madness of the past began to bleed into modern
politics. All bets were off. And in the process, the red heifer suddenly became directly relevant to our times. Allow me to explain:
two days earlier on June 5, 1967, faced with a mounting threat from
Egyptian forces in the Sinai and Syrian forces in the Golan and the
Galilee—numbering an estimated 250,000 soldiers—Israel struck first,
destroying the Egyptian, Jordanian, and Syrian air forces. The famous
Six-Day War had begun.

At 5:00 in the morning on June 7, deputy chief of staff for the
Israeli army, General Haim Bar-Lev, issued an order to take the Old
City of Jerusalem; the attack began at 8:30 a.m. with the paratroop
commander, Colonel Mordechai Gur, chasing behind the tanks in his
half-track urging them to go faster and faster toward the wall of the
Old City. Not long before 10:00 a.m. paratroopers and armor broke
through St. Stephen's Gate (the Lions' Gate). Colonel Gur followed
in his half-track, and at 9:50 a.m., a time recorded by his assistant,
Gur's vehicle pushed through the smashed gate and drove onto the
Temple Mount.5 At 10:00 a.m. his immediate commander, General Uzi
Narkiss, Israeli central commander, in charge of the forces that took
the Old City, arrived on the Mount. By 10:15 the Israeli flag was flying
above it. And then occurred an incident where the wisdom of pragmatic politics overcame an emotional eruption of the madness.

General Narkiss relayed the events of a meeting he had with the
chief rabbi of the Israeli army, Rabbi Shlomo Goren—but only on the
condition that nothing he said at the time would be published until
after his death. He died in December 1997; on January 1, 1998, his story
was reported around the world.6 Narkiss explained that minutes after
the Temple Mount was taken, Rabbi Goren, in a state of high emotion,
singing and blowing his *shofar*—a ram's-horn trumpet—approached and
said to him, "Now is the time to put one hundred kilos of explosives

into the Mosque of Omar, and that's it, once and for all we'll be done with it."

"Rabbi," replied General Narkiss, "if you don't stop now, I'm taking you from here to jail."

Rabbi Goren walked away without another word.[7]

Shortly afterward, General Narkiss, General Bar-Lev, Rabbi Goren, and Colonel Gur all stood together at the Wailing Wall, stunned by what they had achieved.

Defense Minister Moshe Dayan arrived at approximately 2:00 p.m., and viewing the Israeli flag flying above the Temple Mount, he ordered it removed immediately. He was not about to fall in with the plans of the hard-line Orthodox rabbis who wanted to annex the Mount. A few days later he returned to the Mount to meet with the Muslim authorities. He agreed that while Israeli forces would hold the Old City, he would grant control of the Temple Mount to the Palestinian authorities with the one condition that Jews enjoy access to it, although he conceded that they should not have the right to pray there. Moshe Dayan wanted peace: when he had first visited the newly captured Wailing Wall, following traditional practice, he scribbled a prayer on a slip of paper and pushed it between the stones; the prayer read, "Let peace reign in Israel."[8]

Moshe Dayan wanted peace, and in that cause he was prepared to trade; he was prepared to oppose pressure from his own people in order to avoid taking the final irrevocable step of annexing the second most holy site in Islam. But after forty years, peace is as elusive as ever, and the Temple Mount has since provided countless flash points for trouble. Would the violent heritage have been lessened if Israel had simply taken the opportunity of Muslim weakness to annex the Temple Mount and remove the mosques? We will never know. We can only judge an action in the context of its own time, and we can recognize that to be magnanimous in victory is a mark of a civilized warrior, whatever future consequences might seem to flow from the action.

With the Old City and the Temple Mount in Jewish hands, the Christian fundamentalist prophecy industry went into overdrive. According to the Christians, the events of June 7, 1967 provided direct proof that their understanding of biblical prophecy was correct and that after two thousand years the final days were upon us.

Lecturing on the apocalyptic events prophesied in the Bible on college campuses throughout California during March and April of 1967 was a fundamentalist preacher, Hal Lindsey. His talks centered on the three great events concerning the Jews that would be major signs of the return of Jesus and the final defeat of the Antichrist: the first event would be the gathering of Jews together to reform their ancient nation. The second would be the possession of Jerusalem and the holy places by Israel. The last would be the rebuilding of the Temple.[9]

The first sign was fulfilled on May 14, 1948, with the creation of the modern state of Israel. One can only imagine Lindsey's excitement when, in June 1967, Israel took Jerusalem and its holy places, thereby fulfilling the second sign. Time was now speeding to its apocalyptic conclusion; the Second Coming could not be far off—only nineteen years had passed between the fulfillment of these first two events— events Lindsey believes were prophesied in the biblical texts. The third and last event could not be far off: nineteen years after 1967 was 1986. Could that be the promised year of divine fulfillment? Or would the long anticipated event be in the new millennium? In the year 2000? Most seemed to go with the latter theory. I suppose round numbers are more divine than odd ones—assuming, of course, that God uses the Gregorian calendar (an assumption rather akin to the old belief that God spoke Latin!).

Would the third event take place? Lindsey had no doubt at all that it would despite his admission that the Dome of the Rock on the

Temple Mount was an "obstacle." But, "Obstacle or no obstacle, it is certain that the Temple will be rebuilt," writes Lindsey emphatically, "Prophecy demands it."[10] All this is of vital significance not only for the Middle East, but for the whole world, explains Lindsey, for Israel is "the Fuse of Armageddon."[11] A fuse that has clearly been lit.

Hal Lindsey's book promising the rapid coming of the end times, *The Late Great Planet Earth*, was published in 1970 and was the first widely popular work of this type. It was a runaway bestseller with more than fifteen million copies in print—although he claims thirty-four million in fifty-four languages.[12] The book opened the field for many other writers, although few actually had much new information or insight to add. They just repeated the message in a thousand different ways. Their underlying message was clear though: watch your back, sinners; Jesus is returning. And this time he is breathing fire.

Fundamentalist preacher and writer John Hagee, in his 2006 book, *Jerusalem Countdown*, speaking of June 7, 1967, breathlessly announced that, "This day is extremely important in prophecy. . . . It was during the Six-Day War and the recapturing of the Western Wall that this prophetic truth became a reality."[13] Tim LaHaye and Jerry Jenkins, authors of the bestselling Left Behind series of novels (with more than eleven million sold!), fantasize about life during the end times and concur on its importance. For the fundamentalists, Israel is "the key to end times."[14]

The relevance of events on June 7, 1967, were not missed by the Muslims either. How could they be—for their traditional enemies were now in possession of the second most sacred site in Islam. As special as this day was for Jewish and Christian fundamentalists, it was traumatic for Muslims. They were instantly aware of the biblical implications.

Muslim writers everywhere began to draw the shattering conclusions: their literature reveals a great change from this time forward.

The total defeat and humiliation of the Arab armies in 1967 brought about a social movement in Islam now known as the "Islamic revival" and ushered in a political version of Islam: radical Islam. As explained by Rice University's Dr. David Cook, an expert in Islamic apocalyptic speculation, the radicals became outraged, "Looking around the world and not seeing any hope in it for them, they realize that they are far from the position Muslims should rightfully find themselves in: the dominant place in the world."[15]

Indeed, Cook explains, "Muslims do not see much hope in the modern world: their culture and values are irrelevant, their opinions and positions are ignored or ridiculed, and many of their best and most promising people either emigrate to the West or take on its culture wholesale."[16]

They all believe in the existence of a great international conspiracy against Islam, one run by Jews, one which runs the world. The only remedy in their minds is for the entire world to be united in a great Islamic state ruled by a caliph. They have absorbed Christian fundamentalist arguments and blended it with Western anti-Semitism.[17] They are all fanatically fixated on Israel and the Jews.

For these Muslims, Jerusalem is "the apocalyptic capital of Islam." From Jerusalem the Islamic messiah—the Mahdi—will rule, and it is also to there that Jesus will return.[18] They are incensed: Muhammad Arif writes in 1996, "Jerusalem was Arabic previous to Islam, previous to Christianity, and previous to Judaism, and that Islam has more rights to it because it is [the] correct [faith] and any other is false."[19]

The Muslims are also well aware of the Jewish desire to remove the Islamic buildings from the Temple Mount. In 1990, author `Abd al-Aziz Mustafa warned, "If the Jews reach the al-Aqsa Mosque and put into action their plots, in the midst of a generation of Muslims reaching a quarter of the inhabitants of the earth, may God help us for the shame. . ."[20]

Several other writers expect that the plans to destroy the mosques on the Temple Mount and rebuild the Temple will be successful, but that this event would set off a series of cataclysmic events culminating in the return of Jesus and the end of time.[21]

As you can see, the madness had found a focus, and it was not going to let go. Even worse, it had become organized, as the modern-day role of the red heifer will soon reveal.

TWO

THE RED HEIFER

After the ecstatic Israeli paratroopers took the Temple Mount during the morning of June 7, 1967, they assigned one of their young
brigade chaplains, Yisrael Ariel, to guard the entrance to the Dome
of the Rock. He later recalled thinking that he was simply minding
the site until a detachment of Israeli army engineers could come and
tear the mosque down.[1] The expectation of the hard-line religious
was that the Israeli state would take this opportunity to return the
Temple Mount to Jewish worship. But the engineers never arrived,
and Moshe Dayan conducted his deal with the Palestinian authorities, allowing them to maintain the site as an Islamic place of worship.
To Ariel, permitting the Temple Mount to continue as an Islamic site
was anathema. He did not care whether the Islamic authorities would
object or preach jihad; the Arab armies were defeated, demoralized
and in disarray in the face of the rapid Israeli victory. He felt—like
Rabbi Shlomo Goren—that now was the moment to act.

Yisrael Ariel not only had an interesting history, but he kept very
interesting company: he had studied under a messianic teacher, Rabbi
Tzvi Yehuda Kook, who saw the influx of Jews into Israel as part of
a divine plan and who was also opposed to the Arabs' holding on to
any of the land that was once Jewish, such as the West Bank towns of
Hebron, Jericho, and Nablus.[2] Like Islamic fundamentalists, Kook was

no democrat; he maintained no distinction between religion and the state. He felt that the time of the Messiah was coming closer and that all of the events in the world about him were a prelude to the end times.

Within a few years a number of Rabbi Kook's followers had established Kiryat Arba, a settlement on the outskirts of Hebron where the Tomb of the Patriarchs stood. Then, in 1974, they organized the West Bank settler movement, the *Gush Emunim*, whose members flooded into the Arab-owned lands on the West Bank and built heavily defended communities. It became the vanguard of religious Zionism.[3] It was one of "his" seminaries—the Mercaz Harav Yeshiva—that was attacked by a Palestinian gunman in March 2008. Eight students died.

Ariel, by then a rabbi, moved even further to the hard right of religious Zionism. In the early 1970s the violent and racist Kach political party was founded by Rabbi Meir Kahane. Kach policy was, at times, not too far away from that of the Nazis—Kach wanted to forbid any sexual relations between Jews and Arabs and proposed that the death penalty should be the punishment for anyone caught in such a mixed relationship. They wanted to expel all the Muslims from Israel and the West Bank and wanted the two mosques on the Temple Mount to be removed.[4] In the 1981 elections for the Israeli Parliament, the Knesset, second on the list for the Kach Party was none other than Rabbi Ariel.

In 1984, the same year that Rabbi Kahane was finally elected to the Knesset, Rabbi Ariel founded a group called the Temple Institute. On its registration documents the Institute states that its long-term aim is to rebuild the Temple.[5] Its founders, apart from Ariel, included a leading Kahane follower and a rabbi named Dov Lior of the hard-line *Nir Yeshivah* in the Gush Emunim settlement of Kiryat Arba. Rabbi Lior also seems to have taken heart from Nazi precedents, writing that any Arab terrorists who were captured by Israel should be used in medical experiments.[6] He considers that all the problems faced by Israel in the world were God's punishment for Israel's failure to rebuild the Temple after the victory of the Six-Day War.[7]

Like his cohorts, Rabbi Ariel is also quite vocal: he angrily wrote in a hard-line journal that the commandment "Thou shalt not kill" refers only to killing another Jew. Any other killing is a different transgression. He despised those Jews who did not want to rebuild the Temple and he stated his belief that Christians and Muslims were idol worshippers who, by Jewish law, were forbidden to live in Israel.[8]

Men like these, their eyes glittering with self-righteousness, acting out what they perceive as the will of God, are dangerous. Whatever religion they might belong to, in their hearts they belong only to their own violent prejudices. Their spirituality is a monstrous fraud, but their madness is infectious, and there are always some lost souls hunting for that certainty given by a rigid and unbending authority. There will always be some who enjoy marching to the beat of the same loud drum.

These Jewish rabbis have their pathologically violent brothers in both Christianity and Islam. Perhaps we should send them all to some icy wasteland or burning desert to fight amongst themselves and leave the rest of us alone. But until then we must watch them closely.

I first encountered Ariel's group, the Temple Institute, in January 1992 while on a short trip to Jerusalem with Professor Robert Eisenman from California State University–Long Beach and Professor James Tabor from the University of North Carolina–Charlotte. While on a break from the cave-exploration work we were engaged in around the high cliffs bordering the Dead Sea where the Scrolls were found, we decided to visit the Temple Institute and listen to what they had to say.

We entered the Old City of Jerusalem through the Jaffa Gate and made our way down the ancient, narrow David Street, lined, as always, with shops selling antiques, leather bags, wooden crosses, metal menorahs, and other tourist mementos, to a narrow street in the Jewish Quarter not so far from the Wailing Wall.

Just beyond a small square where young children often played and kicked a football around was the headquarters of the Temple Institute. It looked like an integral part of the ancient architecture, perhaps unchanged for one thousand years or more, but inside it proved to be restored in a modern style. Rabbi Chaim Richman spoke to us and a number of other visitors. Behind him, as he talked, stood a large glass case that took up most of the wall and contained a collection of gold and silver candelabra, bowls, and other sacred objects destined for the rebuilt Temple of Solomon; for this—as we were soon to learn—was their main concern.

Rabbi Richman spoke with intelligence and lucidity, expounding, with rational erudition, a story that left me utterly shaken by its single-minded ambition. He openly proclaimed that the members of the Institute wished to remove the Dome of the Rock and the al-Aqsa Mosque so that the Temple of Solomon could be rebuilt.[9]

At first, I felt that I was in some kind of shrine dedicated to an alternative reality; I had difficulty taking this man seriously, but serious he certainly was, as well as educated, and apparently well-funded. Whatever my personal feelings were, I had to accept that his actions were at least logical given his basic assumptions and beliefs. It rapidly dawned on me that he and his colleagues were not fantasists; they were going to do it; they were going to destroy the sacred Muslim structures on the Temple Mount.

This seemed to me rather akin to some pagan worshippers who had decided to demolish St Peter's in Rome because they wanted to rebuild the temple of Isis, which had originally stood on that site. It seemed quixotic, and yet such things have happened: in India, on December 6, 1992, Hindu extremists destroyed the Ayodhya mosque, which had stood since 1528. Ayodhya is considered to be the birthplace of Rama, an ancient king of the region and the subject of the great Hindu epic, the Ramayana. Hindus believe that before the mosque was built, Rama's most important temple had stood on that same site, and they wanted to rebuild it. The destruction led to widespread violence, which cost over one thousand lives. It seems inevitable to me that the destruction of the mosques on the Temple Mount would cost considerably more lives; certainly we would see the true meaning of jihad.

Rabbi Richman explained that supporters of the Institute had been exploring under the Temple area—using the many tunnels and perhaps creating a few of their own—so far as it had been possible with regard to *Halacha*—Jewish law. They had concluded that the original Holy of Holies is right beneath the present Dome of the Rock, another reason why this sacred Islamic structure would need to be destroyed.

Make no mistake about it—they are serious; according to their plans, the Third Temple *will* be built. And to serve the Temple they are training priests in the Temple tradition of blood sacrifice. Each priest in training is a descendant of the priestly line of Aaron, the *Kohanim*; each has had a special garment woven just for him. All the required implements, dishes, and other objects are also being created as the funds become available. In particular, four of the sacred trumpets have already been replicated. These are important, Rabbi Richman explained; even the Romans had considered these sacerdotal trumpets as the key to Jewish divine power.

Rabbi Richman carefully expounded on the Institute's mission, telling us that the Temple of Solomon had been the only connection between mankind and God; the ark of the covenant was the point where the presence of God touched the earth. Their plan is not only to rebuild the Temple but also to obtain the original ark of the covenant. This would immeasurably strengthen Judaism, he explained, for in the absence of an operating Temple today, modern Judaism is but a weak reflection of what it was in the past. And then Rabbi Richman added, "The Temple is the sole rectifying force in the life of mankind. . . . The Temple represents harmony; it will bring harmony to the world."[10]

He later elaborated this further, writing that Jerusalem will one day be recognized "as the spiritual centre of all humanity" explaining that "Service in the Holy Temple is meant to be nothing less than an act of purification for all humanity."[11] "Israel," he wrote in 2006 (quoting Exodus 19:6), has the divine mission of being a "kingdom of priests and a holy nation."[12]

Richman and his colleagues believe that every human being on earth today is ritually impure, a belief based upon the Torah. Some types of impurity can be worked through by ritual, but the most severe impurity is that caused by exposure to death. All humans are subject to this, hence all are contaminated. The Temple could not be served by its priests until a universal method of purification is available to remove mankind's contamination. He quoted Maimonides, who said that one could rebuild the Temple even if one was ritually impure; but once it was built, one needed to be ritually pure to serve it.

And this inevitably brings us to their interest in the "red heifer."

In order to build the Third Temple, it would be necessary to invade the Temple area. When the time comes, the Temple Institute activists plan to rush across the Mount with who knows what demolition equipment. But before they can do this, they need to resolve one remaining problem: these deeply orthodox Jews cannot risk rushing across the open Temple Mount in case they inadvertently step upon the site once occupied by the Temple with its Holy of Holies. Since no one knows exactly where this stood in the Temple Mount of Herod's time, they cannot take the chance of setting foot just anywhere on the Mount. But there is one way, requiring the most efficacious purifying method known to ancient Judaism—the ashes of the ritually sacrificed perfect red heifer. As they enter the Temple Mount, having already purified themselves, they will sprinkle the sacred water mixed with the ashes of the red heifer, which will allow them access to the entire Temple Mount in order to complete the demolition of the mosques now standing there.

In the past a container that held ashes drawn from all the previous red heifers was held in the Temple as insurance against a period during which no perfect animals would be born, for the perfect red heifer is defined as one which, by its third year, has only one black hair on its body and no blemishes. No such perfect red heifers exist today. But Rabbi Richman mentioned a cattle-breeding program being conducted in the United States at that time, and he also showed us photographs of the ranch in Louisiana where he said the program was located.

In this breeding task the Temple Institute has the help of those fundamentalist Christian groups that also are waiting for the coming, or second coming, of the Messiah, since for them, the Messiah is Jesus. As stated earlier, the widely accepted belief amongst fundamentalist Christians is that the formation of the state of Israel is the first sign of Jesus' imminent return; another important sign is the rebuilding of the Temple of Solomon as the base from which Jesus will rule. Strangely, this latter belief is also held by the Muslims.

We can only hope that the Jewish Messiah and the Christian Messiah are on friendly terms and do not start competing for the same divine space. Then again, perhaps they are the same being?

But Rabbi Richman is adamant that there is no possibility of the Messiah's being Jesus. In a reply to a letter on the subject from a fundamentalist Christian, he makes a number of points about the Jewish concept of the Messiah:

> Jews do not believe that the Messiah is a part of G-d, or Divine in any way, more than any other person. No indication of this can be found in the Old Testament, since this is not a Jewish concept. . . . We do not accept the notion the Scripture "foretells" that G-d would robe Himself in flesh. We believe that this idea is the very embodiment of idolatry, and we must give our lives to make a stand against it. . . . The reason why Jews like myself do not accept Jesus as the messiah is a very basic one—

we do not see that he fulfilled any of the requirements for the job. If he never qualified, it is not even a question of rejection.[13]

The Christian pastor who posted this letter on the Internet headed it "Rabbi Richman's Antichrist Diatribe Against Jesus As The Messiah."[14] Despite joint efforts between Christian and Jewish fundamentalists to raise the prized red heifer, there is clearly no sense of amity or common purpose expressed here.

And what of the Islamic Messiah, the Mahdi? Where might he fit into the scheme of things? One nineteenth-century claimant in the Sudan led a violent insurrection against Egyptian rule, destroying a large army and, during the capture of Khartoum in 1885, killing the governor, British general Charles Gordon, and then taking control of this remote Egyptian province of the Ottoman Empire; more recently Osama bin Laden has been the focus of a swirl of messianic speculation. Are we facing a trinity of Messiahs—if so, at least we have the symbolism right. But is it three in one; or is it simply three? I must admit that I was confused, and more than a little worried, when I left the Temple Institute.

What I hadn't realized at the time was that this breeding program was well advanced. The key figure was a Christian Pentecostal rancher, the Reverend Clyde Lott of Canton, Mississippi. In 1989 Lott happened to read closely the biblical text Numbers 19:1–22, where the ritual involving the red heifer is described. As a cattle breeder, he was intrigued; what breed of cow could have given rise to this red heifer? There hadn't been any living in Israel since the destruction of the Temple almost two thousand years earlier, but, Lott realized, a red breed of cattle is not uncommon in the United States, the Red Angus. He pondered this question. He was also intrigued at the possibilities a red heifer raised. As a fundamentalist Christian, he believed that Jesus was going to return once the three signs of the end times were fulfilled, the three we have already noted: the gathering of Israel, the city of Jerusalem owned by Jews, and the Temple rebuilt.

In common with other fundamentalist Christians, Lott held that only the third condition was yet to be fulfilled. He concluded that the second coming of Jesus and so the entire fate of all on the earth depended upon the successful breeding of a red heifer, for it was only by the use of the purifying powers of its ashes that the Mount could be entered and emptied and the Temple rebuilt.[15]

He pondered for over a year; then on September 18, 1990, he arranged for a letter containing his ideas to be sent from the Mississippi Department of Agriculture and Commerce to the American diplomat in charge of the export of agricultural products to the Middle East who was based in the U.S. Embassy in Athens. The letter stressed, "Red Angus cattle suitable for Old Testament Biblical sacrifices will have no blemish or off color hair, genetically red will produce red."[16]

The letter was passed from official to official until, approximately three months later, it was forwarded to the director of the Temple Institute, Rabbi Chaim Richman. Richman contacted Lott and invited him to visit Israel; the two men quickly joined forces. During 1991 and 1992 they instituted the red-heifer breeding program, initially on ranches in the United States.

Lott began breeding red heifers, but producing a perfect one was proving difficult. In 1996 a red heifer was finally born in Israel on a farm near Haifa, though it was not connected with Lott's breeding program. It was named Melody. Rabbi Yisrael Ariel and fifteen or twenty colleagues arrived to look at her. They agreed that for the moment she met the requirements.[17] By 1997, however, she had grown a white tail and was pronounced unworthy of sacrifice.

When I recently returned to the Temple Institute, it was apparent that things had changed. The original spacious building was closed up; the door was scruffy and dusty. By the look of it, no one had been there for some time. Across the narrow street, down a few steps, was a small bookshop; this now was the Temple Institute. It sold cards, miniature temple-construction kits for children, souvenirs, prints, and, of course, books in Hebrew, English, and other languages. It all seemed a bit tawdry. The Temple Institute looked like it had fallen on hard times.

A group of Christian tourists or pilgrims from the United States had entered and descended down a staircase to a lecture room where they were listening to a talk about the Temple and the importance of the ancient priesthood and the Temple animal sacrifices.

I paid my fee and slipped down to join the small group. Next to me was Mark from Texas, an enthusiastic Christian who was obviously well briefed on his Old Testament. After smelling some samples of the sacred incense to be burned in the Temple and hearing a long and thoroughly unbelievable tale about the magical qualities of the Jewish priest's breastplate—the sacred stones mounted on it, we were told, would light up to give the answers to questions; but only the high priest could see or read the message—we were taken to a room with a large model of the Temple in it. Our lecturer began explaining the various elements. Meanwhile I noted on the floor, leaning against the rear wall of the room, a framed color photograph of a red heifer—the one called Melody by the look of it. I wondered why it was not hanging on the wall. This seemed oddly disrespectful under the circumstances. And curiously, our lecturer hadn't mentioned the red heifer at all.

As we exited the Temple Institute and were walking up the street, I approached Mark from Texas and asked, "I am a bit confused here. Didn't Jesus' death remove the need for animal sacrifices in the Temple?"

"Yes," replied Mark from Texas with a knowing smile, "He was the sacrificial Lamb of God and stopped animal sacrifice for all time."

Then he added in what I thought directly pertained to the relationship between the Temple Institute and its Christian supporters, "The Jews don't recognize that Jesus stopped the animal sacrifices."

Mark from Texas had expressed a major difficulty that accompanies the Christian support for those groups wishing to rebuild the Temple. The Christians want the Temple rebuilt because this means that the second coming of Jesus is that much closer. The Jewish groups are happy to accept their patronage since it represents backing for Israel as well as significant financial aid for their organizations and for Israel itself. But what is not openly spoken of is the basic conflict that Mark from Texas noted: the Christian supporters do not support the aims of the Jewish restoration groups, which are firmly focused on the renewal of the Temple sacrifices.

This is quite plausibly why I sensed a palpable, albeit unspoken and unexplored, tension during this second visit to the Temple Institute. It appears that the Institute has had to change its public appeal when speaking to such groups, avoiding the subject of Melody and the red-heifer breeding program altogether.

The Christian attitude about such sacrifice is perhaps best expressed in the letter to the Hebrews, contained in the group of letters attributed to Paul although there are many reasons to indicate that it was not written by him. It is, nonetheless, a very interesting text.

It addresses a Jewish Christian audience in the second century A.D., one which is familiar with traditional Jewish learning and Temple practice. It could perhaps date from a time when the Temple was still operating, but this seems far too early for its theology. Nevertheless, it does share similarities of symbolism with the messianic Dead Sea Scrolls, and so it probably emerged out of this messianic fervor, which gave rise to the Christians—it is quite simple: "Christ" comes from the Greek *christos* meaning "the anointed one" (king or high priest), the latter a translation of the Aramaic *meshiah*, which is transliterated as "messiah." Hence a "community of the *Messiah*" and a "community of the *Christos*" are exactly the same community; the messianic community is the Christian community.

The letter is certainly addressed to a Jewish messianic audience, one that still had an expectation that the Temple service might soon be reinstated, but, as the letter points out, such ideas were misguided and focused upon the external and the superficial rather than the inner spirit. In essence, the letter to the Hebrews sought to convert Jews to Christianity.

The letter speaks of Christ's coming as the High Priest and reveals that Christ entered the Holy of Holies not with the blood of sacrificed goats and bull calves but with his own blood, which has "won an eternal redemption for us" (Hebrews 9:12). It also mentions the red heifer specifically, "The blood of goats and bulls and the ashes of a heifer are sprinkled on those who have incurred defilement and they restore the holiness of their outward lives" whereas the blood of Christ, "the perfect sacrifice," purifies our inner self (Hebrews 9:13–14). There is no longer any need for sacrifices according to the Mosaic laws because, "When all sins have been forgiven, there can be no more sin offerings" (Hebrews 10:18).

To render the Mosaic law redundant is to negate all the learning of the rabbis and the value of everything that they believe and teach. The only conclusion one can draw is that the continued acceptance of support from Christian fundamentalists by these Orthodox rabbis who wish to rebuild the Temple is an act of breathtaking cynicism. For the Christian fundamentalist groups to continue to give their support is an act of naïveté, equally breathtaking.

What both groups are choosing to ignore is that the Christians are intent upon converting all the Jews to an acceptance of Christ as the Messiah at the end times. In the minds of these fundamentalist Christians, those Jews who do not accept this will unfortunately die. Hal Lindsey, in *The Late Great Planet Earth*, writes that upon the end of the war and the return of Jesus, "A great many of the surviving Gentiles and Jews put their whole trust in the true Messiah, Jesus Christ . . .

(who will) set up an ever-lasting Kingdom and bring about the spiritual conversion of Israel."[18] And Lindsey becomes more specific still: after the battle of Armageddon, he writes, Jews will be impressed by the power of Jesus, and "the greatest period of Jewish conversion to their true Messiah will begin." Jews will "come to see the name of their true God and Messiah, Jesus Christ."[19]

John Hagee, in his *From Daniel to Doomsday*, echoes this belief, explaining that in the end the Jews will convert to accepting Jesus as the Messiah; in other words, they would convert to Christianity.[20] And describing that Jesus will win the battle of Armageddon at the end of time, he writes:

> The hearts of the Jewish people—warmed toward God because of His intervention—will fully turn to their true God. In that moment, Israel will look upon her Messiah with recognition. . . . Jesus Christ, the true Messiah . . . shall rule and reign forever from the city of Jerusalem, the city of God.[21]

I would like to know what Rabbi Yisrael Ariel thinks of all this—as he accepts money from Christians who believe it.

Each side, Jewish and Christian, has a strong and incompatible agenda, seemingly irreconcilable.

Seeking to escape from the madness, one evening after visiting the Temple Institute, I went on a walk from my hotel into the commercial district of West Jerusalem. I passed a sign that proclaimed, RED HEIFER STEAKHOUSE. I realized that the best thing we can do to delay the eruption of the temple madness is to keep eating the red heifers.

Of course, I ate there that evening.

THREE

DESTROYING THE MOSQUES

Today the Temple Institute denies having any interest in removing the Islamic buildings, yet it is hard to see how the Temple could be rebuilt without doing so. It appears as if this whole field has entered a period of denial and spin. The true motives of these groups seem to have gone underground with the exception of some who still make no secret of their belligerence toward the Islamic holy sites, namely members of the Temple Mount and Land of Israel Faithful Movement headed by Gershon Salomon, a former officer in the Israeli army and former student of Rabbi Tzvi Yehuda Kook. Salomon, who speaks his mind quite openly, has a large number of secular Israelis very worried.

Every year, at Hanukkah—the Jewish festival that is celebrated a few days before Christmas—he leads the faithful on a march to the Temple Mount. They are dedicated to rebuilding the Temple and make no secret of their desire to remove all the Islamic buildings there. As Gershon Salomon has stated, once the Temple has been constructed, "Islam is over."[1]

They consider these Islamic shrines to be pagan; their very presence desecrates the Temple Mount, and until they are removed, the Mount cannot be reconsecrated to the God of Israel. Magnanimously, they suggest that rather than destroying the al-Aqsa Mosque and the

Dome of the Rock, these shrines be dismantled and moved to Mecca where they can be rebuilt for the Islamic faithful.[2]

Just a moment's reflection lets us see how absurd this idea is in the real world: who would let them dismantle the structures? And who would dare transport them? But these are minor details compared to the real problem: the Dome of the Rock is not so much sacred in itself, it is rather the cover, the protective shell of a sacred place. It is what guards the great Foundation Stone from which, according to Islamic tradition, Mohammed ascended to heaven as noted in sura 17, "The Night Journey" in the Koran.

Muslims will point out an elongated depression in the rock itself, which is claimed to be Mohammed's footprint. The same sura states that God has blessed the precincts of the site of the ascension, thereby rendering it sacred to all Muslims. Jerusalem and the Temple are not specifically mentioned in the text, but from the earliest times the site of Mohammed's ascension has been held to be on the Temple Mount. To rebuild the structures in Mecca would be to render them as lifeless as an object in a museum since their sacred nature ultimately derives from the place on which they are built.

So what are the Temple Mount Faithful activists going to do? Ship a thousand tons of rock to Mecca as well? Except that this rock, the Foundation Stone, is also sacred to Judaism, revered as the site of Jacob's dream of the ladder giving entrance to heaven. The logical absurdity of this reasoning would lead ultimately to a proposal that Jerusalem itself be dismantled and rebuilt in Mecca. We can see how foolish this is. Its suggestion is no more than a public-relations cover, a naive attempt to head off criticism and hold the attention of the Orthodox Jews and fundamentalist Christians who support this idea but don't wish to think too hard about its tragic implications.

Ever confident and determined, the Temple Mount Faithful actually carved and consecrated a cornerstone for the new Temple. On October 7,

1998, they carried it around the gates of the Temple Mount beginning at the sealed Golden Gate in the eastern wall. Islamic authorities controlling the Mount threatened riots if this cornerstone were to be laid, and so the Israeli authorities ordered the gates giving access to the Mount to be closed. Ultimately, they were allowed to bring the cornerstone close to the gates and carry it seven times around the walls of the Temple Mount and the Old City.[3] Leading the procession was a priest dressed in the ancient regalia and a group of Levites who played instruments and sang. In an address to the crowd, Gershon Salomon publicly declared his desire to destroy the Islamic structures:

> The public struggle and march of the Faithful will not stop until the Islamic abomination on the Temple Mount and their control of the most holy place of the G-d and people of Israel and of all the earth will be removed.[4]

Because the consecrated cornerstone could not be simply discarded, it was placed in a small site, a traffic circle near to the Damascus Gate, and left, unmarked, waiting until it might be placed permanently in its intended place.[5]

Reading of these events, one is bound to think that all had slipped into some kind of parallel universe where the real world is something of only minor interest. But, fortunately for the sane among us, the real world has intervened.

When in 1996 the red heifer, Melody, was born and rabbis pronounced her "qualified," great excitement erupted both amongst Orthodox Jews and the media, which began reporting that the birth of a red heifer was a sign of the coming of the Messiah. With this came the thought that now was the time to rebuild the Temple. The Muslim community and most of the Jewish population of Israel were deeply worried. The last thing both communities needed was this kind of problem. There was at least one media call for the heifer to be destroyed immediately so that the potential harm she promised could never occur.

This media circus focused Clyde Lott and Chaim Richman on the global political and social consequences of what they were doing.[6] Could this attention possibly account for their current downplaying of the entire program? In 1999 it was reported that the Temple Institute had ceased working on the breeding project with Lott but "declined to say why."[7] Certainly it is hard to take this as a waning interest in the original goal. Richman himself has said that the breeding work continues and that "the Temple Institute has its own plans with regard to red heifers."[8] Could there be other factors at play here?

Journalist Gershom Gorenberg discovered that the immediate cause of the break between Richman and the red-heifer project organization, the Canaan Land Restoration of Israel, Inc., formed in spring 1998 to facilitate the import of cattle into Israel, of which Lott was president and Richman a director, was financial, but it seems that there is even more to the story. Richman himself repeated an allegation that when appearing in a film on the subject, Lott had spoken about "spreading the gospel in Israel."[9] It seems as if with this statement a small quake had hit the fault line, and Richman decided not to await a major tremor.

Since that time a number of other groups have begun breeding programs, and a number of red heifers, apparently correct in every way, have been born; the last reported was in 2002. Unfortunately for the breeders and the rabbis—but perhaps fortunately for the rest of us— all have subsequently proved less than perfect. During the three years required for the heifer to reach the correct age for sacrifice, imperfections appeared in each of them. But the Temple Institute Web site still presses on. In 2007 they made available a long explanation of the importance of the red heifer, commenting that "A perfect heifer, born and raised under a controlled environment, would be fit to be used for the Temple. And that is precisely what is being done today."[10]

Certainly, Muslim writers are well aware of the conspiracies that exist to destroy their sacred buildings, the al-Aksa Mosque and the Dome of the Rock, on the Al-Haram al-Sharif—the Noble Sanctuary, which is the Islamic name for the Temple Mount. In fact, a 2004 report by the Al Jazeera television company, which has a large viewing public in the Middle East and elsewhere, stated as a fact that "Most Israelis believe the Temple must be built over the mosques."[11] This is greatly overstating the case, as there are many Jewish people who do not share the view of the fundamentalists, but it is an indication of what the Islamic world believes, and it is that belief which will translate into action.

This fear has been expressed many times, but the danger surrounding it is most evident when it becomes entangled in Islamic apocalyptic writing. This material, mostly published in Cairo, is as rabid and violent as the Christian writings about the "end times." This parallel is not so surprising when one considers that much of the Islamic material has been drawn from the Christian publications. Academic expert in this field, Dr. David Cook, notes, "the modern Antichrist scenario . . . has become completely dependent upon Christian ideas and sources."[12] To this apocalyptic speculation is added a very generous amount of the very wildest anti-Semitism.

While most of these texts are available only in Arabic, others are translated into English. This is a worrying development since it reveals that the aim of these books is to direct the message at native-born Muslims in the United States and England who do not speak Arabic.

During the buildup to the millennium, in common with many Christian fundamentalist writers, Islamic heralds of the apocalypse began to churn out this material for an ever-increasing audience. In 1996 a book written by Hisham Kamal `Abd al-Hamid was published in Cairo with a title that translates as *The False Messiah (Dajjal) Is About to Emerge*. In it the author explains that after the al-Aqsa Mosque is demolished and the Third Temple built, a series of disasters will be unleashed upon the world. Revealing his debt to Christian writers, he uses Christian dates and is certain about what will happen: "The Jews are planning to destroy al-Aqsa Mosque during the year 2000."[13]

As it turns out, others had already trod on this ground before him: in 1987, Sa'id Ayyub had also warned of the destruction of the al-Aqsa Mosque in the year 2000 in his bestselling book on the Antichrist, *Al-Masih al-Dajjal*.[14] He was, of course, wrong, but the book revealed how this madness had quickly crossed from the Christian and Jewish worlds into the Islamic world. The madness was becoming organized.

In 1998, another writer in Cairo, Fahd Salim, insisted that the Dome of the Rock was going to be demolished on January 1, 1999 and that, exactly one year later, Jesus was going to return.[15] He presented the ideas of the end times as commonly believed amongst Christians, making no distinctions between those fundamentalists who await the end and the vast majority of Christians who view the biblical apocalyptic themes as merely symbolic. The resulting misimpression is akin to the way many Christians fail to understand the differences between fundamentalist Muslims and those who tread a more moderate path. But like fundamentalism in Christianity, the certainty, self-confidence, and aggressiveness of Muslim fundamentalists are shifting the faith's center of gravity toward the rigid edges.

What is increasingly alarming is that this fundamentalist belief in the coming destruction of the Temple Mount mosques is now becoming such an integral part of Western strategic planning. "As is well known," Salim wrote in 1998, "the Masons have set the year 2000 as the outer limit for the implementation of their great plans, and the first part of it will be the destruction of the mosque of al-Aqsa and the foundation of the Third Temple in its place. The West believes in this and aids in its realization."[16]

And there is more to worry about in this story: in ancient times, up to the dissolution of the patriarchate by the Romans in the early fifth century A.D., there was a Jewish religious authority operating in parallel to the Roman civil administration. This Jewish authority, the Sanhedrin, was comprised of seventy-one leading rabbis or sages who dealt with religious disputes. It occasionally would act as a court in order to try false messianic pretenders or claimants to the office of high priest. It was the ultimate authority in matters of the interpretation of the Mosaic law; it even had the power to impose the death penalty for serious transgressions. In addition, according to early tradition recorded in the *Tosefta*—a collection of traditions outside those recorded in the Mishnah, "They may not burn the red heifer save according to the instructions of the court of 71."[17]

The Sanhedrin met in a special room in the Temple and after the Temple's destruction in A.D. 70, the Sanhedrin moved to the first of a series of alternative sites; the last meeting place was Tiberius, on the Sea of Galilee, around A.D. 425.

And so it was in Tiberius, in 2004, that the new Sanhedrin was convened. At its head, serving under the title of *Nasi*, was a highly respected scholar, Rabbi Adin Steinsaltz, who had, among other achievements, translated the Talmud into Hebrew, French, Spanish, and Russian and had written extensively on Kabbalah. A leadership council of seven prominent members was formed. Along with Rabbi Adin Steinsaltz in this select Sanhedrin council was Rabbi Yisrael Ariel, the founder of the Temple Institute.[18] Also on the Sanhedrin, and a prominent spokesman for it, was the Temple Institute's Rabbi Chaim Richman. Joining them was Rabbi Nachman Kahane, whose brother Rabbi Meir Kahane—formerly the head of the Jewish Defense League and the violently racist anti-Islamic Kach Party—had been murdered in New York by an Islamic activist in 1990.[19] The new Sanhedrin is evidently not a home for the religiously tolerant. But then, what liberal Jews would really want to be associated with the revival of a two-thousand-year-old court that could order death by stoning?

Following its initial convening, the Sanhedrin moved to Jerusalem where its leadership council meets once a week. One of the Sanhedrin's aims is to influence the political direction of the state of Israel seeking veto power over any laws passed that it deems incompatible with biblical Jewish law. Its involvement with the politics of Israel is becoming increasingly evident. In 2005 it issued a ruling opposing the removal of the Jewish settler communities in Gaza, declaring that no Jew should cooperate with the process. It added that, with a pro-law Israeli government, the Israeli army would be ordered to reconquer the territory and rebuild the Jewish communities there.[20]

The Sanhedrin sought to flex its muscles: in January 2007 the Sanhedrin Rabbinical Court issued a ruling against Israeli General Yair Naveh, who had issued orders restraining settlers on the West Bank who opposed the closure of their settlements. The Sanhedrin ruled that General Naveh had acted contrary to the Torah in issuing these orders and so "was guilty of crimes punishable by death according to Jewish law."[21] Shortly thereafter Israeli state prosecutors began a criminal investigation of those rabbis who signed this ruling, one of whom was Rabbi Ariel.

It is no surprise then to find, according to Sanhedrin spokesman Rabbi Richman, that "the Sanhedrin is researching ways to renew the deepest roots of our faith—to renew Temple service."[22]

That the Sanhedrin functions in a milieu of messianic expectation is demonstrated further by a press report issued in February 2007 stating that the Sanhedrin had bought sheep for ritual sacrifice during the Passover and that it sought to perform such ritual sacrifice on the Temple Mount itself. One of the Sanhedrin explained that this was "to remind Jews that the Temple rituals will resume when the Messiah comes."[23]

| | | |

Simply put, The Temple Faithful regard the creation of an Israeli state as the first step in a process of bringing redemption to the entire world. Its official policy states that, "Israel is the elect nation of G-d, sovereignly (sic) chosen for His purpose as a vessel through which redemption will be accomplished."[24]

It calls on all other nations in the world to support Israel in this task while reminding us that, "The redemption of the people of Israel is a condition for the redemption of the earth."[25]

This is not an isolated and eccentric attitude, but one held by a number of diverse fundamentalist individuals and groups. For example, Rabbi Aryeh Kaplan, writing in 1976, stated that, "In Jerusalem, the Jewish people will thus become established as the spiritual and moral teachers of all mankind."[26]

He sees Jerusalem not only as the center of the world and as a center of civilization "but also as the very center of creation."[27] He also views the Foundation Stone, now protected by the Islamic Dome of the Rock as "the very first point at which God began the act of creation."[28] And he explains, "Since this spot is where all spiritual forces come together to influence the physical world, this is indeed the 'Gate of Heaven'. . . spiritual channels emanate from the Foundation Stone bringing spiritual sustenance to all the world."[29]

What worries me deeply about all this is its breathtaking arrogance. There is no room here for any other spiritual systems, no room for Christianity or Islam, Buddhism, Hinduism, Taoism, or the many other perfectly valid paths by which spiritually minded people can journey toward knowledge of matters divine.

The concept that no other spiritual sites exist in the world other than the Temple Mount is so naive, so utterly ignorant, as to be laughable were the implications of this type of thought not so disastrous. In fact, we laugh at our own peril; for these people believe what they say, and they are intent upon achieving political power.

Their approach is demanding, dogmatic, and, above all, exclusive. But it will not be the last time that we will encounter such a perspective as we make our journey through this minefield. We must step carefully.

Back in 1992 I had asked Rabbi Richman whether there were any prophetic statements that would give a time frame for the rebuilding of the Temple. He replied that there was no particular prophecy. However, he explained that he believed the gathering of Jews in Israel in the modern world was relevant; he felt that we were in a significant time in history. "The times now are fuel for the fires of redemption," he stated. One gets a distinct whiff of the apocalypse; he clearly believed that he would see, in his lifetime, the rebuilding of the Temple. Although he explained that the rebuilding of the Temple had nothing to do with the Messiah, he admitted his belief that, "if you build it, he will come."

But the rebuilding of the Temple, as we have seen, is inseparably linked with the coming of the Messiah. And, according to both Christian and Islamic tradition, the coming of the Messiah is linked with a great battle to be fought in northern Israel: the battle of Armageddon!

So it is to Armageddon that we must now turn.

FOUR

ARMAGEDDON

For far longer than any cultural memory can recall, Palestine has been the bridge between Africa and Asia; any prehuman or human groups who migrated from Africa to the rest of the world needed to walk this way. Many settled; and when they did, they left their traces. The Dead Sea valley was, in those ancient times, a lush land with numerous fresh-water lakes teeming with wildlife. It became the major route for those moving north, and, as such, it is to this day a great repository of information concerning our evolution.

The human race has quite a few different human ancestors; in fact, at some times in the past, different species of primitive prehumans existed at the same time—two and a half million years ago, for example, there were at least five different species coexisting. And thirty thousand years ago there were two species: Neanderthal and what used to be called Cro-Magnon but is now known by the scientific name *Homo sapiens*, our direct ancestors. The Neanderthals died out around 20,000 years ago, although no one really knows why. Perhaps we saw them as a protein source and ate them. This extinction—or genocide—left only *Homo sapiens* who thereafter slowly came to dominate the world.

Despite all that we know, however, there is still much that eludes us—where, for example, did the sophisticated tool-making prehumans living in Boxgrove, England, 600,000 years ago fit in? And what about the cultural traces found in Bilzingsleben, eastern Germany, from 400,000 years ago, which serve as evidence of a people who seem to have built settled communities?

Because so many of our distant ancestors traveled through Palestine along the land bridge known to archaeologists as the Levantine Corridor, it is here that many archaeologists concentrate their studies, each trying to answer the question such anomalies raise.

At Ubeidiya, a site just south of the Sea of Galilee that had once been the shore of a lake, three teeth, stone tools, and animal fossils were found dating from 1.3 to 1.4 million years ago. The teeth could not be identified but the type of tools found were typical of an ancient, once widespread, prehuman called *Homo erectus*—"upright walking man"—whose earliest remains were found in Africa but who reached as far as China. Paleontologists consider that Homo erectus were our remote ancestors. Similar tools were excavated in Ethiopia and at Olduvai Gorge, the site in Tanzania where so many ancient remains have been discovered. Also at Ubeidiya, excavations that were begun in 1960 by Ofer Bar-Yosef and Naama Goren-Inbar exposed roughly thirty layers representing different periods of occupation.

Stone tools discovered at a later site north of the Sea of Galilee revealed that a second major wave of migrants passed up the Levantine Corridor around 780,000 years ago. To the west of the present lake the caves of Skhul and Qafzeh reveal that very early Homo sapiens were living in the area up to 130,000 years ago. About 70,000 years ago Neanderthals arrived, driven, it is thought, from the north by the increasingly cold conditions as a new Ice Age began. Finally, about 12,000 years ago more settled groups began to inhabit caves in the hills behind Haifa, while others built small stone huts. Both began to deliberately plant and harvest cereals in a move that eventually led to truly domesticated plants and ultimately to the associated settled farming communities.[1]

Such prehuman and early-human achievements invite us to question our assumptions about the line this development took through the millennia. Another of the great mysteries that gives us pause to think involves an ancient piece of carpentry found in the Jordan Valley.

In July 1989 Naama Goren-Inbar and her colleagues were excavating an ancient waterlogged site in the northern Jordan Valley at Gesher Benot Ya'aqov, just south of the Sea of Galilee. A study of the magnetic orientation of the early strata revealed that the sediments holding the objects there dated no further back than 750,000 years, while fossil evidence indicated the most recent date to be 240,000 years ago.[2] Naama Goren-Inbar's site lay somewhere between these two dates. From other indications, however, she narrowed the date to approximately 500,000 years ago, a time when Homo erectus was walking through Palestine, hunting animals with sophisticated but nonetheless primitive stone tools, and living in caves.

It was at the western extension of this site that a mechanical digger lifted up one of the most enigmatic objects ever found in an ancient site of this kind: the digger carried, in its bucket, what proved to be part of a wooden plank. The wood was identified as willow, but not just a rough hewn length of wood; this was straight, with a flat surface and a slightly beveled front edge. This flat surface had been well prepared and bore no evident tool marks. Furthermore, it had been highly polished with an organic substance.[3]

Such an unusual finding raises the question: why would people who live in caves and have no concept of a straight line need a straight plank with a polished surface? It is clear that considerable effort had gone into producing this artifact. So where in a cave would it have been used?

Archaeology has no answer. Not even Naama Goren-Inbar knows the artifact's use. When I asked her, she said as much and added even more curiously that while such sites were generally attributed to Homo

erectus, she was reluctant to identify it with any particular species of
early prehuman since she had not found any bones on the site.[4]

Speaking further to this point, she and her colleagues wrote that
"it is possible that we have underestimated the capacities" of these
unknown early prehumans and that "further 'unconventional' discoveries may cause us to revise our opinion of their abilities."[5] Which
brings me to a crucial point: despite these unanswered questions—and
maybe even because of them—we can be certain that prehumans and
humans have been in Israel for a very long time indeed, a distance
back into the mists of the past immeasurably greater than that which
can be calculated using information in the biblical book of Genesis.
And if Genesis can so easily be demonstrated to be mythology rather
than fact, where does this leave those fundamentalists who take every
word of the Bible as immutable truth?

For just one moment, let us take a passage from the Bible quite literally: Genesis, chapters five to eleven, allows us to calculate the number of years that elapse between the creation of humanity and the rise
of historical records, from the creation of Adam to Abraham, who was
born in the historically existent Mesopotamian city of Ur, the remains
of which still exist in Iraq and about which we know quite a lot since
it has been excavated and texts relating to its history and intellectual
life have been found in ancient libraries.

If, according to Genesis, 1,946 years transpired from Adam to
Abraham, and if Abraham is usually dated to approximately 1800 B.C., then
Adam and Eve would have resided in the garden of Eden around 3,746 B.C.
This is absurd, for it would mean that the creation of humans occurred
later than the remnants found in the caves of the Haifa hills, later than
the paintings we have found in the Ice Age caves in France and Spain,
and after the large urban communities of Jericho and Châtel Hüyük were
built. Were there no humans around to inhabit them? And if not, who
would have lived in them? Tired aliens resting up after a long flight?

This, of course, has a direct implication for another of the funda-mentalist's obsessions—that of creationism as opposed to evolution of the species we share our world with.

Now, no one would deny that there are considerable difficulties with the theory of evolution. But that is the challenge of science; it progresses in its attempt to methodically solve the difficulties raised by its hypotheses. An honest scientist is a humble person, well aware of what his study does not know but who continues nevertheless to seek answers.

The difficulties with the theory of evolution are many and obvious: where are all the intermediate transitional species, the missing links? Why do some species, like sharks for instance, survive for hundreds of millions of years, while others in the same habitat vanish? Why, for example, has no one found a fossil of a giraffe with a medium-sized neck? And how does one explain perhaps the greatest mystery of all, one that takes us back 530 million years to the Cambrian explosion: at this early time almost every known animal body shape appeared. Life seemed to have chosen its basic forms and stuck with them. The animal kingdom as we know it today is divided into phyla, and it is generally agreed that there are thirty-seven phyla in total, all of which emerged during the Cambrian period. Why should these ancient body forms have proved so stable? No one knows for sure.

If evolution progresses by physical changes allowing for a greater chance of survival in a given habitat, then how do part structures help? How does half an eye, or half a jaw, or half a wing impact things? So far as survival advantages are concerned, it is all or nothing. Darwin himself said that thinking about the evolution of the eye gave him a cold shudder.

But we don't discard the theory of evolution just because of the difficulties understanding it poses; rather, we look at what other mech-anisms might be at work: for example, rather than looking only at the evolution of species, perhaps we should also look at the evolution of ecosystems where feedback from the environment can potentially cause unexpected effects, effects that would not necessarily need to be viewed as advantageous to a single species' immediate survival. And then there is the interesting thought that perhaps the universe is goal directed: if astronomical theory is correct and the sun has moved from an initial huge molten fireball to the solar system we have now, then we can see this as evidence of a progression where inherent potential is unfolded. Could evolution be somewhat similar?

Supporters of creationism believe that the world was created a few thousand years ago and that—for example—the dinosaurs were wiped out by the flood and all of the fossils we find date from this time and are evidence of that disaster. According to the dating given in the Old Testament, this would mean that dinosaurs were roaming the earth in approximately 2000 B.C. And this leaves hanging the question of why Noah didn't fill his ark with them so that they would survive along with all the nice furry animals with big eyes he transported? Perhaps he thought that he, and the furry animals, might end up as lunch? We will need to return to this great question later.

Still others think that dinosaurs probably did survive the flood: creationist leader Tom Willis stated in an interview in 2000 that the large beasts Behemoth and Leviathan mentioned in the biblical book of Job "clearly are dinosaurs."[6]

So if Tom Willis is right and dinosaurs were around in the Middle East in approximately 500 B.C., where are all their skeletons? Why do images of them not appear in the very detailed Assyrian battle and hunting scenes that were carved in relief on stone panels in the royal palaces and which can now be seen in many museums? Apart from the enigmatic long-necked creature carved on several early Egyptian palettes— which might be a representation of the *Mokele-mbembe,* a mysterious Likouala river-and-swamp-dwelling creature, which the inhabitants of the northern Congo jungles claim lives there still—there is no evidence for the existence of such monstrous animals, and certainly nothing to support Willis's argument of dinosaurs roaming through the Persian Empire and coming to the attention of Job.[7] If there had been, we can be certain that we would know about it, given the large number of letters and official documents that have survived from that epoch.

Clearly the Bible cannot be taken literally. It is a collection of myths and hero stories gathered together to serve a religious function—firstly that of Yahweh, the jealous god, and then that of Jesus, the Messiah.

In fact, it is worth seeing just how wrong the Bible is here because those who take its teachings literally are part of the great Christian fundamentalist movement who are also taking another mythological text literally—the book of Revelation—a literal reading that is spilling dangerously over into our politics and foreign policy. While it is a good idea to be suspicious of statistics, polls estimate that 59 percent of Americans believe that the disastrous events depicted in the book of Revelation will come true.[8] That represents more than half the U.S. population. So just how many of these fundamentalist believers are in positions of power or in the armed forces serving in the Middle East? Given the widespread implications of the situation, we must consider the book of Revelation more closely for ourselves. We must also return to our study of the Levantine Corridor to help us establish context.

One of the earliest known towns, Jericho, sits in the Jordan Valley close to where the Jordan River flows into the Dead Sea. It was here that some of the earliest indications of a settled agriculture were discovered. Later, civilizations developed in Egypt, Anatolia, and Mesopotamia as well as farther afield in Persia, Pakistan, India, and China. Roads were developed for trade, aiding the constant movements of people from one country to another. Egypt needed timber from Syria and, importantly, lapis lazuli from Afghanistan;

Mesopotamia needed wood as well. In time, a number of major routes had developed; a great road passed down the coast from northern Syria to Egypt. Another curved across from Harran—the home of Abraham—and passed through the Orontes River Valley before joining the coast road. The coastal route was by far the easiest except for one barrier that needed to be crossed—the hills stretching inland from Haifa had proved to be a choke point.

Driving inland from Haifa, immediately to the north of the Carmel hills, but south of the coastal plain and the Jezreel Valley, one can easily see the great difficulty faced by travelers. The hills are steep and rocky, punctured by narrow wadis that reach deep into them. They are also littered with numerous low but impenetrable cliffs and covered with thick forest broken only by scree slopes. Certainly small groups of agile people, moving carefully and carrying light loads could, given time, make their way across on foot, but horses and wheeled vehicles—the carts of traders or warrior's chariots—would find it impossible; they were restricted to the few passes.

There was one main pass, however, which ran through to the south. Obviously any town that had authority over this pass would gain enormous power from the control of movement along it and would rapidly grow in wealth from the tolls that could be extracted from the travelers and traders reliant upon it. Inevitably such a settlement developed: the large fortified city of Megiddo. Seated upon its high mound at the very edge of the hills, Megiddo overlooked the flat Jezreel Valley stretching out before it and, just a mile south, the entrance to the Musmus pass through Wadi Ara, the most direct and major route through the Mount Carmel range linking the northern and southern coastal routes.

Megiddo also dominated a lesser but still important route, that which moved east through a narrow corridor of flat land to the Jordan River near Bet She'an and then south down the Jordan Valley to the Red Sea.

The mound of Megiddo—in Hebrew *har Megiddo*—was rendered by the author of Revelation as Armageddon. He wrote—as translated in the King James Version of the Bible—that the vast army led by the different "kings of the world" were brought together into one vast host:

> He gathered them together into a place called in the Hebrew tongue Armageddon. And the seventh angel poured out his vial into the air; and there came a great voice out of the temple of heaven, from the throne, saying, It is done.
>
> —REVELATION 16:16–17

If we refer to the original Greek text, we find slight, but important, differences worth noting: the place of assembly is called *Harmagedon*, which is closer to the Hebrew; the angel pours the troubles out of a bowl rather than a vial, which may be making an allusion to the bowls of sacrificial blood poured out by the priests of the temple; the great voice issues not from the temple in general but from the *naos*—which in the New Testament usually refers to the central sanctuary, the Holy of Holies.9 The voice proclaims: "It has occurred." This denotes more of the beginning of an ongoing process rather than "It is done," which, on the contrary, suggests that the event is all over.

But whatever the differences between the original and the translation, there is no escaping the fact that the book of Revelation is predicting a fierce battle on the plains beneath Megiddo, a battle where a great military coalition of the armies of many kings will gather to fight the forces of God. It is hard to avoid the thought that this description echoes a real battle fought almost 2,500 years ago; and almost certainly entangled with it is a memory of the later destruction of a Jewish king, Josiah, at the same site.

The first point to note is that for a first-century messianic Jewish writer to choose the symbol of a great and definitive battle at Megiddo and the Jezreel Valley is not at all unlikely: the area has seen numerous conflicts, some of which would have seared themselves into the cultural memory of the inhabitants of Palestine. Archaeologist Eric Cline has recorded a total of thirty-four such conflicts over the last four thousand years, and six of those were specifically centered upon Megiddo.

The first recorded battle was in 1479 B.C. when Egyptian pharaoh Thutmosis III fought the Canaanites.[10] Thutmosis, "Son of the god Thoth," fought a great army led by many kings, which leads one to ask, has some dim memory of this disaster for the Canaanites been included in the description in Revelation? Surely we should be open to the possibility.

The story of this Egyptian victory is to be found carved in hieroglyphs on the wall of the great Egyptian temple of Amon-Re at Karnak, on the southern edge of the modern city of Luxor. And for the next 350 years the Egyptians controlled the Jezreel Valley and the trade routes down the coast as well as the Jordan Valley with their administrative centers at Megiddo and Bet She'an to the east near the river Jordan.

In the twenty-third year of his reign, 1479 B.C., Thutmosis, seeking to extend Egyptian influence, invaded Palestine with a large army. The chronicle of his campaign states that the king of Kadesh had arrived at Megiddo and had "gathered to him the princes of every foreign country which had been loyal to Egypt" along with others from much further afield.[11]

Thutmosis deceived the Megiddo garrison as to his intentions. He took his army along a narrow and dangerous path through the hills. This path was so dangerous that the Megiddo defenders did not even consider the possibility of his taking it. Consequently they failed to defend themselves properly. So narrow was this pass that when Thutmosis, who had personally led the army, reached the Jezreel Valley with his vanguard, much of his army was still on the other side of the hills waiting for their chance to move across. In all, it took seven hours for the entire army to gather beneath Megiddo.

Viewing this huge and unexpected Egyptian force, the defenders who were outside the city on the flat land, were caught out. Thutmosis, standing in his gilded chariot, charged forward with his troops. The fighting was so close and intense that when the defenders saw that the Egyptians were getting the better of them, they rushed to the walls of Megiddo, where they shed the weight of their armor, reached for garments their comrades on the other side of the wall had let down for them to be used as makeshift ropes, and survived only by being pulled over the wall to safety. The Egyptian army could have taken Megiddo then, but its soldiers were too distracted by the huge amount of plunder that had been abandoned by the defenders and which now lay all about for the taking.

Thutmosis ultimately besieged Megiddo, digging a ditch around it and building a wooden stockade so that none could escape or enter. Megiddo fell shortly thereafter, and the huge booty taken was recorded: 2,041 horses, 924 chariots plus two worked with gold, weapons, cows, goats, and 20,500 sheep, but only 340 living prisoners and the hands of 83 dead.[12] Perhaps the battle was much smaller than the chronicle—which sought to record glory for Thutmosis—suggests.

This battle was no doubt at the heart of local memory, lingering for at least a thousand or more years. But there was one further formative incident in Jewish history regarding Megiddo that has a bearing on its reputation as the center of great upheaval: the death of King Josiah in 609 B.C. The story is related in two places in the Old Testament: 2 Kings 23:29 and 2 Chronicles 18:28–34. The first, probably the more accurate ancient record, simply states that the pharaoh Necho II killed King Josiah at Megiddo, whether by battle or treachery is not specified; the second gives an account of a battle before the walls of Megiddo in which an Egyptian arrow mortally wounded Josiah, who died later in Jerusalem. Because of this latter description's similarity to other stories, experts have little confidence in its veracity.[13]

But John of Patmos, the author of the book of Revelation, would have been familiar with these two descriptions and would have had no reason to doubt that they were accurate history. Certainly it was treated as such by the pro-Roman Jewish historian Josephus, who repeated the story of the arrow in his account of Jewish history.[14] True or false, it did not matter, it was taken and used by John of Patmos as it suited his purpose.

What *is* important is that this story, focused upon Megiddo, became part of the cultural heritage of the worshippers of Yahweh and was included in the Old Testament. What is also important here is the very symbol of Josiah, for he was a reformist king noted for having removed the cult objects of Baal and Asherah and the house of male sacred prostitutes from the Temple that his predecessors had placed there. The Old Testament stresses that, unlike his father and grandfather, he "did what is pleasing to Yahweh" (2 Kings 22:2), though unfortunately this did not save him.

After Josiah's sudden death, his son reverted to the ancient pagan worship as did his brother Jehoiachin who became king in turn. Jehoiachin reigned for only a short time before the Babylonians invaded in 598 B.C., besieged Jerusalem, looted the Temple, and took the king back to Babylon in exile. Much of the ruling class of Judah accompanied him in exile.

Nine years later, Nebuchadnezzar's troops returned to complete the destruction. They besieged Jerusalem, which fell in the early summer of 587 B.C. They burned down the Temple and the royal palace and exiled many more inhabitants to Babylonia; others fled to Egypt. Judah became part of the huge Babylonian Empire. It was a deeply traumatic period, explained as Yahweh's having angrily abandoned his people because of their sinful worship of the Canaanite gods and goddesses. It is not surprising that the death of Josiah, the destruction that befell Jerusalem in the wake of his death, and the sins that caused it would have all been powerful symbols invoked by John in the book of Revelation, a book whose basic theme is the destruction visited upon sinners. Another such powerful symbol is that of the Canaanite Mother Goddess worshipped in the Temple by all the later Jewish kings, except Josiah, who turns up in Revelation as a model for one of the terrible figures of John's vision, "the great whore" (Revelation 17:1).

Megiddo today is a huge but rather sad collection of low stone walls, for the most part complicated by the many different periods of its history now exposed. The most dramatic remains are the great gates of the main entrance, still approximately twelve feet high; but perhaps most interesting for the less casual visitor is the area where the city temples were placed; in all, seventeen levels of temples have been excavated. One early Bronze Age structure is a circular stone altar reached by seven steps, apparently for holocaust offerings, as animal bones were discovered in the vicinity, which remains otherwise enigmatic.

Nearby are remains that seem to be traces of the grandest temple ever found at this early date, around 130 feet long. It is very ancient; strata excavated from the top of its three successive temples would place the primary one to approximately 2500 B.C., in the era of the Great Pyramid. The first temple at Megiddo then must be creeping perilously close in time to the era assigned by Genesis to the creation of Adam and Eve and their expulsion from the garden of Eden.

But what struck me more and more over the several days I spent at Megiddo was its lack of what I might call "spirit"—there is no one word that more fully describes the intense feeling that often rushes over me when I visit sacred sites or sites turned sacred by sacrifice: churches, synagogues, mosques, temples, or battlefields where young men or women gave their lives to the soil. It is hard to articulate: I experience it as a surge up my spine and an instant clearing of my head as though somehow what has passed there has reached out and embraced the whole of the horizon. It is sacred; it is timeless; and it is connected to everything that lies beyond. There are much better ways to explain it, I'm sure, as this depiction seems inadequate; nevertheless, many will immediately recognize the ineffable feeling that I am struggling to express, as it is likely that at some time in all of our lives, we have visited a place that sent a glow or a chill through our hearts.

I have visited—and lingered in—many historical sites in many different countries, and I have become used to feeling a deep spirit at quite a few of them; perhaps not always over the complete site, but often localized in a temple area or in the remains of a chapel or some darkened internal or subterranean chamber. One can sense that the original inhabitants were drawn to the site by something they felt deep within the soil and rock, something they recognized as emerging from the living earth they revered. I have noticed many times that those who feel it seem to automatically take off their shoes and sit quietly, breathing evenly, treading that internal road toward high noon.

But we should not think that only ancient sites bear such spirit: a good modern example is New York's Ground Zero. This is a place that has been turned sacred by a sudden destructive sacrifice. It is fair to say that the whole world shared the horror of New York that morning, stared at their television screens, and knew that they would never forget that moment. The feeling that infuses the ground there is very tangible; it is real. People arrive, become quiet, and walk around and stare into the rubble-filled site as if visiting a sacred place—which, of course, it now is.

On a visit to New York, my wife and I wanted to visit Ground Zero to pay our respects; we felt that it was important. But when I got out of the taxi and walked across the street to the protective mesh fence around the site, the sadness was so intense that I had to fight to stop crying. I could not talk; there was nothing to say. The old church of St. John nearby, in its small tree-filled park, certainly gathered to itself some of that spirit and honored those who died; but the focus lay at Ground Zero. I felt that it was tragic that there were plans to build on it; I could not imagine who would ever be able to work in a building placed on that site.

But at Megiddo, the apparent site of great battles before and the great battle to come—between the divine forces of good and the demonic forces of evil—which ushers in the end of time and the return of Jesus, I felt nothing. That alone was interesting. I think that I looked closely at every stone on the entire site completely lost in the past, thinking of the glories this city had seen, but it was an intellectual appreciation. It seemed to me that it was a dead site, a residual monument to power, to trade, and to money, proof that all greatness passes, that all glory is fleeting and only dimly remembered in legends now twisted and spun to serve a later cause. The inhabitants and proud rulers of Megiddo had their day, and that day passed a long time ago.

I sat on an ancient stone on the edge of the ruins and gazed out over the flat Jezreel Valley below. It was hard to see how the terrible events promised for the battle of Armageddon could fit themselves there. The battle described in the book of Revelation, despite its obvious setting in a world of chariots, swords, and metal armor rather than some technological future, is just far too large and destructive, with too many participants, to be anything other than fantasy.

The battle involves thunder and lightning, a huge earthquake, the fall of cities and a hail storm of huge stones that brings down a plague with it, and birds of prey that swoop down to gorge themselves on the flesh of the dead (Revelation 19:21).

But if this was literally fantastic, what are we to make of the modern version? It comes in a number of variations, but there is general agreement that Russia and its Arab allies move on Israel and the battle soon turns nuclear with its epicenter at Armageddon. And the Muslim writers have picked up the same theme. Bestselling Egyptian apocalyptic writer Muhammad Da'ud, whose works are sold in large numbers throughout the Middle East, explained in 1995 that the Mahdi would be fighting in the battle at Armageddon and would release a number of nuclear bombs in the Jezreel Valley.[15]

How he thinks that Jerusalem—only about sixty miles away—would be inhabitable afterward is a mystery to all, to say nothing of crowded West Bank Muslim communities such as Jenin only ten miles away. Da'ud's nuclear bombs are very selective: they kill only the Jews in Israel; Muslims are not affected. Rice University's Dr. David Cook remarks in bemused amazement at such ignorance,

> And yet we find the Mahdi setting up his capital in Jerusalem and rebuilding the country. Da'ud has enough realism to understand that it would be totally destroyed, but not enough to comprehend that it would be uninhabitable. . . . One should note that God does not apparently interfere . . . except that he causes the nuclear winds to blow the other way so that they do not kill Muslims.[16]

I suppose Da'ud would answer that God can do anything, even produce an atomic bomb with radiation that only kills Jews, and perhaps Christians, yet produces no fallout.

We are back to wondering about the point of the great effort God seems to be making to kill so many people through technology when surely it would be far simpler for him to hurl down a few thunderbolts. Surely such divine projectiles would be much more accurate and less likely to incur "collateral damage."

But how the Sermon on the Mount can be squared with atomic warfare in the Jezreel Valley is something I leave to the fundamentalist theologians. "Blessed are the merciful," said Jesus, "Blessed are the peacemakers" (Matthew 5:7, 9).

Where modern preachers like John Hagee get the idea of Jesus' coming to "trample His enemies until their blood stains His garments" is, at first sight, one of the great mysteries of fundamentalist religion. It has nothing in common with the Christian religion that, one presumes, is derived from the words of Jesus reported in the New Testament.[17]

In fact, the idea derives from Isaiah (63:3) where a figure, whose heart is filled with the desire for vengeance, in fury tramples his enemies until their blood covers his garments. The text of Isaiah makes the identity of this figure quite clear: it is Yahweh, the jealous and ruthless God of Israel to whom the sacrifices in the Temple were made; it is not Jesus at all. The author of a detailed commentary on the book of Revelation, Oxford's Professor George Caird, was aware of this clash and noted that there was an, "embarrassment for the Christian reader in those prayers for vengeance which are found in both Old and New Testaments."[18]

Today buses arrive at Megiddo and disgorge tourists who straggle in a tight group through parts of the ruins before filing obediently back onto their buses and heading off for some other pile of stones where a prophet once stood or Jesus once walked. One thing is certain however: a big attraction for Christians is the battle at the end of time, and so big is this that the Israeli Antiquities Authority is prepared to entertain it—without mentioning the return of Jesus, of course. The small museum joined with the shop and restaurant at the base of the mound has a sign that reads:

> Right here, beside you and around you, man's most important conflict will take place in the last days—the greatest and final war. In the New Testament, St. John predicts that the decisive battle between the forces of good and evil, to end all destruction and persecution, will take place at Megiddo, or in its other name, ARMAGEDDON.

But, of course, there are those who have been promised that they will avoid all the disasters of Armageddon and its aftermath: the true believers who will be "raptured" away and watch from their comfort-able seats in heaven while the disastrous events unfold on earth. John Hagee, writing in 1999, has no doubts:

> Without warning, Jesus Christ . . . will appear in the heav-ens in a burst of dazzling light . . . all over the earth graves will explode as their occupants soar into the heavens. Marble mausoleums will topple as the bodies of resurrected saints rise to meet the Lord in the air. In the next moment, empty cars will careen down the highway, their drivers and occupants absent. Homes of believers will stand empty with supper dishes on the dining table, food bubbling on the stove, and water running in the sink. . . . The next morning, headlines will scream, "MILLIONS ARE MISSING!" The church of Jesus Christ—which includes every born-again believer—will be completely absent from the earth."[19]

And Hagee, not one to miss a snide comment about his pet peeves, adds:

> A few politically-correct pastors, New Age church members, and secular humanist religious leaders will remain, and they will be hard-pressed to explain why they didn't vanish with the true saints of God.[20]

Actually, I think they would be rather relieved that Hagee and his "saints" had all gone.

Still, we do need to take a look at this—if only to be prepared for a time when suddenly the motorways are filled with driverless cars, and the skies with pilotless airplanes that begin dropping out of the sky. The Christian fundamentalists show no sympathy for the terrified passengers. Why should they, I suppose, since along with the "believ-ing" pilots, all other "believers" will have been plucked out of their seats to watch the coming mayhem from the idyllic vantage point of heaven; the rest can die! Certainly they play no further part in Jesus' new fundamentalist thousand-year reich. Not only are the Christian fundamentalists childishly simplistic with their idea of heaven in the clouds, but more dangerously they are completely ruthless. They do not believe in the sanctity of all life; they believe only in the sanctity of some lives—their own. We cannot look to the Christian fundamentalists for compassion, love, or forgiveness. That central message of Jesus has long been discarded in favor of something much darker and much more destructive.

Perhaps the vehicle-licensing authorities, responsible as they are for public safety, should withdraw the licenses of all those who expect to be raptured away? Perhaps airlines should only employ pilots who are atheists, Buddhists, Hindus, Taoists, ancestor worshippers, shamans, or adherents to various South and Central American cults; in particular, perhaps they should recruit politically correct New Age secular humanists since they apparently have the best chance of remaining at the controls when Hagee's Jesus comes.

All in all, it is best that we know what we are dealing with. Let us look now at the book of Revelation itself and see what it has to say about Armageddon and the rapture. A large number of people believe it to be the literal truth about humanity's future. Could they be right? And if so, should we believe it too?

FIVE

John of Patmos

Cultural memory is surprisingly retentive. It carries the imprint of events for hundreds, even thousands, of years, imprints stabbed into the heart of a culture like a great lance hurled by the gods themselves. And, at the same time, such memories serve as proof that the healing takes a long time.

Some memories have become more distorted than others; what they have lost in historical reality, they have gained in religious or political influence as we find today with events still measured against the ever-distant past. For no matter how distant this past may be, we can see that our culture is shaped by a number of core myths that reverberate down through history via the sacred narratives.

Approximately ten thousand years ago, at the end of the last Ice Age, following several millennia of slow temperature rise and the melting of vast ice caps, a critical geographical shift occurred: according to the evidence gleaned from ice-core samples taken in Greenland, there was a rapid and catastrophic collapse of the ice caps. For the next thousand years, at least, the sea levels rose relentlessly, in all, over four hundred feet.

The remains of animals and plants that once lived on dry land have been found lying deep beneath the sea. Fishermen have often dredged up such remains from what were evidently fertile plains and valleys. Off the west coast of Canada and southern Alaska, for example, pine cones have been found buried in peat at a depth of 465 feet, proof that the waters have risen by at least this much. That humans as well as animals roamed these now-flooded lands is revealed by a stone hand tool that was dredged up from 175 feet below the surface.

Off the east coast of the United States similar evidence is much more widespread. What is now the continental shelf was once a vast forested territory teeming with wildlife. Fishermen dragging the ocean floor for scallops have brought up the teeth of mammoths and mastodons from as far as 190 miles from the present coastline and at depths of up to four hundred feet. Remains of horses, tapirs, musk ox, and giant moose have been discovered too. That there is nothing geographically unique about these finds is shown by similar finds across on the other side of the Pacific where mastodon teeth have been found three hundred feet below the surface of Japan's inland sea.[1] Europe's North Sea, too, once part of a great plain embracing Ireland, England, and mainland Europe, also has given up animal and human remains from its depths. Archaeologists have learned to dive and excavate underwater after finding the remains of sunken settlements.

For low-lying areas such as exist in the Middle East, this rise in sea levels must have been seen as a very real disaster for the increasingly sophisticated human settlements there as the rushing waters swallowed mile after mile of land every day for generation after generation. It is no wonder that the region maintained the memory of a great flood that covered the world. We can be sure that the cultural scars from these great floods ran very deep indeed. It should come as no surprise really that this theme finds an echo throughout early myths across many different cultures.

Writing developed at least as early as the fourth millennium B.C.; we have found the first stories discovered in Mesopotamia dated around 2600 B.C., written texts that almost certainly first existed in the

oral tradition. One of these early stories, which we have from clay tablets dated to the early second millennium B.C., is the epic adventures
of Gilgamesh, a king of Uruk, a Babylonian hero figure who set out
into the underworld to find the secret of immortal life. On his journey he meets a wise survivor of the great flood, which had been sent
by the gods, a survivor who was able to pass on this antediluvian wisdom to Gilgamesh.

We can see by the many parallels that this chronicle of a destructive worldwide flood became transmuted into our own Old Testament
story of Noah and his Ark. But with the latter, the flood has been given
a moral purpose; instead of being a result of the melting of the ice caps,
it is the result of God's—Yahweh's—disgust at the corruption, wicked-
ness, and violence of humans, particularly in their cities; it is the result
of his decision to wipe the earth clean of humanity with the exception
of Noah, his wife, his sons, and his son's wives, whom he allowed to
ride out and ultimately survive the flood in a great ship.

A more recent example of cultural memory can be found in the
stories of King Arthur. It is generally agreed that the heart of the story
concerns a late Romano-British military commander fighting to stave
off foreign invaders following the withdrawal of the Roman legions
from Britain, which began in A.D. 407. The English monk Bede com-
piled a chronicle of events in England from the Roman invasion to his
time, the late seventh and early eight centuries A.D. He recorded that
after twice seeking help from Roman legions, the Britons emerged
from their collective trauma at the rapid disintegration of their society, and a leader called Ambrosius Aurelianus, said to be of Roman
ancestry and noble connections, commanded the Britons in a victory against the invaders in A.D. 493.[2] His chief captain led the British
forces to their last great victory at the battle of Badon Hill. Writing a
little later than Bede, another monk, Nennius, identified this victorious military leader as Arthur.[3]

Whatever the truth, and these old chroniclers were much closer to it than we are, the story of Arthur was later placed into a magical and mystical context by combining elements of Celtic and Christian belief with codes of medieval chivalry, creating what were subsequently known as the legends of the Holy Grail.

A more specific example can be seen in the annual festival of Iraqi Shiites that maintains the memory of the battle of Karbala, a battle fought in A.D. 680 in which the last of the descendants of Mohammed, his grandson Husayn, was slaughtered by the army of the Umayyad caliph from Damascus, a formative event in the history of Shiite Islam. This battle is still being invoked to inspire opposition to what the Shiites regard as illegitimate authority: it was used against the Shah of Iran, the Israelis in Lebanon, and the death squads of Saddam Hussein.[4] The death of Husayn is recalled by the great Shiite period of mourning and collective atonement, the *Ashoura*, a religious festival banned by Saddam Hussein and not reinstated until after his fall in the Second Gulf War of 2003. But the holding of this festival is anathema to Sunni Muslims who are deeply indignant at its occurrence and who, to this day, barely recognize Shiites as true Muslims at all.

In February 2005 a suicide bomber, a Sunni Muslim from Jordan, blew himself up amongst a large group of Shiite recruits for the Iraqi security service: 125 Shiite Muslims were killed and 150 more were wounded. Yet in his hometown back in Jordan this bomber was celebrated as a martyr, an indication that for him, his family, and supporters, the Shiites he killed were infidels whose destruction was fully authorized.[5]

In the Kingdom of Saudi Arabia, a bastion of puritanical Wahhabi Sunni Islam, Shiites are subjected to considerable prejudice. The leading religious figure in Saudi Arabia, Abdul-Aziz ibn Baz, has issued a number of rulings, each a *fatwa*, that proclaim all Shiite Muslims to be apostates to Islam. Incredibly, in the face of calls for Muslim unity, a member of the Higher Council of the Ulama—the religious scholars—

in Saudi Arabia, went further, issuing a fatwa that allowed Shiites to be killed, an injunction repeated until as late as 2002. In Saudi Arabian schools, children's text-books were not only anti-Semitic but equally anti-Shiite—this faith was a heresy, the texts explained, one that was worse than Christianity or Judaism.[6]

We can see that the events of a war almost 1500 years ago are still directly and dangerously affecting politics in the Middle East today. The much discussed issue of the Palestinians, while a tragedy for moderates in both Gaza and West Bank as well as those Israelis who also want nothing but peace, is but a distraction from the real battle, which is over the Shiite-Sunni divisions, a battle that is becoming more and more obvious as each side struggles to gain advantage in the Middle East. Professor of Middle East politics Vali Nasr explains: "The Shia-Sunni conflict is at once a struggle for the soul of Islam—a great war of competing theologies and conceptions of sacred history."[7]

He is well aware of the direct modern relevance of this ancient event: "It is not just a hoary religious dispute, a fossilized set piece from the early years of Islam's unfolding, but a contemporary clash of identities."[8]

Ultimately, he explains, the final form of the Middle East will not be decided by some version of "Arab Identity" or by one or another type of national government, whether democratic, royal, dictatorship, or some other. It will be defined in the "crucible of Shia revival and the Sunni response to it."[9]

Left to itself, the Middle East—indeed Islam in general, pushed as it is by extremists from both camps—will implode along its own deep fault line until some resolution emerges that will have nothing to do with Western-style political or financial structures. Islam has its own Armageddon to face, one quite separate from anything the Christian fundamentalists might cook up.

But the battle at the end of time has not been forgotten: according to Islamic apocalyptic writers, the Messiah—the Mahdi—will be returning along with Jesus to take over Jerusalem, which will become the messianic capital. This will involve a huge battle between the forces of good and evil—the forces of Islam against the forces of the West—the battle of Armageddon. All Jews will be killed, and all the technology of Europe and the United States will be given to the Muslims.[10] The worldwide caliphate will be established—including all of Europe, which has converted to Islam—during the course of which the Catholic Church will be completely annihilated.[11] The coming of the Mahdi is the beginning of the Muslim domination of the world.

Dr. David Cook points out that there is, amongst Muslim supporters of the apocalyptic predictions, a deep hatred of the Western countries coupled with an envy of their great power. He comments,

> Although many Arabic-language Muslim apocalyptic writers may hate the West and envy its power, there is no question they are impressed with the success of modern technological societies. [Apocalyptic authors] seek to explain to their audiences how exactly this awesome power is either going to be nullified in the immediate future or is going to be transferred in its entirety to Muslims.[12]

Many Muslims cannot understand why Islam seems to have little importance in the wider world: if Allah is the one true God, and if Muslims are faithful to him, why is it that Islam does not rule over the world? President Mahmoud Ahmadinejad of Iran, a Shiite, who is struggling to develop the nuclear components that could create a nuclear bomb and who wishes for the complete annihilation of Israel, is waiting for the Mahdi. Like many Christian fundamentalists, he seems to hold that the chaotic and widely destructive end time is coming soon, but for him there is a very different outcome: for Ahmadinejad, it will finally confirm and establish Muslim dominance. But his dream ignores the social pressures caused by hard-line religious rule, especially in Iran itself. Ahmadinejad was re-elected president in June 2009 by what can only be described as a severely manipulated vote. Almost immediately the streets of Tehran—and, it appears, several other large cities—were filled with opponents to his aggressive rule; their anger was greater than their fear of violence. This provided dramatic proof of a deep and probably irreconcilable split in Iranian society, one which can only intensify. Such a split potentially lies at the heart of every society where an inflexible and repressive religion rules over the politics.

It has been reported that a widespread belief in Iran claims that Ahmadinejad and the other members of his cabinet have sworn to "work for the return of the Mahdi" whom he believes to be the hidden Twelfth Imam.[13] This hidden Imam was the last of a line, succeeding his father in the late ninth century when he was only five years old. He disappeared in A.D. 874, and Shiites believe that his return will be the precursor to the end time.

There was an influential messianic society in Iran dedicated to the Twelfth Imam, the *Hojjatieh*, and Mahmoud Ahmadinejad was prominent within it. Shortly after he became president of Iran in June 2005, he proclaimed that the true ruler of Iran was the hidden Imam and that the aim of his government should be to speed up the Imam's return.[14]

In his speech to the United Nations in September 2005, Ahmadinejad concluded by appealing to God for the rapid appearance of "the Promised One," meaning, of course, the Mahdi. Delegates were astonished. Ahmadinejad felt that he had captivated his audience with a divine presence, which he felt over him. Delegates reported, however, that their open-mouthed amazement was because "they couldn't believe what they were hearing from Ahmadinejad."

The diplomatic editor of the English newspaper the *Daily Telegraph* explained what the delegates actually were thinking: "Their sneaking suspicion is that Iran's president actually relishes a clash with the West

in the conviction that it would rekindle the spirit of the Islamic revolution and—who knows—speed up the arrival of the Hidden Imam."[15]

We have every reason to worry about presidents and prime ministers who have the messianic gleam in their eyes, for their gods normally demand constant sacrifice.

We cannot dismiss either cultural memory or its power to shape
the present as well as the future. It is evident that if we can find in this
mythology elements that parallel recorded historical events, we will
understand better the beliefs that inform the narrative. And through
understanding, we can seek some way to defuse the bitterness and
anger that keeps these ancient wounds bleeding.

Having seen the length of time through which real historical
events, however distorted by myth, can survive, it is entirely plausible
that the Egyptian pharaoh Thutmosis's battle against the coalition of
kings, leaders of city-states, at Megiddo in 1479 B.C. should turn up
1500 years later in the book of Revelation as a contributing factor to
the gathering of forces and the battle of Armageddon. It is a time span
no longer than the memory of the battle of Karbala has been maintained by the Shiites.

Like all good stories, Revelation is drawing not only from cultural memory but also from the writer's own experiences and creative
imagination in order to provide images to illustrate and emphasize the
points he is trying to make. And the point that the author is trying to
make concerns the terrible and inevitable punishment for sin and the
urgent need for repentance if these horrors are to be avoided.

The book of Revelation was written by a Christian, John "the
Divine," who was not the apostle of the fourth gospel but, as all indications suggest, a convert from Judaism, though further details of his
life remain mysterious. As we shall see, John had a good grasp of
Hebrew culture and language, far better than his grasp of Greek culture and language. It has been argued that his writing comes from a

man writing in Greek but thinking in Hebrew.[16] He clearly expected his audience to possess as strong a knowledge of the Hebrew language and Jewish history as he possessed, since many of his symbols are drawn from the Old Testament. He explains at the beginning of his book that he had a divinely inspired vision of things "which must shortly come to pass" (1:1) For John, it is a matter of some urgency, since he quickly adds, "for the time is at hand" (1:3).

He explains that he was in exile on the island of Patmos because of opposition to his Christian beliefs. There is no reason to doubt his assertion: the Romans used islands such as Patmos as places of banishment for those who had offended the emperor or transgressed the laws of the Empire.[17]

One "Lord's Day"—a Saturday at that date—John had a vision. He was, he said, "in the Spirit" (1:10). He heard a great voice behind him, like a blast from a trumpet: the voice demanded that he write down all that he saw and send this account to the seven churches in "Asia" (1:4)—the Roman province that covered much of modern southwestern Turkey ruled from its capital, Pergamum.

Asia included the city of Ephesus, the site of the huge Temple of Artemis, one of the seven wonders of the ancient world. Ephesus was not only one of the largest cities in the Empire and the most important seaport in the region; it was also one of the cities in Asia Minor to which Paul traveled while preaching the gospel around A.D. 54 or 55.

Paul spent, in all, three years in Ephesus, and by the time of John the Divine, the most important Christian church stood there. As each new governor—always a proconsul—entered the province of Asia, he was required to do so through the port of Ephesus; it was, for that reason, quite literally the gateway to Asia for the Romans. All in all, it is not so surprising that John chose to send his first letter there.

He was writing to these churches of Asia with a message from God, from the "seven spirits which are before his throne" and from

Jesus, "the faithful witness . . . and the prince of the kings of the earth"
(1:4–5).

That John was expecting the events he saw in his vision to occur
during the latter part of the first century A.D. is proved by his comment
that when Jesus returns from the heavens, riding upon the clouds, he
will be visible to everyone, including, significantly, those who helped
crucify him! (1:7). We can see that any participant in the crucifixion—
which most likely occurred in A.D. 36—could not possibly still be living
much beyond the first century A.D.[18]

We do not know exactly when Revelation was written. The pro-
Roman theologian Irenaeus, bishop of Lyons around the end of the
second century A.D., knew of the work and recorded that it was written "towards the end of Domitian's reign," which began in A.D. 81 and
ended with his murder in A.D. 96.[19] In his Revelation, John revealed
himself to be bitterly opposed to the Roman Empire and clearly would
rejoice at any destructive reverse of Rome's seemingly limitless power
on earth.

However, John never specifically identified the great Empire
whose end he predicted; neither did he name its great city, which he
called Babylon—a coded reference indicating perhaps that such accu-
sations were life threatening.

It was also a safe argument at the time because Mesopotamia, the
land centered on the twin rivers Tigris and Euphrates, where Babylon
was situated, was under the control of the Parthians who were no
friends of the Romans and whose armies could consistently defeat the
Roman legions.

Rome had feared the Parthians ever since the traumatic and decisive defeat of the Roman general Crassus with his seven legions at the
battle of Carrhae (previously called Harran, the town where Abraham
lived for a time) in 53 B.C. A decisive role was played by the huge corps
of mounted archers for which the Parthians were famous; the Romans

feared them from that time onward, and we will see that this fear found its way into the book of Revelation.

Furthermore, in a humiliating event during A.D. 62, which must have reverberated throughout the Roman Empire—and perhaps gave encouragement to those who sought to defeat the Romans, such as the Jewish rebels in Judaea who exploded in revolt four years later—another Roman army was defeated by the Parthians on the banks of the river Euphrates. But what made this even worse was that this army lost its nerve, succumbed to fear, and simply surrendered; they were then allowed to leave under shameful conditions. The commander, General Paetus, fled, abandoning his wounded, even though reinforcements were but three days away. The historian Tacitus commented that he succumbed to "a panic-stricken flight as disgraceful as running away in battle."[20]

Parthia was not taken under Roman control until A.D. 117 by the emperor Trajan. So on the face of it, around A.D. 95, we can say that John's enemy was also Rome's enemy; John could get away with his apocalyptic vision without being arrested for subversion. In any case, being a Christian brought trouble enough, and we cannot really blame John for wanting to disguise the object of his attack somewhat. Although, it is fair to say, he did not disguise it very well!

But John was not referring to the past; he was referring to his own times, since he was expecting the events of Revelation to occur shortly. But neither was he referring to the Parthians when he denounced Babylon. To help his readers glean the true object of his anger and derision, he gave a clue later in the text: he described Babylon as a woman, the "Mother of Harlots" drunk with the blood of Christian martyrs—which is certainly not relevant to Parthia since it was unlikely that any Christians were there (17:5). And specifically flagging this image as an important clue, he explained that the Mother of Harlots was sitting upon seven mountains (17:9). The identification could not be clearer: by Babylon, John meant Rome and, by extension, the Roman Empire. For hundreds of years Rome had been known as *urbs septicollis*, the city of the seven hills; each year in December a great festival was held to celebrate this, the "Feast of the Seven Hills."[21]

Furthermore, in Christian circles Rome was spoken of as Babylon. We need only look at the first letter of Peter: "The church that is at Babylon. . . ," meaning Rome (1 Peter 5:13).

John wrote after the persecutions of Christians in Rome under Nero in A.D. 64, after the destruction of Jerusalem and the Temple in A.D. 70, after the fall of Masada in A.D. 74 and the end of resistance in Palestine, and at the end of a period of violent persecution not only of Christians and Jews but also Romans by the emperor Domitian—whose cruelty was ended in A.D. 96 when he was stabbed to death by four assassins in his bedroom, to the delight of the Roman Senate. John certainly would have no reason to love the Romans. But who could oppose their power?

Rome seemed invulnerable and impregnable. Nothing could upset its control over the known world. In fact, the Roman Empire was reaching its peak around this time, its armies were highly motivated, its leadership was militarily competent, and its wealth was growing by the day. It seemed that nothing could possibly bring about its downfall. And yet John was predicting its destruction. How might this occur? There was only one way: by divine intervention. Even the strongest legions of Rome could not fight and win against the gods. And John would have known of a dramatic example, when, just a few years earlier, it seemed that divine intervention brought total destruction upon a Roman city.

In A.D. 79, following violent earthquakes, Mount Vesuvius near Naples exploded and destroyed the large coastal city of Pompeii so rapidly that many were killed in the act of fleeing. Flowing lava and falling rocks and ash covered Pompeii so completely that the city was lost for the next 1700 years. During the eruption volcanic debris crashed into the sea, which was rendered almost impassable by thick floating pumice. For the Romans, the gods had punished Pompeii and in a few hours wiped it from the face of the earth.

Can we see a memory of such a destruction of a city which, to John of Patmos's mind, would have represented all the corruption and license he was opposing? John tells us "a great mountain burning with fire was cast into the sea" (Revelation 8:8), which is a good description of the red-hot lava flow and the superheated debris blown out of the mountain to fall in the sea. He described the fish dying, ships being destroyed, and the sea turning red like blood. It was all very quick, John records, "in one hour is she made desolate" (18:19).

He later returned to the same image, reporting that in his vision he saw that, "a mighty angel took up a stone like a great millstone, and cast it into the sea, saying, Thus with violence shall that great city Babylon be thrown down, and shall be found no more at all" (18:21).

The rocks hurled into the sea and the total disappearance of the city again recall an eyewitness account of the destruction of Pompeii. Roman writer Pliny "the Younger" witnessed the eruption and destruction from across the Bay of Naples; his uncle, Pliny "the Elder," was to die suddenly on the beach at Pompeii, choked by the dense fumes. Pliny "the Elder" was in command of the Roman fleet based in the bay, and he sailed it across to Pompeii to rescue the inhabitants of that increasingly dangerous city. His nephew reported that as the ships approached the beach,

> Ashes were already falling, hotter and thicker as the ships drew near, followed by bits of pumice and blackened stones, charred and cracked by the flames; then suddenly they were in shallow water, and the shore was blocked by the debris from the mountain.[22]

Could John have witnessed these events himself? Or might he have heard about them from sailors who were there? There are certainly elements that seem to best indicate sailors' talk.

> Every shipmaster, and all the company in ships, and sailors, and as many as trade by sea, stood afar off, and cried when they saw the smoke of her burning, saying, "What city is like unto this great city!" And . . . they cried, weeping and wailing.
>
> —REVELATION 18:17–19

It seems reasonable to conclude that John was drawing from the experience of Pompeii to illustrate what he hoped would be the fate of Rome itself. And all of this was expected to occur in the lifetime of those who were active participants in the crucifixion.

Unfortunately, by the end of the first century A.D. the predictions of Revelation had failed. Rome still existed and was stronger than ever.

But the point is that the book of Revelation was not revealing the future. On the contrary, it was revealing, in a highly ornate and symbolic manner, John's hopes for the future, a desperate longing that whatever it was that caused the destruction of Pompeii would also destroy Rome. And that cause, John thought, was divine anger. A lot of pagan Romans thought the same way.

Needless to say, this has nothing whatsoever to do with events in the Middle East in our time, two thousand years later—whatever the Islamic and Christian fundamentalists might say—however hard they may protest against the thought that any part of the book of Revelation might be symbolic.

Authors of lurid books on the battle of Armageddon such as Hal Lindsey simply take it as a given that the descriptions in Revelation are to be taken literally. "The Bible," wrote Lindsey, "contains clear and unmistakable prophetic signs. We are able to see right now in this Best Seller predictions made centuries ago being fulfilled before our eyes."[23]

Tim LaHaye and Jerry Jenkins at least address the issue. "In recent years," they write, "a number of teachers have concluded that prophecy should usually be interpreted symbolically."[24] This is, naturally, an erroneous teaching to them. Their position is clear: when reading the Bible, "take every word at its primary, literal meaning unless the facts of the immediate context clearly indicate otherwise."[25] Perhaps this is a good approach, since the "facts of the immediate context" of the book of Revelation demand that we should read it symbolically.

John Hagee takes, as one would expect, a more aggressive approach to his dismissal of any talk of symbolism. He explains that the biblical prophets "were not creating allegories or fables" and that John, scribbling away on Patmos, was not trying to tactfully disguise the object of his ire, "nor was he being metaphorical when he described Armageddon with great and vivid detail." Vivid details are clearly a mark of truth to this preacher.

"No, my friend," insists Hagee forcefully, allowing no room for any alternative view, "Armageddon is an actual battle."[26]

John of Patmos wished the Roman Empire to be utterly destroyed, but why? Why would he wish what happened at Pompeii be visited upon Rome and its whole empire?

To answer this, we need to look not to the future but to the past; for the previous century Rome had persecuted and destroyed the Jews, and latterly, the Gentile converts to messianic Judaism, the Christians. The troubles had begun in A.D. 6 with the rise of the violently messianic Zealot movement and gradually increased until widespread revolt and war broke out in A.D. 66. This was ruthlessly suppressed, ending in A.D. 74 with the fall of Masada; Jewish prisoners were thrown to the wild animals in public arenas from Judaea to Rome.

John was not to know—and it would have horrified him to know—how comprehensively wrong his vision would prove to be. In fact, not only did Rome not fall, but it and its empire had further horrors to visit upon the Jews and the Christians. In A.D. 115 the Jewish community in Alexandria, for centuries a strong, influential, and wealthy community, rose in revolt under a messianic leader known only as Lucuas. It was put down after two years; the entire Jewish community in Egypt was destroyed and never again held any significance. Then in early A.D. 132 a second revolt erupted in Judaea and Galilee under the highly competent leadership of another messianic contender, Simon bar Kochba—"Son of the Star." This revolt was initially successful, and the Romans were driven out of Israel for three years, leaving behind shattered or annihilated legions. During these three years the Temple was rebuilt or renovated sufficiently for sacrifices to be reinstated.

But ultimately the revolt failed. The Parthians, who were expected to invade Roman territory and draw north those legions that might be used to attack Judaea, neglected to lend the support they had been counted on to provide. Despite the large and influential Jewish community in Persia, the attack they expected to lead never occurred, and the Jewish revolt collapsed under the weight of the armor the Romans unleashed upon Judaea in A.D. 135. It was the end. Judaism settled upon another path, which had no links with the land or the Temple in Jerusalem.

And it was around this same time that the impossibly self-righteous Justin Martyr was arguing the superiority of Christianity and a divine Jesus with a Jewish philosopher, Trypho. Justin was teaching in Ephesus, one of the seven churches that had received John's description of his revelation. Justin certainly had read it, for he makes reference to John's vision in his own writings: "There was a certain man with us," Justin explained, "whose name was John . . . who prophesied, by a revelation that was made to him, that those who believed in our Christ would dwell a thousand years in Jerusalem; and that thereafter the general . . . resurrection and judgement of all men would likewise take place."[27]

Justin's words seem to hint that John was released from his exile and moved to Ephesus, where he played an important part in the life of the church there.

We should note that in this rather sanitized summary, Justin has stayed well away from criticism of the Romans. In any case, he preferred to save his abuse for the Jews who, in his opinion, were responsible for killing Christ. Indeed, it is curious—and an insight into his thinking—that, after all the troubles of the preceding 120 years or so, he blamed the Jews. By doing so, he reveals that the strand of messianic Judaism that later became Christianity and maintained a belief in a divine Jesus was essentially anti-Semitic and pro-Roman. Perhaps this is not so surprising given its Gentile roots. Indeed, it is perhaps also not so surprising that Justin moved from Ephesus to Rome, where he continued teaching. We should remember that it was the version of Christianity supported by Justin that approximately two hundred years later became the official Christian faith of the church of Rome and has remained so since that time. One wonders what Justin thought about John's predictions of the destruction of Rome; then again, Justin at least knew that they had failed.

The Romans were tolerant of alternative beliefs so long as those beliefs were tolerant of the Romans'. But the God of Israel, Yahweh, by his own admission, was a jealous god and would not recognize or share space with any others. And Justin, in his arguments with Trypho, made an assertion that must have been extremely insulting for Trypho: Justin made it very clear that the Christians were now the "true Israelitic race."[28] In many ways this is curious, for by asserting this, Justin was taking upon himself and his supporters all the historical enmity that Rome, with its many gods, had long maintained against Judaism, which recognized only one God. The Romans saw Judaism as a heresy and, due to its opposition toward sacrificing to the divine emperor, grossly disrespectful. Justin was to pay for this.

It is curious that Justin should be writing this just after the violent end of the Bar Kochba revolt. But perhaps it is not too strange; Justin's dispute reads like a piece of opportunistic propaganda aimed at establishing a gulf between the Christians and the Jews. The reason is not difficult to find. When Justin was resident in Rome, he wrote his first *Apology*; this was dedicated to Emperor Antoninus Pius. Evidently Justin wanted imperial acceptance for himself and Christianity.

But he failed; for the Romans, one God was never going to beat many gods, thus Justin was judged as subversive. Justin was beheaded around A.D. 165, along with some of his colleagues, for refusing to sacrifice in the Roman manner, that is, to the gods.

For John the Divine, exiled on Patmos, sacrificing in the "Roman manner" was idolatry and one of the great sins for which humanity was to be punished by terrible plagues, famines, wars, earthquakes, and, ultimately, by the great battle of Armageddon. John was living in a world of constant divine intervention where earthquakes, erupting volcanoes, and wild storms were a result of the anger of the gods—or God. There was no need to seek anywhere else for an explanation.

It is now time to see just what John wrote as he sat in exile on Patmos, consumed by bitterness and a strong desire for revenge against those who had wronged him, and his God—whose divine messenger was Jesus. John began his book by stating,

> *This is the revelation given by God to Jesus Christ so that he could tell his servants about the things which are now to take place very soon.*
>
> —REVELATION 1:1

Let's take a look at it.

REVELATION

For a writer who is said to have been poorly educated in Greek, the tongue in which he wrote, John performs his literary task with considerable dramatic skill; he wastes no time seizing our full attention with an impressive preamble:

"This is the revelation given by God to Jesus Christ" (Revelation 1:1).

The revelation he was reporting, John explained, was then passed directly to him from Jesus one Saturday during his period of exile on Patmos. We must be clear: John was claiming access to some very high-level connections; they were warning him of "things which are now to take place very soon" (1:1). Furthermore, there was great urgency about the message, a demand that its meaning be taken to heart without further delay, because, John informed his readers, "the Time is close" (1:1–3).

There is a curiosity here: we have to remember that John was writing over two hundred years before the Council of Nicaea, where, in a famous vote, Jesus and God were made the same. John, we find, had a rather different approach. For him, Jesus was a kind of messenger of God, rather like the Roman Hermes or the Egyptian Thoth, both of whom were bearers of revelations from the gods to men and women who had prepared themselves to receive them. Often these gods would bring their messages at night, in dreams. They were taken very seriously just as John took his own revelation.

That John's revelation was not entirely free from his own background is easily seen, for its symbolism, as stated earlier, draws heavily upon the Hebrew scriptures and its expressed hatred of John's enemy, Rome; in this manner it reveals more about John than it does about God—or Jesus. It also reveals that, despite his clumsiness with Greek, John was by no means uneducated. In fact, he has an impressive knowledge of the Old Testament prophetic tradition and, we can say, events of the Roman Empire over the preceding century. He was not unaware of events in the world he inhabited.

That Saturday on his Greek island when the spirit took him over, the first thing John experienced was a sudden blast of sound from behind him, a voice "like a trumpet," he wrote. This voice commanded him to record all he was about to see, "and send it to the seven churches of Ephesus, Smyrna, Pergamum, Thyatira, Sardis, Philadelphia and Laodicea" (1:10–11). John followed these instructions exactly; in his letters he informed his brethren in those churches that he had been shown his vision by Jesus himself, who had received it directly from God. At the very least, John wanted his brethren to know that he had powerful friends.

Upon hearing the commanding words booming behind him, John turned. He saw Jesus surrounded by seven gold lamp-stands or candlesticks and holding seven stars in his right hand; from his mouth stretched a sword, its blade sharp and double-edged.

John recorded that he fainted in fear.

But Jesus revived him; reaching down, he reassuringly touched John with his right hand, telling him not to be afraid while describing himself as the "First and the Last", the "Living One" who was once dead and now is living forever; "I hold the keys of death and of the underworld," he explained, again revealing the parallels with the Greek Hermes or the Egyptian Thoth, both of whom guide the dead to the underworld—or, more correctly, the "Netherworld."[1] He then commanded that John should write "all that you see of present happenings and things that are still to come!" (1:17–19).

Jesus then revealed that what John had witnessed was symbolic: the seven stars were the angels of the seven churches in Asia, and the seven candlesticks were the seven churches themselves (1:20).

This, of course, indicates that John did not expect his audience to take his revelation literally. John wanted his audience to seek behind the symbols for the meaning hidden there.

Here, at the very beginning, one particular type of symbol dominates, the symbolism associated with the number seven. In fact this permeates the entire text of Revelation. In many languages written letters also represented numbers; this meant that any particular word or phrase could also be depicted numerically. This was the science of *gematria*, and there was a strong tradition of its use in Judaism, especially in Kabbalah.

The immediate source of John's first vision of the seven candlesticks is from the Old Testament prophet Zechariah who had a vision himself. Zechariah saw a gold lamp-stand with seven lamps on it (Zechariah 4:2). This is clearly related to the great gold candlestick—the menorah—in the Temple in Jerusalem, which had seven branches. This image is depicted on the triumphal Arch of Titus, which dominates the short road leading from the Colosseum to the Forum in Rome and shows the treasures taken from the Temple in Jerusalem. It is known that these seven branches on the menorah represented the planets: the Jewish philosopher, Philo of Alexandria (*ca.* 20 B.C.–*ca.* A.D. 50) wrote that the, "seven candles and seven lights being symbols of those seven stars which are called planets . . . the sun, like the candlestick, being placed in the middle of the other six."[2]

Philo further explained in the same text that this candlestick was a symbol of heaven, while the altar of incense where offerings were made symbolized the things of the earth.

Significantly, given the importance of the number seven for John, it was also the most important number for both the ancient Egyptians and the Mesopotamians. The Egyptians linked the number seven with perfection, and it was said that the god Re had seven souls—*bas*—and certain gods and goddesses had seven forms. Seven is also often associated with Osiris, the Lord of the *Duat*, the "Far World," which was the parallel but invisible world to our own, inhabited by the gods, goddesses, and the dead—in other words, the "underworld" over which John's Jesus claimed dominion. The number seven, undoubtedly due to its association with the powerful divine world, was also a very significant number in Egyptian magic.[3]

Seven was also a powerful number in Assyrian and Babylonian magic: spells had to be said seven times, rituals conducted seven times, seven demons expelled, and seven gods called upon by the magician; seven seals were placed as a protective necklace about the neck of the person who had requested the help of the magician.[4] There were, too, seven gates to the underworld; when Inana—Ishtar to the Assyrians—descended to that kingdom, she had to give up one of her seven veils at each gate.

In Judaism, as well, the number seven was primal: together with the day of rest, it represented the seven days of creation, which made the number seven a symbol of the underlying harmony of all creation. It is the number of days in the week, the seventh being the Sabbath, and, in accordance with the discoveries of Babylonian and Assyrian astrology and astronomy (the two were not separate), it was the number of the celestial guardians—Sun, Moon, and Mercury, Venus, Mars, Jupiter, and Saturn—all of which could be seen by the eye and all of which seemed to move independently against the background of the fixed stars. The number seven underpinned all creation; accordingly, John made it underpin all the events of his revelation. But for him, above all, the number seven was the symbol of completeness, his events all end with the seventh occurrence.[5]

In addition, Judaism had a pattern of special years: every forty-nine years—that is 7 x 7—there occurred what was termed a Jubilee Year. "The Book of Jubilees," an apocalyptic Jewish work from the second century B.C., which was discovered in Ethiopia and parts of which have been found amongst the Dead Sea Scroll fragments in Cave 4 at Qumran, claims to be a record of secret knowledge given to Moses on Mount Sinai. It is dominated by the symbolic use of "seven": Adam, it explains, was seven years in the garden of Eden; the flood was caused by the opening of the seven "flood-gates of heaven" and seven great openings in the sea, and the water had completely disappeared after seven years; God appeared to Moses on the seventh day on top of Mount Sinai.[6]

With one of the greatest Jewish apocalyptic works dominated by the number seven, we should not be surprised to find that the greatest Christian apocalyptic work is similarly dominated. John wrote his seven letters to the seven churches. The preambles were not identical, but they all had the same general thrust: as he said to the members of the church at Ephesus, "Repent, . . . or I shall come to you and take your lamp-stand" (2:5).

On the face of it, this does not seem like much of a threat; in fact it seems downright pathetic. But what John was actually meaning was, "Repent, or I shall take away your church." It seems that all of the churches had members of the congregation who were not true believers or who had fallen away from whatever John held to be true belief, and John was threatening these sinners with a direct attack by Jesus unless they changed their ways completely and immediately.

And this was the meaning behind the symbol of the sharp sword issuing from Jesus' mouth—it represented the power of the Word of God. It was a symbol obvious to John's ex-Jewish audience who would know their Old Testament: Isaiah described the birth of the "servant of Yahweh," the savior of Israel, whose mouth was a sharp sword (Isaiah 49:2). Former Oxford professor of Holy Scripture Dr. George Caird explains, "This is a symbol of the prophet, whose utterance has a cutting edge to it."[7]

So, John's strategy is clear: his Revelation is a manual for frightening sinners back to the fold. It probably worked; it certainly works now since hundreds of preachers—perhaps thousands—have made lucrative careers out of it by engendering a fear of the future in millions of people. But their confident preaching doesn't prove them right of course.

At this point in the narrative John led straight into a series of fearsome images: a door opened in the heavens, and he was taken through in order, the booming voice informed him, to see "what is to come in the future" (4:1). He then saw God on his throne, surrounded by twenty-four other thrones, each with an elder sitting on it. Lightning and thunder came from the throne, and in front of it were seven great lamps burning and the seven angels. Around the throne itself were four animals: the first like a lion, the second like a bull, the third with a human face, and the last like an eagle. Each of these monsters had six wings and eyes all around its head. They constantly sang hymns to God (4:1–8).

We have here another image that Jews would recognize since it, too, derives from the Old Testament, from visions reported by Ezekiel and Isaiah; John clearly saw himself as following in the same tradition—he saw himself as a prophet—but now to the Christian community, not the Jewish.

Ezekiel reported being touched by the hand of God and then having a vision of God on his throne out of which shone fire and light. Below were four animals, each with four wings and four faces: each animal had the face of a human, a lion, a bull, and an eagle (Ezekiel 1:26–28). Apart from the wings, this is clearly the source for John's description, which leads us to suspect that his revelation, however it might have begun, was revised in the light of the prophetic tradition. It seems rather more deliberate than spontaneous. Perhaps John felt that he had to write his vision in accordance with what previous prophets had reported in order to gain credibility with his audience, which would have been familiar with the works of these two Old Testament prophets.

The small matter of the discrepancy over the number of wings is solved by a passage from one of the prophetic visions of Isaiah: he saw God on his throne, and above him were divine beings, each with six wings (Isaiah 6:1–2).

With the scene set in the divine throne room of Yahweh, presumably in heaven's great palace—a kind of Christian Valhalla or Asgård—from where the world was ruled and the future determined, John, placing himself in the role of a courtier to the divine and royal presence, begins his story of destruction and woe. He reported that God held in his right hand a great scroll, which was sealed with seven seals (Revelation 5:1). This is reminiscent of the protective seven seals used in Babylonian magic to keep away evil influences. Only Jesus "the Lion of the tribe of Judah, the Root of David" (5:5) was fit to break these seals and read the scroll.

And disasters were about to be unleashed onto an unsuspecting world.

One by one the seals were broken, and with each, John saw a new vision, a portent of the future. At the breaking of the first four seals, like Babylonian magicians invoking the gods or demons, the four strange creatures would cry, "Come!" At each call a horse and rider would appear; first came a white horse, secondly a red horse, then a black horse, and lastly, with the fourth seal, a "deathly pale" horse arrived; its rider was called "Plague" (6:8). John reported that each rider was granted control over a quarter of the earth, "to kill by the sword, by famine, by plague, and wild beasts" (6:8). Things were beginning to heat up, but we must realize that all this killing was merely priming the system for even greater destruction.

The breaking of the fifth seal brought out the souls of all who had been executed for their belief in God; they cried to God for revenge, "How much longer will you wait before you pass sentence and take vengeance for our death on the inhabitants of the earth?"

There were no innocents so far as they were concerned. With this, John was getting into his stride. God asked these martyrs to be patient for a little longer until a few more believers had been killed (6:9–11).

With the sixth seal came a destructive earthquake; the sky was blackened—perhaps from volcanic ash—and the moon became as "red as blood." The stars then fell out of the sky; mountains and islands were rocked by earthquakes. All the population of the earth ran to the mountains in an attempt to hide amongst the rocks and caves. They knew, said John, that the day of vengeance had arrived (6:12–17).

Four angels stood at each corner of the world about to unleash the four winds upon an already-devastated earth. But another angel held them back temporarily, asking them to wait until a seal had been placed upon the foreheads of all believers—twelve thousand from each of the tribes of Israel, a total of one hundred and forty-four thousand.

This, too, is drawn from the Old Testament prophetic tradition. The prophet Ezekiel described a vision he had of God sending a group of men into Jerusalem and the Temple to utterly destroy all the sinners, those who have abandoned the worship of him and returned to the worship of the pagan gods. God instructed these killers to "show neither pity nor mercy; old men, young men, virgins, children, women, kill and exterminate them all. . . . Defile the Temple; fill the courts with corpses" (Ezekiel 9:5–7).

Yahweh was not only a jealous god; he appears here to have also been a psychopathic one.

This does, in passing, give us some idea of how revolutionary Jesus' message of love, compassion, and forgiveness was to Jews raised in this violent and dogmatic perspective. It does, too, give us an inkling of how dangerous Jewish fundamentalism can be if it takes passages like this from the Prophets to its heart. Unfortunately, many of them do. This particular passage is, by any standard, the equal to the Koran's demand of death for unbelievers. There is little humanity to be found in Middle Eastern fundamentalism. And this is the direction that Christian fundamentalism is heading as fast as it is able. It is time we recognized the extreme dangers in this.

But not all were to be slaughtered by this group of divine assassins. God delegated a scribe to pass through Jerusalem marking a cross on the foreheads of those who were still believers. These people, God instructed, the assassins should not touch.

They were joined by countless people from all races, believers all of them.

Then Jesus snapped the seventh seal: "And there was silence in heaven for about half an hour" (Revelation 8:1). It was the calm before the storm.

It was here that the trouble really started.

The seven angels were given seven trumpets—and here John is echoing the story of Joshua's attack on Jericho. Joshua marched his army around the city for six days. Leading the march were seven priests blowing upon seven trumpets.[8] Then on the seventh day they marched around the city seven times and upon a command, the trumpets blew, the invading Israelites gave a great shout, and the walls of Jericho collapsed. With the exception of a prostitute, a supporter of the Israelites, the only one who was spared, all the others, including men and women, young and old, together with all the animals, were slaughtered in this early example of genocide. The God of Israel, Yahweh, evidently was not in the mood for taking prisoners (Joshua 6:1–21).

In Revelation, the seven angels blow their trumpets one by one, and one by one, terrible disasters strike the earth—hail and fire mixed with blood scorches the earth, a great mountain drops into the sea, the sea itself turns to blood, and a third of all creatures in the sea are killed while a third of all the ships are smashed, a third of all drinking water is poisoned, a third of the light from the sun, moon, and stars is lost, and then, with the fifth trumpet, the doors to hell are opened, and destructive scorpion creatures erupt onto the earth under the command of an evil leader called in Hebrew *Abaddon* (9:11).

The sixth angel sounds his trumpet, and a huge mounted army from beyond the Euphrates River of "twice ten thousand times ten thousand mounted men" (9:16) attacks, and a third of the earth's population is destroyed. But the survivors, not realizing by this slaughter that God was trying to tell them something, continued worshipping their idols.

Then the seventh trumpet is blown.

This announces the time for God's own anger; the dead are to be judged, and those who believed are to gain their rewards. The Holy of Holies in heaven is opened up, and the ark of the covenant is seen within; a huge storm erupts with lightning, thunder, hail, and an earthquake (11:18–19). Despite the natural mayhem, it is all but an introduction to the appearance of two great monsters.

It is worth looking a little closer at this extravagant and murderous introduction to see where it is coming from, for here we have yet another example of the Hebrew background of John coupled with his expectation that his audience would share this.

Abaddon, the leader of the demonic forces issuing from hell, is a word used six times in the Old Testament to refer to *Sheol*, the most commonly used ancient Hebrew name for the underworld, the world of the dead.[9]

This focus on death is also seen in John's description of the great mounted army from beyond the Euphrates River. This very clearly refers to the Parthians and their greatly feared massed regiments of mounted archers. But the number of those invaders mentioned is far beyond anything feasible or believable—it amounts to two hundred million men. An unbelievable figure, that is, to all except the Christian fundamentalists who find a place for it in their scheme of end-days destruction.

Hal Lindsey in his bestselling book, *The Late Great Planet Earth*, is almost hyperventilating as he hits his readers with the revelation that this army is going to arrive and that it is a vast Oriental army. He appears to think that his logic is impeccable since he proudly explains it in his book. His argument is this: the other side of the Euphrates is the East; Orientals live in the East; the Chinese are Orientals; therefore the army of two hundred million is Chinese. Having established his credentials in logic, Lindsey decides to frighten us: "A terrifying prophecy is made about the destiny of this Asian horde. They will wipe out a third of the earth's population."[10]

The natural inclination is to fall about in laughter at such faulty logic, specious argument, idiotic conclusions, and unrealistic politics; what would the Chinese want with two hundred million of its men in the deserts of Iraq and Jordan? Presumably they would be heading for Megiddo and the Jezreel Valley. Whether the valley could hold them and their campfires is very doubtful. But we need to take this very seriously indeed, because this prediction has been repeated many times and is still being repeated today in Christian fundamentalist quarters. We can only hope that it is not believed by any members of the U.S. army or air force serving in Iraq.

The publication in 1959 of Herbert W. Armstrong's *The Book of Revelation Unveiled at last!* by the Worldwide Church of God reveals that the idea was around before Lindsey. Armstrong warned us that a Communist Eurasian army of two hundred million is coming.[11] He coyly omitted to say where it is heading; one is simply expected to assume that it is up to no good, wherever it goes.

Evangelist John Hagee naturally has an explanation for the invasion of this horde: it will be an army of two hundred million men "advancing from China to capture the oil-rich Persian Gulf."[12] Quite how this huge army would make its way through the Gobi Desert, through the mountain pass beyond Kashgar and into Uzbekistan, then across the deserts of Turkmenistan into Iran is anybody's guess. At the very least they would need around ten million trucks just to carry the soldiers and their immediate survival and fighting kits. And that is not counting the gas tankers slowly trundling along behind or the trucks that break down during this trip of up to three thousand miles. Who indeed would be confident enough to predict how much food to pack? Or engine oil? And what would happen if hostile aircraft began attacking this long column of trucks?—a column that, if the trucks drove two abreast in convoy, would need to be about 120,000 miles long, not counting the gas tankers. On the face of it, even if it could be done, which seems very unlikely, what would the Chinese army do, coil the convoy like a snake in central China? In any case it is clear that the whole venture would be more of an exercise in self-destruction than invasion.

There is another crucial impediment to such an invasion: the Chinese government would not want its army to be far from China. We only have to look at the turbulence of Chinese history to realize that. It reveals, down the centuries, an oscillation between a huge unified state governed by rigid central control and, upon the loss of control, a fragmented land torn by widespread civil war. Modern China remains vulnerable to this fragmentation: every year thousands of riots break out in China, some involving tens of thousands of men and women. In 2003, for example, Chinese journalists estimated about 58,000 riots erupted involving upwards of three million people. Higher figures have since been indicated in later years. It is hard to believe that the Chinese government would wish their army to be anywhere but close at hand.

However, despite the confident predictions of Lindsey, Hagee, and others, the authors of the Left Behind series of bestselling apocalyptic novels, Tim LaHaye and Jerry Jenkins, can at least see the flaw in the argument:

> There is no way the communist government [of China] could risk committing *all* its military and armament to the Middle East, for they know their freedom-hungry citizens would revolt before they returned. Besides, the logistics of moving an army of 200 million from the Orient to the Euphrates and the Arabian Desert to the little land of Israel seems impossible.[13]

No, they conclude, apparently quite seriously, "The 200 million . . . are not humans but demons."[14]

It looks like these two American writers are operating in a generally similar frame to the Egyptian Islamic apocalyptic writer Hisham Kamal `Abd al-Hamid. In a book about the Messiah and the Antichrist published in 1996, he raised the subject of UFOs; his firm belief was "that the people of flying saucers are demons in human form."[15]

John then reports a vast vision: in the heavens appeared,

> A woman, adorned with the sun, standing on the moon, and with the twelve stars on her head for a crown. She was pregnant, and in labour, crying aloud in the pangs of childbirth.
>
> —REVELATION 12:1–2

She also, despite protestations from the Catholic Church, has been taken as an image of the Virgin Mary, and many later images of her depict her standing upon a crescent moon and crowned with twelve stars. Many of the images do, subtly it is true, seem to show Mary as pregnant. It all appears to be a bit sensitive theologically for some reason because the church's official position is that, "It does not seem probable that John had Mary in mind or intended any allusion to the physical birth of the Messiah."[16]

It does seem a curious point to take issue with. On the contrary, it seems likely that John had Mary very much in mind, especially since a later passage informs us that her male child, once born, "was taken straight up to God" and that his destiny "was to rule all the nations with an iron sceptre" (12:5). This, of course, fits nicely with the depiction of the ruthless Jesus in Revelation.

However, it is clear that her role is also seen in a broader context: John mentions the "rest of her children" being "all who obey God's commandments and bear witness for Jesus" (12:17). So the woman is not only the Virgin Mary, the mother of the Messiah, but she also assumes the role of mother of the entire messianic community—in other words, the Christians. Is this an early hint of the cult of Mary in the Catholic Church? Significantly, the city of Ephesus—the church to which John's letter was addressed—was the site of the church council in 431 that declared Mary the "God-bearer," thus justifying the development of the powerful cult dedicated to her.

But the troubles of this woman were not solely those of childbirth. Just as she was giving birth, a huge red dragon dropped from the sky, a dragon with seven heads; each of these seven heads held a crown. This dragon sat in front of the woman intending to devour her child as soon as it was born.

While the dragon is clearly a symbol for Satan and is specifically identified as such (12:9), we have here from John yet another allusion to ancient Canaanite gods.[17] In this case it is to the seven-headed Canaanite creation deity, the ocean dragon or Leviathan, the memory of which reached back into the Old Testament. For example, Psalm 74:14 mentions the many heads of this monster: "You crushed Leviathan's heads."

This image could easily have entered Jewish religious tradition during the exile in Babylon after which much of the Old Testament was gathered together. A seal, now in the University of Chicago, found at Tell Asmar—east of modern-day Baghdad—depicts a god, or gods, attacking a seven-headed dragon; elsewhere a plaque was found showing a crowned god killing a seven-headed dragon, which seems to be emerging from a river.[18]

John described the satanic red dragon as having ten horns as well as the seven heads. This is an addition that would appear to hark back to a vision of the prophet Daniel while he was in Babylon; in a prophetic dream he described seeing four great beasts, the last of which had ten horns; out of these horns sprouted another smaller one (Daniel 7:8).

Daniel, seeking advice from a mysterious companion, was told that the ten horns represent ten kings; the small horn being a king after them who was different and who would gain power over the "saints of the Most High" and the Law (Daniel 7:24-25). It is hard to see this as anything other than an allusion to the Temple and its priests. If this is correct, this points to the king of Syria, the aggressive Antiochus Epiphanes who ruled 175-164 B.C. and who took the Temple in Jerusalem. We will see that Daniel in particular was an important source for the ideas and symbols that John used in his Revelation.

The Catholic editors of the *Jerusalem Bible* supply an explanation for Daniel's vision: the ten horns represent the kings of the Seleucid dynasty who, after the death of Alexander the Great, had been given rule over Syria—which, at its greatest extent, included Asia Minor and Mesopotamia.[19] The reigning king of that dynasty at the time Daniel was writing was Antiochus Epiphanes, who, invading from his Syrian base three times between 170 and 167 B.C., took Judaea, slaughtered the population of Jerusalem, looted the Temple in Jerusalem, and finally, in 167 B.C., set up an altar to Zeus in the Holy of Holies. It was as a result of this chaos that the Maccabees emerged as saviors of the Jewish religion and nation. John would expect his audience to understand this mingling of ancient legend and Old Testament prophecy.

John then reported that the child was taken to heaven for protection and that the woman escaped to a safe place that had been prepared for her in the desert. The dragon was defeated in a battle in heaven and cast down to the earth where he first unsuccessfully tried to capture the woman and then, enraged at his inability to do so, departed to cause trouble for all believers. Satan, for John, was unleashed upon the world, and it was his influence that lay behind all the persecutions of Christians and John's own exile on Patmos.

And with this we might think it would be a good place for John's visions to end; after all the mayhem, Jesus was in heaven with God, the Virgin Mary was safe in her desert refuge, and a defeated Satan was a broken force restricted to meddling in affairs of the earth, vulnerable to all who fought in Jesus' name.

But no, John wanted vengeance. His own rage, reflected in the rage of God, was only just getting into its stride.

So we enter upon the day of the beast.

SEVEN

THE DAY OF THE BEAST

"I was standing on the seashore," John recalled with a disarming simplicity.

After all the mayhem he had described, this change of tone comes as a welcome relief; John sounds at peace with himself and the world about him.

Certainly it would be nice to think of him in this state of mind, lost in wistful thought, gazing quietly across the ocean toward that hazy line where the sea meets the sky, while above him the day fades and slight waves lap tenderly over his sandals. Yes, it would be nice to think of John as someone whose heart was no stranger to quiet contemplation and a love of the natural world, for Patmos is, in many ways, the perfect Greek island, and as places of exile go, John could consider himself fortunate. Roman historians regularly describe places of banishment to uninhabited or barely inhabited rocky islets where those who have fallen from favor are left to rot.

It would indeed be nice, but unfortunately such calm does not seem to be John's way; before we even have a chance to catch our breath, he immediately informs us, "Then I saw a beast emerge from the sea" (Revelation 13:1).

So, after the briefest of respites, the horrors begin again. The peace was merely an illusion; just the eye of a hurricane passing overhead.

Before John's eyes—according to his account—a great ugly beast dragged itself out of the sea and across the shore. It had seven heads and ten horns and on each horn was a crown. So far, so familiar; we have met this beast before. We can recognize the lumbering Leviathan of Mesopotamian legend, with its many decorated horns, which—as we have already noted—to John undoubtedly symbolized the Syrian kings of the Seleucid dynasty. But John now gives us more detail: he explains in outrage that Leviathan's seven heads were marked with blasphemous names, and one of its heads, he added, had an injury that should have proved fatal but which, in fact, had healed (Revelation 13:3).

As this beast emerged, John notes that it looked like a leopard with a bear's claws and a lion's mouth and that it had been given all the authority and power of the dragon—that is, the one also with seven heads and ten horns that fought against the pregnant woman who has been identified with the Virgin Mary. We now know that for John this dragon represented Satan, so we can assume that this new beast is simply a new form of that great adversary. And we are correct to do so since John later confirms that the beast and the dragon are the same (20:2).

As John continued to watch, perhaps immobilized with shock and awe and unable to flee, a second beast emerged, but this time it came out from the ground. This beast had only two horns and was, according to John, the servant of the first satanic beast from the sea.

This second beast held great authority throughout the world. It performed miracles and could call down thunderbolts from the heavens; furthermore, it forced all humanity to worship Satan, the sea beast. All those who saw the miracles this demonic creature could perform were deeply impressed, and in this way the world's population was won over to Satan's cause. In fact, they were persuaded to erect a statue to honor the sea beast; the latter then, explained

John enigmatically, breathed life into this image, which allowed it to speak (13:15).

This is an extremely revealing scrap of information. We can learn a lot about John himself from this stray fragment, for here again we have a direct drawing from ancient Middle Eastern thought: the ancient Assyrians, Babylonians, and Egyptians believed that a god's divine presence could be enticed into an image of itself whether that image be a painting, a relief carving, or a statue. And to maintain the divine presence in that image, offerings were to be ritually presented to it on a daily basis.

But it wasn't that the ancients thought the statue or image was the god itself. What they believed, in fact, was that the image was simply infused with the power and glory of the god or goddess it depicted.[1] These images weren't actually the deities themselves but more like proxies. Putting it very directly, we could view the statue or image as a kind of lens through which the divine world might be approached and through which the divine world might spill out into the terrestrial.

The same general principle applied to the idea that the sun, moon, and planets were conduits to gods and goddesses. They contained and expressed divine presence.[2] This can be seen, for example, in the ancient Sumerian word *utu*, which indicated the sun and the divine power animating it—the power of the sun god was seen as immanent in the stellar body, the sun, itself.[3] It is this belief that is one of the important concepts that contributed to the development of astrology.

The breathing of life into statues was a recognized technique of the ancient priesthood; it was also an important symbol associated with the pharaohs. The symbol of the breath of life was the *ankh*, and many painted reliefs in the temples depict the gods touching an *ankh* to the nose or lips of the pharaoh, imparting the breath of divine life. The ritual basis to this animation of statues was revealed by the enigmatic

Roman period text *Asclepius*, which was attributed to Hermes, the Greek equivalent of the ancient Egyptian God *Tehuti* (Thoth)—guardian of the mystery traditions, initiator into secret knowledge, and guide to the dead. The excerpt from *Asclepius* reads as follows:

> Those gods are entertained with constant sacrifices, with hymns, praises and sweet sounds in tune with heaven's harmony: so that the heavenly ingredient enticed into the idol by constant communication with heaven may gladly endure its long stay among mankind. Thus does man fashion his gods.[4]

We can fairly conclude, then, that when John wrote of the statue of the seven-headed beast, he was revealing his knowledge of the more secret side of the ancient religious traditions. Since this would have been knowledge forbidden to the public, even in the first century A.D., we need to ask ourselves where John might have acquired such knowledge. Is there more to him than we have suspected? Is his apparent Jewish background just one part of his heritage? Like many other converts to Christianity, had he formerly been part of the pagan priesthood before becoming disillusioned? It is a very small but telling point, which does demand some explanation. But with the paucity of evidence at our disposal, such an explanation must, for the moment, remain elusive.

For now, however, it is important to note that according to John's account, all those who refused to submit to the statue of the sea beast were executed. And the servant beast forced all people to be branded on their foreheads or on their right hands with the name of the sea beast or "the number of its name." These branded people were the only ones permitted to be involved in any commercial activity whatsoever. We can clearly see at work here the arcane art of gematria, where every letter, every word, and every name has a number, and, in the event one misses it, John spells it out for us:

If anyone is clever enough he may interpret the number of the beast: it is the number of a man, the number 666.

—REVELATION 13:18

Of course, Christian fundamentalist writers and preachers have made much of this number. They have searched for it in all kinds of unlikely places and in so doing have managed to induce a kind of public hysteria. Such paranoid speculation can go to absurd lengths: some supermarket bar codes have come under suspicion, and even the American apocalyptic authors Tim LaHaye and Jerry Jenkins admit to being bemused by the story of a U.S. Air Force officer who lost his career because of his refusal to accept a numerical identification label; he feared that accepting the numerical ID would mean that he had accepted the brand of the beast. LaHaye and Jenkins gave him full marks for devotion but low marks for understanding prophecy.[5]

This officer was clearly living in fear, but not the fear for which he had been trained to deal with, that was raised by the Cold War's doctrine of mutually assured destruction—a principle similar to the one at work when two gunslingers, with their pistols jammed in each other's eyes, wait for the other to blink or tire. Rather, the officer's far greater fear seems to me to be fear of the vengeance of Revelation's Jesus, fear of the mounted god with a sword and bloodied robe who protects the gates to heaven.

The creation of such fear, of course, helps preachers to increase the level of sectarian cohesion within their fundamentalist congregations and among readers of their apocalyptic books; for the beast is the Antichrist, and by this logic, any use of the number is a secret revelation that the Antichrist is alive and well and meddling in daily life even today. Its implications turn up in almost every book on the subject.

But the number of the beast is quite simple to decipher, and it again places us back in John's time or, to be truthful, some years before he was sent into exile on Patmos. The question is: what man could the number 666 symbolize?

Once more we're returned to gematria. Using the principles of this decoding method, we first need to be aware that the number 666 occurs early in church tradition. It is mentioned by the late-second-century theologian Irenaeus. Although a variant reading puts the number at 616, the former is considered the more authentic tradition. Certainly Irenaeus thought so.[6] Using gematria, we find that if we transliterate the Greek for "Emperor Nero"—*Neron Kaisar*—into Hebrew, we get the number 666.[7] Nero, the beast from the city of the seven hills! But note that this would only make sense to an audience familiar with Hebrew.

And this brings us an answer to the curiosity of the blasphemous names that John said were borne by the seven heads of the amphibious satanic Leviathan. The coins of the Roman emperors carried the word, in Latin, *Divus*; in the eastern parts of the Roman Empire, where Greek was the official language, coins instead carried the word *Theos*.[8] Both mean "god."

Since the time of Augustus, 27 B.C., the emperors had considered themselves to be deities; temples were built to them, and sacrifices were offered to their images in temples throughout the Empire—including the Temple of Jerusalem; it was this that caused so much trouble between the Romans and the fervently nationalistic Jewish groups, the messianic Zealots.

At the time of John's exile, Domitian was emperor; early in Domitian's reign he had assumed, in his writing and speech, the title of *Dominus et Deus*, that is, Lord and God.[9] For John this most certainly would have been utter blasphemy and reason enough to condemn Domitian and his predecessors.

If one excludes the chaotic period after Nero's suicide in A.D. 68, during which three temporary emperors came and went within the span of one year, and counted only Nero and the other deified Roman emperors to follow, one would note that the number of these emperors was seven—exactly the number associated with John's symbolic seven-headed beast. They were emperors Augustus, Tiberius, Caligula, Claudius, Nero, Vespasian, and Titus. Domitian was still alive and so, strictly speaking, was not a full member of the pantheon of gods, however much he may have exalted his status on earth.

For John the end was coming, and he expressed this view forcefully in his Revelation. It would not be long. But there were a number of preliminaries: John saw 144,000 people with the Lamb (Jesus) and "his Father's" (14:2) names written on their foreheads as had been described earlier. However they all seem to have been male, since John explained that they were all virgins and have "not been defiled with women" (14:4). John was evidently on the same rocky road traveled one hundred years later by the misogynous Tertullian, a road that leads, in time, to those theologians of the present day who still refuse to grant full spiritual worth to women and thus refuse to countenance women priests and bishops.

John also described an angel flying above, announcing that the time of God's judgment had arrived; then a second flew by saying, "Babylon has fallen, Babylon the Great has fallen" (14:8). A third angel arrived, announcing that all those who had worshipped the beast or his image and who had accepted his branding would face the fury of God. They would be tortured in the presence of Jesus and the angels "for ever and ever" (14:11). It seems rather like a kind of eternal interrogation by the Inquisition.

Finally, Jesus is portrayed as coming down in a white cloud, wearing a golden crown and carrying a sickle—with the intent to harvest the earth: in other words, to kill without mercy in carrying out God's judgment. According to John the blood that was thereby spilled would reach up to the bridles of horses for two hundred miles (14:20).[10] Of course, this must be a huge exaggeration on John's part for dramatic effect, but there are many who nevertheless take his words to be literally true.

Then seven angels brought seven plagues, after which the seven angels poured out seven bowls filled with God's rage. The sixth bowl was emptied over the river Euphrates, which dried up, allowing the invaders from the east, led by their kings, to cross. With them, from the dragon, the beast, and the false prophet came three demons who gathered all the kings of the world together for a great battle.

They assembled the kings and their armies at Armageddon.

Next the seventh angel emptied his bowl, and a voice cried out from the Holy of Holies in heaven, "The end has come" (16:17). The usual effects of John's vision then ensued: lightning, thunder, and earthquakes. And, as usual, Rome and other cities fell.

Then John was taken by an angel and shown how the "famous prostitute" (17:1) met her end. On her forehead was written "Babylon the Great," and she rode upon our beast with seven heads and ten horns, the Leviathan. John, leaving aside all restraint, described her as, "the mother of all prostitutes and all the filthy practices on the earth. I saw that she was drunk, drunk with the blood of the saints, and the blood of the martyrs of Jesus" (17:5–6).

Then John reminds us again that we cannot take these visions literally—as so many insist that we do—and he emphasizes that they are symbolic.

> Here there is need for cleverness, for a shrewd mind; the seven heads are the seven hills, and the woman is sitting on them. The seven heads are also seven emperors. . . . The ten horns are ten kings. . . . The woman you saw is the great city which has authority over all the rulers on earth.
>
> —REVELATION 17:9–18

Rome! The lair of the beast; the home of the whore—how John avoided crucifixion for his blatant sedition is a true miracle, for John's Revelation could be viewed as more of an act of heresy than prophesy—especially by a Roman administrator having a bad day.

And this great city will be burned—just as it was during the great fire of Nero in A.D. 64, when ten out of Rome's fourteen districts were destroyed during the six days that the conflagration raged. This disaster was blamed upon the Christians, who then suffered in the arenas, torn to pieces by dogs or crucified, or made into living torches and burned at night. Nothing was too terrible for Nero. Even the Roman historian Tacitus, no friend of Christians, expressed his horror at what had been done to them and implying that he was not alone in his outrage. It was obvious to him that they were being tortured and butchered to satisfy Nero's thirst for blood rather than for the crime of being Christians.

> Despite their guilt as Christians, and the ruthless punishment it deserved, the victims were pitied. For it was felt that they were being sacrificed to one man's brutality rather than to the national interest.[11]

John would have been well aware of Emperor Nero's reputation, and it was most likely, in his mind, symbolized as the head with the healed wound, reminding us of Nero's suicide. Perhaps such wounds heal in whatever Valhalla deified emperors went to after death.

John's description of this destruction of Rome again—as we saw with descriptions of Pompeii—hints at the actual reports of seamen who witnessed the burning of Rome from their ships:

> *All the captains and seafaring men, sailors and all those who make a living from the sea will be keeping a safe distance, watching the smoke as she burns, and crying out, 'Has there ever been a city as great as this!'*
>
> —REVELATION 18:17–18

But for John this destruction was what he and "all you saints, apostles and prophets" had been waiting for; "God has given judgement for you against her" (18:20). John could hear rejoicing in heaven over this destruction.

There is another popular modern interpretation of the ten kings and their identification with Rome. Christian fundamentalists today assert that ancient Rome could not possibly be the object of these prophecies as it has long been gone. They posit the view that there must be some modern equivalent, some reincarnation of Rome. And they have found it, or at least they think they have found it, although they play fast and loose with the facts to support their assertion. They currently identify the beast or "the new Rome" as the European Union, primarily because it reached its modern form by virtue of the Treaty of Rome in 1957 and because it is ruled by a nonelected junta—called the Commission—in an attempt to hide its nondemocratic status.

We should let John Hagee explain the general position adopted by these preachers, for his understanding of it is typical: the ten kings, according to Hagee, represent the ten countries that form the European Union, and they are supremely dangerous. The beast represents the Antichrist, who will come from the European Union or, he explains, from some country that was once part of the Roman Empire "which stretched from Ireland to Egypt and included Turkey, Iran and Iraq."[12]

Through such statements Hagee exposes the lack of historical knowledge typical of the great majority of these Christian fundamentalists. He has no idea, for example, that Ireland was never part of the Roman Empire. Similarly, his ignorance extends to the Middle East: Iran was never part of the Roman Empire; it was within the empire of the feared Parthians. Furthermore, Assyria and Babylon were only part of the Roman Empire under the emperor Trajan, who conquered them in A.D. 115, and even then, they did not remain part of the Empire for long. The next emperor, Hadrian, abandoned them as too difficult to hold militarily. So we must be very careful when we consider Hagee's interpretations of the symbolism in Revelation. We need to be mindful of his historical ineptitude, an ineptitude that is unfortunately quite common amongst Christian fundamentalist writers.

Jerusalem, the Dome of the Rock rising above the Temple Mount. (Photo by Michael Baigent.)

Jerusalem, the Old City. The Western Wall of the Temple with the golden Dome of the Rock visible behind it. (Photo by Michael Baigent.)

Israeli army's Chief Rabbi Shlomo Goren carries a Torah scroll and blows a shofar, a ram's horn trumpet in celebration of taking the Temple Mount from Jordanian forces during the June 1967 Middle East War. (Photo by Newsmakers © Getty Images.)

Gershon Salomon, leader of the Temple Mount Faithful, marches with a model of the Jewish Temple the group wishes to build on the al-Aqsa mosque complex. (Photo by Menahem Kahana © Getty Images.)

Christian farmer and preacher Clyde Lott, who began a special breeding program in the United States to help Rabbi Chaim Richman and the Temple Institute in Jerusalem obtain a perfect red heifer for the purpose of ritual sacrifice as detailed in Numbers 19, pictured here with one of his cattle.

The base of the enigmatic circular temple in Megiddo with seven steps leading up from the left. Seventeen levels of temples have been excavated, the first dating from around 3300 B.C.

(Photo by Michael Baigent.)

Megiddo, Israel. View from the ruins over the Jezreel Valley, where, according to Christian Fundamentalists, the great battle of Armageddon is to be fought. The rainbow, according to scripture, is the sign of the covenant with Noah that humanity will never again be destroyed by a flood. (Photo by Michael Baigent.)

The remains of the great entrance gates of Megiddo dating from the Late Bronze Age. They are wide enough to allow war chariots to pass through. The Egyptian Pharaoh Thutmoses III conquered the city in 1479 B.C., capturing 926 chariots. (Photo by Michael Baigent.)

The overgrown mound or Tell, of Megiddo, rising above the edge of the Jezreel Valley. (Photo by Michael Baigent.)

Ruins of Megiddo looking over the flat Jezreel Valley with the symmetrical shape of Mount Tabor in the distance. (Photo by Michael Baigent.)

Patmos: the Greek island where John the Evangelist lived in exile and where he wrote his Revelation that predicts the great battle of Armageddon. View from the site of the monastery, which is dedicated to his memory. (Photo by Michael Baigent.)

One of the gates of Pompeii, near Naples, destroyed by the eruption of Mount Vesuvius in A.D. 79. A memory of this may be contained in the destruction recounted in *Revelation*. (Photo by Michael Baigent.)

Small temple of Isis in the ruins of Pompeii. (Photo by Michael Baigent.)

Rome: the remains of the Forum area, political center of the Roman Empire. (Photo by Michael Baigent.)

Rome, detail of the triumphal Arch of Titus, raised on the route from the Coliseum to the ancient Forum. The carving shows some of the treasures taken by the Roman army from the Temple in Jerusalem. Prominent are the seven-branched candelabra and two of the sacred trumpets. (Photo by Michael Baigent.)

View of the Forum ruins, which are surrounded by the present-day city of Rome. (Photo by Michael Baigent.)

Painting of the "Rapture" when, prior to the battle of Armageddon, all true Christians, according to Fundamentalist theology, will be swept up to heaven, leaving their cars, boats, and airplanes driverless and out of control. (Painting © Chris Anderson.)

Nevertheless, Hagee purports that this part of Revelation is directly relevant to modern affairs and that the Antichrist will ultimately rule over the "ten-kingdom federation." Hagee is certain: the ten horns on the beast represent "the European confederation which will produce the Antichrist." Hagee elaborates by saying that they are "members of the European confederation that arises from the old Roman Empire."[13]

Hagee may believe that the European Union is comprised of ten countries but, in reality, it is comprised, as of this writing, of twenty-seven: Germany, France, Netherlands, Denmark, Belgium, Luxemburg, United Kingdom, Ireland, Italy, Spain, Portugal, Austria, Slovakia, Czech Republic, Finland, Sweden, Latvia, Lithuania, Estonia, Poland, Hungary, Romania, Greece, Slovenia, Bulgaria, Malta, and southern Cyprus.

Hagee also fears the advent of the euro as it might challenge the dollar; for some reason devaluation of the dollar is, for him, the mark of the Antichrist.[14] This dominance of the euro, he explains, will be the forerunner of a cashless society, which fits in with the threat that no one lacking the mark of the beast will be able to buy or sell (13:17). So Hagee has found more to scare us with: "Without the mark, no one will be able to buy a loaf of bread or a drop of milk. They may not be able to buy homes or make rent payments. They may not be able to hold jobs."[15]

Another aspect of the beast's rule is "one-world government," and Hagee points ominously at the United Nations. For preachers like Hagee, the United Nations represents only one aspect of the nefarious schemes of the Antichrist to rule the world. A universal religion is another of its schemes. Fundamentalists become apoplectic if anyone suggests that there is one god whom all religions worship under different names. This will not do at all. Only the Christian God is the true God; in this notion, incidentally, they find strong support in the current papacy. Writers Tim LaHaye and Jerry Jenkins are adamant,

The idea that all religions point to the same god is blasphemy. So is the idea that there are many ways to God. . . . Just one was God's "only begotten Son," and only He gives us access to God through prayer.[16]

There is no ecumenical understanding in such an approach, which is far too rigid to acknowledge the deep spirituality to be found in all religions.

This leads to another very sensitive point for the fundamentalists: even though they support Israel, they certainly do not support Judaism. Make no mistake about it, they are expecting Jews to convert to Christianity—or be killed at the end of days. John Hagee, for example, is extraordinarily dismissive toward Judaism and the Israeli government despite his constant refrain of support for Israel. When speaking of the Antichrist, Hagee adds in a revealing aside, "I wouldn't be surprised if, in a show of false humility, he visits the temple himself, accompanied by the Jewish leadership of Israel."[17] Unless I have misunderstood him, Hagee seems to want Israel to be Christian in the final hour, not Jewish.

In Hagee's end-of-times scenario, the Jews will be supporters of the Antichrist who, in a flamboyant gesture, will allow the temple to be rebuilt and the Jewish daily sacrifices to be reinstated. Hagee is getting very close to a cynical, disparaging, and ultimately destructive attitude toward Judaism. We have seen it all before; especially when the war drums sounded loudly all over Europe in the mid-twentieth century. Such people's love of Israel is not derived from a love of Judaism but rather from a belief that its creation as a state actually proves the accuracy of their interpretation of prophecy and is the first within a series of events ending with the Second Coming, which, with Jesus ruling from Jerusalem, will bring the conversion of Jews to Christianity. Given these beliefs, Israeli supporters of these fundamentalists are playing a very dangerous game indeed. The financial support they now receive may very well turn out to be a grave expense later on.

Revelation, as noted earlier, also reveals that after the destruction wrought by God's judgment, heaven throws open its gates, and a rider on a white horse appears. His cloak is already soaked in blood and his name is "The Word of God." He is at the head of a great army, "the armies of heaven," all similarly riding white horses. He has a sharp sword coming out of his mouth, which reveals that he is the figure from the very beginning of Revelation. He is Jesus, and he was angry. An angel appears and calls out to all the birds,

> Come here. Gather together at the great feast that God is giving. There will be the flesh of kings for you, and the flesh of great generals and heroes, the flesh of horses and their riders and of all kinds of men, citizens and slaves.

> —REVELATION 19:17–18

The narrative here returns to the battle of Armageddon. The beast is arrayed with his army at Armageddon, but his army has been defeated; the beast and the false prophet have been taken prisoner. They were both hurled into a lake of burning sulfur. His army was slaughtered "and all the birds were gorged with their flesh" (19:21). Clearly, John's unhealthy obsession with death and destruction had not been tempered.

Then an angel descends from heaven, carrying a huge chain and the keys to the underworld. He takes the dragon—which John usefully confirms for us is Satan—and chains him up for one thousand years (20:2). He throws him into the underworld and seals the entrance. He would not be released for one thousand years, a millennium during which Jesus would rule over the world following his second coming. And this was to bring yet another battle.

After the thousand years had passed, Satan was to be released, and we are confronted by a huge invading army that besieges Jerusalem.

And here we have the first mention in Revelation of the enigmatic Gog and Magog. Fundamentalist writers make much of these two.

The initial impression is that these two are a ferocious pair of warrior leaders, but this is not an accurate reading of the sense of John's statement, which seems to imply that both are large territories out of which the great army emerges.

These two words are first mentioned in Ezekiel, when one of the enemies of Yahweh is referred to as "Gog and the country of Magog" (Ezekiel 38:1–2) according to the Greek Bible, or "Gog, country of Magog" in the Hebrew Bible.[18] So we don't even know whether Gog or Magog is the leader or the country. In Genesis, Magog is listed as one of the grandsons of Noah along with the Medes, a nation living in what today is northwest Iran (Genesis 10:2). But no matter; the important thing is that this leader and his people are enemies of God, and the implication of the Genesis reference is that they come from the north and the east, beyond the Euphrates, for what seems a rerun of the battle of Armageddon.

In Revelation the two names have been transmuted from a leader and his country into two groups of peoples. Again John shows his debt to Jewish culture: this rendering of the names is common in the Talmud, where Gog and Magog are identified with the plotting kings and princes who revolt against Yahweh and his "Anointed"—that is, his Messiah, who are described in Psalm 2:1–2.[19] The result of all this is that we can be sure any mention of Gog and Magog is intended to emphasize how the many enemies of the God of Israel are converging on the Holy City, seeking to conquer the last redoubt of Jesus in order for Satan to rule the entire world.

But fire rains down from heaven and destroys them all. Satan, again captured, was this time thrown into the lake of fire and sulfur where the beast and the false prophet already resided in their eternal damnation; "and their torture will not stop, day or night, for ever and ever" (Revelation 20:10).

Then God appeared on a throne; all the dead were resurrected and were judged. Those who failed the test were thrown into the burning lake along with Satan.

Then, seamlessly, in the blink of an eye, the heavens parted and in a blaze of light the new Jerusalem descended looking like a glistening diamond (21:1–11). It settled down on the parched and blasted landscape of Judaea complete with high city walls built of glittering diamond 144 cubits high—approximately 228 feet—and with twelve gates. The city itself was polished gold and it had no need of the sun or moon since the entire city was illuminated by the radiant presence of God (21:23).

The new eternal rule of God and Jesus had begun. A rule where Jesus would throw off his blood-stained robes and an era of peace and sanctity would exist not simply for a thousand years but forever.

It is Jerusalem's defensive wall that strikes the sour note. If there is to be an eternity of peace, why would Jerusalem need walls and gates? John doesn't explain. And there is another oddity about John's vision: there is no temple in the new Jerusalem. This would seem an extraordinary omission.

But John is explicit: "I saw that there was no temple in the city since the Lord God Almighty and the Lamb [Jesus] were themselves the temple" (21:22).

The importance of this statement cannot be overestimated: John is stating that the Jewish Temple is irrelevant to the coming period of eternal peace. Nothing, of course, is said about a mosque, which Revelation would, were it truly giving insight into the future, surely comment on. As further proof that John's vision is a child of its times, Islam is never once mentioned. And in the real world, how could that be? Mohammed was not to arrive, with his own vision of things to come, for another five hundred years.

But both Christians and Muslims agree: Jesus is coming back to rule the new world from his capital in Jerusalem. The fact that the

Christian sacred writings specifically state that there will not be any Jewish Temple in Jerusalem will be a great comfort to those Muslims who fear for their mosques. Perhaps this is one of the reasons that Muslim fundamentalists can happily draw so heavily upon the Christian Revelation for their own interpretation of the end times. And, as we have already noted, both the Christians and the Muslims see, at this time, the end of Judaism—by means of a conversion to Christianity or a conversion to Islam. There is room for a bitter argument here, which Jesus will have to sort out.

From what we have looked at, it is clear that John's vision is related strictly to his own times; any events he predicted for the future were to be sought in the world of A.D. 95–100, not to the modern world as countless fundamentalist preachers try to convince us, day and night.

In so many ways, John's entire work seems irrelevant to the modern world except perhaps when viewed from this possible perspective: perhaps John's vision is intended to be metaphorical. Perhaps it's *really* a vision of the kingdom of heaven, a kingdom at which one arrives after a great struggle; a kingdom that might be visited at any time, by anybody. Perhaps the kingdom John wrote about is the same kingdom Jesus described in the Synoptic Gospels (Matthew 13:11; Mark 4:11; Luke 8:9–10).[20] "Behold" Jesus said—according to the gospel account— "the kingdom of God is within you" (Luke 17:20–21).

Unfortunately few people actually read Revelation for themselves. They rely on the loose interpretations of others. And those who do actually set out to read it rarely, if ever, get past the battles and other horrors described at length to truly look at what John is saying at the very end of the text.

John speaks in the end of those who have purified themselves sufficiently enough to have earned the right to enter the kingdom of heaven and who, having done so, are, unlike Adam and Eve, permitted to eat the fruit of the sacred tree: "Happy are those who will have washed their robes clean, so that they will have the right to feed on the tree of life and can come through the gates into the city" (Revelation 22:14).

And John continues a few lines further on: "Then let all who are thirsty come: all who want it may have the water of life, and have it free" (22:17).

As has long been said, the first battles are those fought against one's own inner demons. Could the events described in Revelation possibly be an amplified and richly embellished metaphor for the internal struggle each of us must endure to become free enough to enter the gates of the Holy City and drink from the eternal flowing river of life?

It seems so to me.

But history is often an enigmatic study. Events occur that defy logical analysis, and John's vision exposes one such anomaly, which we might want to ponder further before we so neatly wrap things up: at the heart of Revelation is the great battle of Armageddon, one involving a huge army led by the "kings of the east," an army that crosses the Euphrates River and meets its end in a huge battle on the plains beneath the walls of Megiddo, a city we've discussed before.

In a very curious twist of history, these events actually occurred. A great army led by kings of the east poured down from the north, crossed the Euphrates River, and fought its final battle beneath the gaze of Megiddo—at Armageddon. We even know that this momentous battle commenced on the morning of September 3, 1260. It was one of the most important battles in history, yet few today remember it.

So what should we make of all this?

Well, one thing is clear: if we insist upon concluding that John's prophetic writing is true, then we must accept that the events he predicted actually occurred eight hundred years ago and thus can have nothing to do with events today.

So close are these actual historical events to the description given by John that if we reject them as the true focus of his prophecy in Revelation, then we must also reject any later example that may also seem to fit the events. In fact there are none. Put simply: if John was indeed making an accurate prophetic statement, then this prophecy came true in 1260.

This certainly does not support the current position of the fundamentalists who believe in John's prophetic gifts and who are expecting these apocalyptic events to occur in the near future. Unfortunately, it is too late; it has already happened. And neither Jesus nor the Antichrist appeared.

These events of 1260 had their beginning in the empire created by the Mongol leader Genghis Khan. About thirty years after his death, one of his grandsons embarked upon the conquest of the Middle East. He led a vast army of about 120,000 eastern warriors from the north through Iran. But their leader at the time, the Great Khan, died in 1259, and most of the troops were withdrawn to Azerbaijan. The depleted Mongol army continued its invasion under a Nestorian Christian general, Kitbuqa, for the Mongols were ecumenical in their religious attitudes—there was only one God whom people could worship as they wished.

Under the leadership of Kitbuqa, Baghdad, the Arab capital and seat of the caliph, was besieged and destroyed in 1258 and the caliph executed. Christians all over the Middle East celebrated and proclaimed the fall of the second Babylon.

The Mongol army crossed the Euphrates River and in 1260 captured Aleppo and Damascus; Kitbuqa entered Damascus in triumph accompanied by the Christian king of Armenia and the Christian prince of Antioch. The three great cities of Islam were in Mongol hands, but ruled by Christian allies.

In late summer 1260 the Mongol army crossed the river Jordan and were soon upon the plains of the Jezreel Valley near Megiddo at a site called Ayn Jalut—today Ein Harod, a small community on the road from Megiddo to Bet She'an. About to meet them was an Islamic army, which had rapidly marched up from Egypt.

Battle was commenced in the morning of September 3. The Islamic forces inflicted a decisive defeat upon Kitbuqa and his army. Kitbuqa's head was severed and sent back to Cairo for display. The Mongol invasion was repelled; they were never to return.

While most of the modern Islamic apocalyptic writers support the fundamentalist Christian position that the events of Revelation are to occur in our own time and that the invasion of Gog and Magog is a symbol for an impending invasion by Russia or China, one writer, Muhammad al-Tayr, stated in 1986 that the invasion of Gog and Magog was in fact the Mongol invasion of 1260.[21] But he has remained a lonely voice.

Such interesting consideration of actual battles aside, I still consider it more likely that John intended the battles in question as a metaphor for one's own personal battles. I also am of the opinion that the book of Revelation should never have been included in the New Testament at all. It provides no stories about the life of Jesus or the apostles. It provides absolutely no moral statements or advice; essentially it concerns vengeance. In this respect, it has more in common with the Old Testament prophets like Daniel or with the texts found in the Dead Sea caves. The Jesus it portrays is not the preacher of love, compassion, and forgiveness found throughout the rest of the New Testament. Rather, the Jesus it portrays is the deliverer of a harsh and brutal judgement, one which is resolved at the point of a sword not with the love of an embrace. In fact, many early Christians did not regard this text as canonical.

Few people realize how late in the history of Christianity the books in the New Testament were officially established. In fact, it was not until the very end of the fourth century A.D., almost 350 years after the crucifixion of Jesus. It was fixed at two church councils: the Council of Hippo in 393 and the Council of Carthage in 397. And it had been only two years since the emperor Theodosius had banned the pagan religions—those religions that recognized many gods rather than just one.

As late as the fourth century, important figures in the church refused to accept the book of Revelation as authentic. The situation is well summed up by bishop of Caesarea, Eusebius, a friend of Emperor Constantine, in his *History of the Church*, which dates from about 325, the same time as the Council of Nicaea was being held, at which he played a prominent role. When speaking of what he called the "recognized books," he said, "To these may be added, if it is thought proper, the Revelation of John."

It is clear that he was uncertain and was not, himself, prepared to take a definitive position. He evidently considered it optional whether one accepted Revelation or not, because when he gave his list of "spurious books," he also included, "the Revelation of John, if this seems the right place for it: as I said before, some reject it, others include it among the Recognized Books."[22]

It appears that in the West, amongst those theologians who were oriented toward Rome or toward Roman theology—such as Justin Martyr, who began a Christian theological school in Rome around the middle of the second century and who was executed around A.D. 165; the North African theologian Tertullian, who was writing and teaching during the late second and early third centuries; and Hippolytus, who, during the same period, was active in Rome—the book of Revelation was accepted, but it was not accepted by many theologians of the East. Origen, head of the theological school in Alexandria until A.D. 231; Cyril, bishop of Jerusalem from around A.D. 349 until 386; John Chrysostom, bishop of Constantinople A.D. 398–404; and his friend Theodore, bishop of Mopsuestia, southern Turkey, A.D. 392–428, who had begun his career as a theologian in Antioch, all refuted its authenticity.

A canon of accepted texts issued by the mysterious Council of Laodicea around A.D. 365 also omits it. But the Council of Hippo, the North African town, which is in modern Algeria, in A.D. 393 did record it as part of the canonical books of the Christian New Testament, and there it has stayed ever since.[23]

But these are not finer points considered by fundamentalist proselytizing hardliners. Confronted by the mess and muddle of their dogmatic assertions of a coming apocalypse, certain points reach a sufficiently high humor to stand out. John Hagee, in a classic revelation of where his thinking really lies, gives a list of "What will we do in eternity." This is, of course, a good question; one doesn't want to get bored with all that time to kill.

"No," he tells us, "We're not going to sit around heaven and pluck on harps all day." Heaven is rather like a country club with many activities; and like a country club, the talk evidently comes around to property and its value: "Heaven is a place of unbelievable real estate. Jesus taught, 'In My Father's house are many mansions'"[24] (John 14:2).

I prefer the plucking of harps in the clouds. The thought of dealing with real-estate hustlers in heaven is not my idea of a contented eternity. Hagee thankfully makes no mention of used-car dealers, and there is no record of Jesus' ever considering the subject. Though surely, in Hagee's heaven, there will be those who want their Porsches and Corvettes to park outside their unbelievable real estate?

But, aren't we still missing something?

The crashing aircraft, the uncontrolled automobiles; what has happened to the rapture? Where is it? Did we read Revelation too quickly and miss it?

The truth is that Revelation doesn't mention it at all. Yet it must be somewhere since it forms such an important part of the fundamentalist doctrine of the end times.

So where *does* it come from?

EIGHT

CARRIED AWAY BY THE RAPTURE

The rapture: it is a very simple concept; if you are on the side of Jesus, then you get whisked away by God before the troubles start. If you are somewhere else in the vast realm of religious aspiration—a Jew, a Muslim, a Buddhist, or Hindu or Taoist or a worshipper at shrines to ancestors or to deities unknown beyond your village bounds—then you don't get whisked away but have to go through the ordeal of "the tribulation," the destructive and bloody period when the seals are broken, the trumpets sounded, and the bowls emptied by the seven angels who afterward must surely have a lot to answer for.

When you get whisked away, there is no warning, no preamble that allows you to park your car, land your airplane, or finish brushing your teeth. No, according to the writers on the subject, God grabs you and you are gone. The sinners are left behind to cope with the disasters if they can, but their abilities and success are no longer your problem. Implicit in the story is that those left behind actually deserve whatever happens, for they are sinners who must be punished. The rapture does not "do" compassion.

In the novel *Left Behind*, the first of an immensely popular series by fundamentalist writers Tim LaHaye and Jerry B. Jenkins, the moment is powerfully described: an airplane in midflight is suddenly missing a large number of passengers. Only the missing passengers' clothes remain upon the empty seats. And this plane is not the only one to experience such a disturbance. It is soon revealed that:

> Thousands were dead in plane crashes and car pileups. Emergency crews were trying to clear expressways and runways, all the while grieving over loved ones and coworkers who had disappeared. . . . Cars driven by people who spontaneously disappeared had careened out of control.[1]

Such, then, is the effect of the rapture, the calling up to heaven of Christians before the end of time. An estimated 40 percent of all American Christians believe that this is precisely what is going to happen.[2] Many of those people believe that it will occur in their lifetime.

But, as we have noted, this rapture event, as such, is never mentioned in John's Revelation even though one would expect it to be, were it truly an important part of the last days. So where does it come from, this escape from the seven years of trials and tribulations leading up to the cataclysm of Armageddon and the return of Jesus?

There is no such standard teaching in Judaism despite the long-desired appearance of the Messiah. Similarly, Islam is silent on the subject, even though it does carry an expectation of the return of Jesus. And, perhaps surprisingly, even mainstream Christian churches make no mention of it, neither the Roman Catholic, Orthodox, nor mainstream Protestant theology contains its precepts. The comprehensive listing of significant people, events, and teachings in Christianity, *The Oxford Dictionary of the Christian Church*, also omits it. Only the fundamentalist version of Protestant Christianity has an obsession about it. Indeed, the rapture appears to be one of its core defining beliefs. And those who speak of it claim biblical support for their position. So why the silence amongst the oldest Christian churches?

It is a curious thing that whenever we begin looking at odd sectarian meanings put upon the recorded words attributed to Jesus, all roads lead to Paul. For Paul not only passed on accounts of Jesus the man to all who would listen and to the future generations who would read his words, but he also passed on an interpretation—or spin—of Jesus. One could argue that in his time he was actually producing a more sophisticated version of the politically active messianic Judaism that gave rise to Jesus, a version that looked far beyond the limited theological boundaries and political struggles of Judaea, beyond the dispute with the Romans. But this spin, in effect, also helped create the perspective within which Christianity, as we know it today, evolved.

Essentially, the Jewish message of the man Jesus died in Paul's arms, and the story of the Gentile Christ took over his journey. It was in Antioch (now Antakya in Turkey) that Jewish refugees from the persecutions in Judaea first formed a community intent on preaching about Jesus, especially to non-Jews; it was there, too, that the disciples were first given the name of "Christians" (Acts 11:26). Before that, like the people who wrote the Dead Sea Scrolls, according to the Acts of the Apostles, they were called "followers of the Way" (Acts 9:2).[3]

In Paul's first letter to the Thessalonians he broached the subject of the "last times" and the second coming of Christ:

> At the trumpet of God, the voice of the archangel will call out the command and the Lord himself will come down from heaven; those who have died in Christ will be the first to rise, and then those of us who are still alive will be taken up in the clouds, together with them, to meet the Lord in the air. So we shall stay with the Lord for ever.
>
> —1 Thessalonians 4:16–17

Paul was using symbolism well established in Jewish tradition here: for example, whenever God appeared to his people, the account of these appearances always included dramatic physical events. When Moses led the Israelites to meet God at the foot of Mount Sinai, the day was opened by "peals of thunder on the mountain and lightning flashes, a dense cloud, and a loud trumpet blast" (Exodus 19:16).

The same type of symbolism was placed in a New Testament context by Matthew when he described the return of Christ following a period of false prophets and destruction. Then "after the distress of those days," the sun and moon will be dimmed, and stars will fall from the sky,

> And then the sign of the Son of Man will appear in heaven, then too all
> the peoples of the earth . . . will see the Son of Man coming on the clouds
> of heaven. . . . And he will send his angels with a loud trumpet to gather
> his chosen from the four winds.
>
> —MATTHEW 24:29–31

It is fair, then, to say that John, scribbling away on Patmos a generation later, must have had this passage in mind—or, at least, some early document, which the later compiler of the gospel also had access to.

So we can accept that there is some New Testament support for the idea of the "chosen" being carried away following a difficult period at the end of days. This is indeed a possible source for the rapture, yet there is no suggestion in the New Testament Gospels of Armageddon or of the thousand-year rule of Jesus; nor is there mention of the term *rapture* itself.

To try to better understand the origins of the rapture as the fundamentalists portray it, we must return to Paul's first letter to the Thessalonians (4:17) to see what we can unpack from its language. The Catholic Jerusalem Bible translates the concept as the chosen being "taken up." The King James Version uses the term "caught up together." In fact the original Greek term is *arpagesometha*, meaning, "they shall be seized." The root term is *arpagee*, "to steal," and as a noun, it indicates a hook or grapnel. It has the meaning of being yanked up like a fish from the sea. But the term we are looking for comes from the Latin translation of the Bible, which equates to the

Greek term *rapiemur,* from *raptus,* "to seize" and *rapere,* "to snatch." This gives rise to our English term "rapture."

So far, then, the fundamentalists seem to be on somewhat solid biblical ground.

But are they really? To be sure, we need to ask ourselves, what did Paul actually mean? Did his statement indicate that chariots would rumble suddenly driverless about the Circus Maximus? Or that carts would be found hitched to oxen meandering through the olive groves and treading their absent owners' clothes into the soft soil? Or that ships would crash upon beaches and rocks as their Christian captains suddenly vanished into the clouds? Of course not. This is not what Paul meant at all.

The exploration of what Paul meant is very dangerous territory to enter for sure—two thousand years of theology has failed to provide agreement on its landscape, and this uncertainty is well covered by religious spin, the dark art we call theology. But we can at least make some investigation of the context within which Paul was speaking.

Firstly, what is his letter to the Thessalonians really about? Can we approach it without recourse to theology? Well, the simple answer is that we can; there is no one to stop us. We have the right to approach any ancient text we like in order to seek its meaning. What we are looking for is what this text is trying to express when it is cut away from any social or historical context.

Imagine, for example, that Paul was a stranger you met in a local cantina in Corinth while waiting for your children to come back from the market, a friendly stranger who turned to you, ordered two drinks, and then started to talk.

As described in the letter, the stranger spoke gently and began by praising the community he had founded some years earlier:

> They were special; I had come to them and taught about how they should break with the idolatry they saw around

them and, despite the opposition they found about them, they should accept God's message. And to their great credit, they did. They became chosen representatives who were an example to the rest of Greece. And they did all this despite the pressures against them.

And putting down your drink, apprehensive as to where this apparent intimacy might be leading, you tentatively asked after these pressures. It seemed to you that the stranger had become reflective, sad, as though he were an old soldier remembering close comrades who had fallen on the battlefield:

> There was great opposition which took many forms. I, myself, was teaching north of here in Macedonia, at Philippi, and I was very roughly treated in the streets and insulted publicly, accused to all and sundry of being boastful, or of inventing doctrines in order to deceive the listeners and to make as money as I could out of the gullible.

And he explained that there were problems all over; indeed in Judaea itself things were even worse. The "churches of God in Christ Jesus which are in Judaea" were relentlessly persecuted by the Jews (1 Thessalonians 2:14).

This struck you as an odd thing to say, since you could be forgiven for thinking that the stranger was himself Jewish. Certainly his god seemed to emerge out of the Jewish scriptures. But as you listened, you realized that it was not just his god he was talking about, but a son of his god, and despite his Jewish heritage, he was expressing a dislike, even a hatred of the Jewish religious leaders because it was they, "the Jews, the people who put the Lord Jesus to death." (2:15). Then the stranger warmed to his theme, and began slipping into a rant:

And now they have been persecuting us, and acting in a way that cannot please God and makes them the enemies of the whole human race, because they are hindering us from preaching to the pagans. . . . They never stop trying to finish off the sins they have begun.

—1 THESSALONIANS 2:15–16

He looked darker, as though storm clouds had drifted in, and he passed into some deep recess of his mind that made the thought of revenge attractive despite his message of brotherhood and peace. He muttered across his tightly clenched fists, "but retribution is overtaking them at last" (2:16).

These persecutors of the infant church were all going to receive their comeuppance; God was going to strike them as he has always struck those who refused to listen to his message. But, he added more brightly, those good people of Thessalonika are chosen; they would be "the crown of which we shall be proudest in the presence of our Lord Jesus when he comes" (2:19).

At this point most people would probably use the first sighting of their children down the street as an excuse to leave. But, intrigued as you were, you chose to stay. The stranger explained that there were many troubles at the present times and he had sent a colleague, Timothy, to Thessalonika to help, for he could see that the great persecutions now happening elsewhere were bound to reach there very soon. About five years earlier Christians had rioted in Rome.[4] And under Emperor Nero the position of Christians was deteriorating. Official opposition from the imperial authorities was now added to the persecution by the Jews and the Greeks. A time of troubles was coming—a time when there would be many killed, martyrs to their faith in the new religion.

The stranger then said he was trying to reduce the deaths that would be coming by asking all the Christians to make a concerted effort to live quietly and unobtrusively, "attending to your own business and earning your living, just as we told you to, so that you are seen to be respectable by those outside the Church" (4:11–12).

But even this would not be enough to prevent all the tragedies that would surely occur in the very near future. And, he explained, he had been asked by members of the church about the fate of those who had died for their belief or who would soon do so, martyred in the streets or arenas by those with too many gods to love only one. The stranger was adamant, he spoke toughly, and without any semblance of doubt or hesitation he had replied to them:

> We want you to be quite certain, brothers, about those who have died, to make sure that you do not grieve about them. . .We believe that Jesus died and rose again, and that it will be the same for those who have died in Jesus; God will bring them with him.
>
> —1 THESSALONIANS 4:13–15

For Jesus was going to return very soon, the stranger informed you. He explained that he had no idea exactly when this might happen, but the day would come "like a thief in the night" (5:2). It would be a very peaceful time, and people would note how quiet the world was when suddenly the return of Jesus, accompanied by his "saints," his chosen ones who are saved, would be announced. The time of great persecutions from the Jews, Greeks, and Romans would be over, and the new faith would be vindicated as the true faith as the chosen received their reward:

> The Lord himself will come down from heaven; those who have died in Christ will be the first to rise, and then those of us who are still alive will be taken up in the clouds, together with them, to meet the Lord in the air. So we shall stay with the Lord for ever. With such thoughts as these you should comfort one another.
>
> —1 THESSALONIANS 4:16–18

So those who are still living, said the stranger, would be gathered up by our Lord with the martyrs and believers, those who have "died in Christ," and taken to the heavenly abode for ever.

"*Is he coming soon then?*" you might well have asked of this stranger whose intensity was likely to have made you a little nervous. He may seem somewhat crazy, but what if he were right?

"*Yes, in our lifetime,*" replied the stranger, "*As I said, some of us will still be living.*"

We can now understand what Paul was talking about. He was giving courage and reassurance to his young Christian church, already persecuted in Judaea and Greece and soon to be openly persecuted by the imperial authorities. He was clearly worried for the many backsliders in his nascent community and for those who were wondering about what they had committed themselves to. Perhaps, too, as a Jew born a Roman citizen in Tarsus, now living in southern Turkey and not in Judaea at all, and as one with links to the Jewish ruling class, Paul could better see the rapid deterioration of society in Judaea, which was to culminate in the great war of A.D. 66–73 and the destruction of the Temple. Perhaps, armed with this prescience or solid intelligence from his Roman and Herodian contacts, Paul feared the effect that this growing instability might have throughout the Empire. In such a case, it would be entirely logical to put as much clear water between his Christian church and Judaism as possible.

One move was to openly blame the Jews for the death of Jesus, thereby absolving the Romans. This was a difficult bit of spin, since the Jews never indulged in crucifixion, quite apart from the fact that this type of execution was specifically used as a punishment for political crimes.[5] But he managed it nevertheless.

It helped that he is described in Acts as being arrested to answer charges made by an intemperate Jewish mob, which brayed for his execution and sent assassins after him. This has been dated to A.D. 58. As a

Roman citizen, Paul appealed to Caesar, and so to Rome he was taken.

The latter part of Acts portrays the Sanhedrin, the priests, and the Jewish religious leaders, together with the Jewish people, as being opposed to the followers of "the Way" amongst whom Paul counted himself. In other words, the proto-Christians were being opposed by the Jews. But hovering in the background is the clash between Jews and pagans, which also lay at the heart of the ruinous war that would come eight years later.

The original accusation had been that Paul had departed from strict observance of the law and had brought pagans into the Temple (Acts 21:28). He had gone to the Temple to allay the suspicions of the leader of the messianic party in Judaea, James, the brother of Jesus, who had heard that Paul was teaching pagans that they did not have to obey the Jewish law—which was the beginning and end of Judaism for James and his fellows. Judging by Paul's letters, this charge was perfectly true.[6]

Whether he had misbehaved in Jerusalem as he was charged we will never know, since Acts is not history but theology; it exists to justify Paul's version of Christianity and to show the opposition he faced from the population of Jerusalem, from the group who appeared to be zealots, the original supporters of Jesus led by his brother James. But the point is clear: Paul was placed under Roman protection and taken out of Judaea to the safety of Rome where he was placed under what is described as house arrest. In fact, his situation looks more like one of house protection. And after this we hear no more about Paul.

The pious legend is that he was released around A.D. 63 and went to Spain, a place he had promised to visit (Romans 15:28). Why not? The absence of evidence has never been seen as an impediment to Christian legend—or Jewish, or Islamic.

But we should note that there is no suggestion whatsoever here that Paul's statements have anything to do with years of fighting, a battle of Armageddon, the rule of Jesus over the earth for one thousand years or the end of the world. What we have here is the promise of a reward for constancy of faith in the face of relentless persecution.

For modern Christian fundamentalists to drag this passage of Paul into the service of their apocalyptic vision is not only a mistake, not only a misunderstanding of Paul's letter to the Thessalonians, but perhaps more important, for a Christian at least, grossly disrespectful to the memory and teaching of Paul himself. They have spun his words to suit their own meaning, a modern meaning that has no place in the events of that winter of A.D. 50–51 when Paul wrote his letter to the Christians of Thessalonika.

So just who were the offenders who distorted Paul's message in this way? The modern concept of the rapture as a sudden disappearance from motorways and aircraft actually has its origins in two sources: the first is the writings of John Nelson Darby (1800–1882), the founder of the Plymouth Brethren.

In a paper called "The Rapture of the Saints," part of his *Collected Works*, which began appearing in 1867, Darby explained how this rapture was to occur. The clear implication was that it was yet to come and was tied in with the Second Coming, an event they hoped was not too distant. With this attitude he reveals that he was not too far removed from the modern fundamentalist position. For Darby, the saved members of humanity were going to meet Jesus even before he appeared on earth, before the Second Coming in other words: "We go up to meet Christ in the air. Nothing clearer, then, than that we are to go up to meet him, and not await His coming to earth."[7]

Lest we have not quite got the point, Darby soon elaborates on this statement; Christ receives the saved by means of, "His coming, and causing them, raised or changed, to come up and meet Him in the air; this is the rapture of the saints, preceding their and Christ's appearing. . . . So that at their rapture He has not appeared yet."[8]

Like many modern fundamentalist writers, Darby clearly considered that this rapture takes place before any of the tribulations and destructions. And though there are glints of commonality between their telling of it and New Testament accounts, this is the key point in which Darby and modern fundamentalists depart from the writings of the New Testament. John of Patmos makes it clear that Jesus comes again before the tribulations and destruction and that even the chosen have to live through some horrors first.

In fact, he is emphatic in his Revelation that at the end of the destructive "tribulation" period only those who have been martyred will be raised to live and rule with Jesus for the ensuing thousand-year period (Revelation 20:4–5). Paul's accounts, which were written earlier than John's, are even further afield from Darby and the others in that Paul's text makes no mention of the seven years of horrors or the thousand years of Jesus' reign at all, though his description does include martyrs and those still living. And neither John's nor Paul's account includes any suggestion whatsoever of automobile drivers—or chariot drivers—suddenly disappearing into the sky.

Perhaps the description closest to those offered up by Darby and the modern fundamentalists is that of Matthew, who details Jesus' arriving on the "clouds of heaven" while angels with trumpets draw together the saved ones from all over the earth (Matthew 24:30–31). But Matthew offers no suggestion of the "saints" being raptured up off the earth to meet Jesus. Rather, the traffic in his account is the reverse of the traffic in Darby's. In Matthew's version, it is Jesus who comes to earth in the Second Coming to gather his people, and not his people who rise to meet Jesus.

The second origin of the notion that the rapture occurs before the horrors strike all but the saintly is, like the Darby misimpressions, a relatively recent source: it comes from the many explanatory commentaries of the Reverend Cyrus Ingerson Scofield (1843–1921) that appear in his widely read edition of the King James Version of the Bible, *The Scofield Reference Bible*, first published in 1909.

Within this work, Scofield speaks of a period of horrors, which he calls "the great tribulation" and which he states, contrary to other commentators, lasts for a three-and-a-half-year period. At the center of these troubles is Jerusalem and Israel and "the people of God who will have returned to Palestine in unbelief"—that is, those who have not converted to Christianity—meaning, it is clear, the Jews. Furthermore, the Jews, he says, will have a covenant with the "beast of the sea," allowing them to reestablish worship in the Temple, which is presumably rebuilt by this time. But the beast will break this deal and demand to be worshipped. This period will be immediately followed by the return of Jesus and his thousand-year rule.[9]

Scofield follows Revelation closely, saying, "the martyrs of the tribulation . . . are raised at the end of the great tribulation," but adds that, "the bodies of living believers will, at the same time, be instantaneously changed."[10] He is evidently drawing from Paul's promise of the redemption of their bodies (Romans 8:23). However, Paul was not speaking of the end of the world but rather of the transformation of individual aspiration from things of the world to things of the spirit—for Paul's is a mystical approach. The King James Version of the Bible does not exactly provide support for the Reverend Scofield's explanation: in the Bible Paul wrote, "For if ye live after the flesh, ye shall die; but if ye through the Spirit do mortify the deeds of the body, ye shall live. For as many as are led by the Spirit of God, they are the sons of God" (Romans 8:13–14).

And then Paul further comments, "For I reckon that the sufferings of this present time are not worthy to be compared with the glory which shall be revealed in us" (8:18).

As one can readily see, Paul is explaining that joining with the Spirit brings about a transformation of the physical circumstances of life, a redemption of the body. There is absolutely nothing here to support a view of anything happening at the end of the world, let alone the idea of the rapture.

Sadly, this is not the only place in Scofield's writings where he takes such liberties. Whenever he leaves the comfortable certainty of his dogmatism behind, he exposes his inability to comprehend the wider reaches of spirituality. At one point, he actually attempts to convince us that eternity is somehow bound by time, a misunderstanding of the very meaning of the word. He writes: "The life is called 'eternal' because it was drawn from the eternity which is past unto the eternity which is to come."[11]

Through such a ridiculous statement we can see that Reverend Scofield is coming from a clearly defined position in which all history is linear, progressing, of course, toward some apocalyptic end. There is no distinction between the infinite and the eternal with him.

In his understanding, Christ is the Master of the progression through time, which is described, he says, perfectly in the Bible—both Old and New Testament.

> "The Old Testament is the *preparation* for Christ; in the Gospels he is *manifested* to the world; in the Acts he is preached and his Gospel *propagated* in the world; in the Epistles his Gospel is *explained*; and in Revelation all the purposes of God in and through Christ are consummated. . . . From beginning to end the Bible has *one great theme* the person and work of Christ."[12]

Cute, but absurd! How could we have expected Scofield to possibly understand Paul's notion of transformation from things of the world to things of the spirit when he misses the point so completely in these other ways? But at least Scofield has been honest enough to reveal where he is coming from. The fact that such extraordinary bias is common among dogmatic Christians does not excuse it, but it does explain it. He evidently didn't expect anyone to disagree with his fatuous speculation.

We are left, then, to conclude that the idea of the rapture has been good business for many Christian fundamentalists and that bits of scriptures have been cherry-picked from all over the Bible, both Old Testament and New Testament, taken out of context, and shoehorned into service to justify an idea that really only arose in the early twentieth century.

In fact, the fully formed picture of the rapture with its crashing cars and airplanes and its chosen ones vanishing up to heaven where they can view the horrors from ringside seats within some great coliseum in the sky, was fashioned as recently as the 1950s and was first launched to a large public audience by Hal Lindsey in 1970 with his book *The Late Great Planet Earth*. In this book Lindsey writes:

> God's Word tells us that there will be one generation of believers who will never know death. These believers will be removed from the earth before the Great Tribulation—before that period of the most ghastly pestilence, bloodshed, and starvation the world has ever known.[13]

That this entire idea is contrary to the biblical text and to that extent is demonstrably fraudulent seems to have gone over the heads of the very large number of people who believe it to be a legitimate understanding of the Bible and a very real prediction of events yet to happen. They believe it, and this belief affects their behavior. As all belief systems do of course.

Perhaps this would not matter so much if I believed, for example, that a rock behind my house was sacred and it told me things that made me a better person. Then there would be no reason for others to become too alarmed. But if I decided that the Bible was secretly saying that a huge war was going to take place between the United States and, say, Mexico, and that this war would occur in my lifetime, then there might be some problems. In that eventuality, though, there is probably little damage I could cause, before I was locked up by some border marshal.

But if I *did* believe all that, and if I were the president of the United States—what then?

NINE

FIGHTING FOR GOD

I suppose we should all feel rather sorry for the late Reverend Jerry Falwell.

All his life he pounded the war drums for Armageddon and the return of Jesus whom he believed would then preside over a thousand-year Christian reign. A thousand years during which Falwell and his colleagues naturally expected to play important supporting roles. A thousand years to get rid of all abortion clinics, homosexuals, and unbelievers.

Clearly Falwell relished the task before him; his enthusiasm was undeniable. And then there was the rapture! What revenge that would be—to suddenly fly upward to the heavenly coliseum, leaving pretend Christians and non-Christians behind to slaughter one another. He delighted in the shock value of the rapture. At a dinner for born-again Christians, which included his friend George Bush Sr., Falwell famously let rip:

> You'll be riding along in an automobile. You'll be the driver,
> perhaps. You're a Christian. . . . When the trumpet sounds,
> you and other born-again believers in that automobile will be
> instantly caught away . . . the car suddenly crashes. . . . Other
> cars on the highways driven by believers will suddenly be out
> of control and stark pandemonium will occur.[1]

Yes, I believe we could almost feel sorry for the Reverend Falwell. He died in May 2007 without having seen either the rapture or the return of Jesus. And since he didn't die a martyr, according to the stipulations in Revelation, he was not going to be resurrected until *after* the thousand-year Christian reign. So he will never have the pleasure of being a big man in Jesus' administration. All his effort with presidents Reagan, Bush Sr., and Bush Jr. was wasted effort.

In the face of this evidence that mortality is still shared by all, the advice to John Hagee, Tim LaHaye, and others who aspire to being corulers with Jesus must be to go and get martyred: preaching in the middle of Basra one Friday afternoon would probably be a good start.

Falwell saw the world in black and white; for him there was no grey. His future was that of Armageddon and the battle against evil. Yet, despite such a simplistic theology his influence on political figures was unquestionable. The first president he directly influenced, as we have seen, was Ronald Reagan. But he was preaching to the converted, for as early as 1971, one year after Hal Lindsey's *The Late Great Planet Earth* appeared, Reagan was expressing an approach to the future centered upon the battle of Armageddon and the return of Jesus.

What was significant about this was that Reagan allowed this approach to influence his foreign policy. To see this, we just need to be sensitive to the coded references. Armageddon, as we know, is the first great defeat of evil by the forces of Jesus, the beginning of the process that will see his return and thousand-year rule.

Reagan saw this battle coming in his lifetime, and in a now-famous speech he introduced the Soviet Union as the "Evil Empire." This was not mere rhetoric. This was drawn from his personal beliefs—we should remember that the fundamentalists held that the evil forces of Gog and Magog in Revelation refer to Russia and its allies.

Significantly, the metaphysical had been integrated into foreign policy. Furthermore, this approach was picked up by Margaret

Thatcher, who also introduced the idea of fighting "evil" into her rhetoric. Military adventures ensued, and Reagan's support for Israel remained steadfast, but he was only briefly drawn into fighting in the Middle East: provoked by the murder of 241 U.S. Marines in the terrorist bombing of their base at Beirut International Airport, he sent a battleship to shell Lebanon like some nineteenth-century despot.

But Reagan was just probing. The full crusade wasn't actually mounted until President George Bush Sr. took office. And crusade it certainly was: reportedly the computer technology used in the Florida headquarters that ran the first Gulf War was called "Templar"; if true, this would be a reference that no military historian or Middle Eastern warrior would miss. The Knights Templar were the first of the standing armies that protected the European Crusader State in the Holy Land throughout the medieval period. They were monks following the Cistercian Rule, but they were also dedicated warriors; they lived in monasteries that were strongly fortified castles. They were formidable and feared by the Islamic forces; even the mighty Assassins paid them a tribute in the thirteenth century.

When the famous Cistercian abbot, St. Bernard, gave them their Rule, he spoke of their importance as "Knights of Christ" dedicated to kill in Christ's name. The Templars then were the first group of Christian monks who were licensed to kill by the church.

The allusion would not have been misunderstood either by the American military or their Middle Eastern opponents. George Bush Sr. was indeed on a crusade.

So, too, was George Bush Jr., though he managed well to avoid the word until after the events of September 11, 2001. On September 16 he mentioned it in public for the first time, at a press conference in which he stated that, "This crusade, this war on terrorism is going to take a while."[2]

And he was to repeat this message again in the weeks and months to follow. It did indeed "take a while."

But Bush went even further. In his view, according to many commentators, the world was engaged in a war between absolute good
and absolute evil.[3] The evil he perceived was not just that of human
failure or perversion but had a deeper cause—it was the direct effect of
Satan, who, to all indications, was alive and well, at least in the minds
of some of his commanders and top officials. It was Satan who was
causing all the problems in the Middle East, they believed, and with
the U.S. president and commander in chief evidently happy with this
viewpoint, one can clearly see U.S. foreign policy happily cuddling up
to the predictions of Armageddon.[4]

In June 2003, Lieutenant General William Boykin, the recently
appointed deputy undersecretary of defense for intelligence, gave a pre-
sentation at a church in Oregon at an annual service honoring church
members who were serving or had served in the military. Boykin
appeared in full combat gear and gave a well-scripted audiovisual presen-
tation. After relating some anecdotes about his active military service, he
showed some dramatic images of the destruction of the Twin Towers on
9/11 followed by a photograph of George W. Bush. Boykin asked the congregation "Why is this man in the White House?" and then he answered,
"God put him there to lead not only this nation but to lead the world."[5]

After showing images of Saddam Hussein, Osama bin Laden, and
others, Boykin stated as a fact—drawing authority from his uniform and
senior position in military intelligence—that the enemy faced by the
United States was not focused upon these specific people. In fact, "The
enemy is a spiritual enemy," he boldly stated, "It's called the principality
of darkness." And he then laid his vision out before the congregation:
"We . . . are in a spiritual battle, not a physical battle . . . the battle this
nation is in is a spiritual battle, it's a battle for our soul. And the enemy
is a guy called Satan. . . . Satan wants to destroy this nation."[6]

It's important to note that Lieutenant General Boykin has a bit of a
history, more than most. He was first commissioned in 1971; at the age

of twenty-nine he joined the special operations group, Delta Force. In 1980 he was in the Iranian desert as operations officer for the unsuccessful Delta Force attempt to free the United States Embassy hostages. In 1983 he was wounded during the invasion of Grenada. In 1989 he was in Panama with the operation to capture President Noriega; in 1993, now a colonel, he was in Colombia with Delta Force, chasing Pablo Escobar, the wealthy cocaine baron who was soon killed. In April that same year Boykin was an adviser on the fatal confrontation with the Branch Davidian religious sect at Waco, Texas, and by October he was in Somalia, commanding the Delta Force group chasing down an Islamic militia leader and was present during the battle of Mogadishu, where he was again wounded. This battle was later the subject of the book and film *Black Hawk Down*.

Following the recovery from his wounds, he was appointed head of the Special Operations Division at the Pentagon and then moved to the CIA as deputy director of special activities. By now a general, from 1998 to 2003 he was based at Fort Bragg, North Carolina, initially in charge of the United States Army Special Forces Command and then head of the John F. Kennedy Special Warfare Center. In 2003–2004 he was involved with the notorious Abu Ghraib prison in Baghdad. His task was to introduce methods of interrogation tried and tested at the Guantanamo Bay prison in Cuba, specifically, the use of the U.S. military guards to soften up the prisoners before being questioned.

High-ranking officers in the U.S. military's legal division were sufficiently outraged at this maltreatment of detainees and the failure to observe the Geneva Convention that they approached the head of the Committee on International Law at the New York City Bar Association. These concerns were ignored by the Pentagon.[7]

As a result of Boykin's mingling of the religious and the military, the organization that lobbies for religious liberty and the importance of the separation between church and state in the United States,

Americans United for Separation of Church and State, pushed hard for Boykin to be dismissed by the secretary of defense, Donald Rumsfeld. But Rumsfeld declined to act.[8]

Boykin was the kind of man Donald Rumsfeld liked—a courageous special-ops commander with plenty of hands-on experience of warfare's black arts, able to act "off the record" and around opposing officers in order to get results. He was the kind of officer to whom Rumsfeld gave important missions and promotions. Both Rumsfeld and Bush liked the use of special forces and "private security companies" or mercenaries as they used to be called before our military language was sucked dry and sanitized.[9] Rumsfeld and Bush placed great faith in secret operations conducted with little or no oversight in order to avoid any problems with legal niceties that might reduce their effectiveness. This was of particular importance when it came to the interrogation techniques they employed—the "pain-based information extraction protocols."[10] Or "torture" by most definitions, remembering that there are international laws opposing it, laws that the United States officially supports.

In fact, Rumsfeld, according to Pulitzer Prize–winning journalist Seymour Hersh, had set up a secret unit called the "Special Access Program." It was well organized with its own aircraft, helicopters, and secret interrogation facilities in foreign countries where a flexible attitude toward information extraction was encouraged. This secret group began operating in Iraq around the fall of 2003. Under the name of Task Force 121 it was made up of men from the army's Delta Force, the navy's SEALs, and paramilitary members of the CIA. The Pentagon also sought help from Israeli commando and intelligence forces.[11] Hersh understood from his research that "this unit was given *carte blanche* to do whatever was necessary."[12]

General Boykin revealed in his presentations to Baptist and Pentecostal churches in 2003 that the Christian Right's attitudes had become an integral part of the war, that the U.S. military was in the process of "recruiting a spiritual army that will draw strength from a greater power to defeat its enemy."[13] That he was there, in the church, "to recruit you to be warriors of God's kingdom."[14] He was reported as explaining that the opponents of the United States such as Osama bin Laden and Saddam Hussein would "only be defeated if we come against them in the name of Jesus."[15]

Boykin was not a lone and eccentric fanatic; we have every indication that this fundamentalist sentiment was widespread at least amongst certain sections of the U.S. Army. When, in 2004, Lieutenant Colonel Gareth Brandl was leading his men in an assault on Falluja, in central Iraq, he inspired them by proclaiming, "The enemy has got a face. He's called Satan. And we're going to destroy him."[16]

Just, in fact, like Jesus is apparently planning to do at the battle of Armageddon. Lieutenant Colonel Brandl was evidently seeing himself doing some of Jesus' work, not the least of which included getting the measure of this guy "called Satan." It is simplistic and medieval, and such sentiments coming from men of leading rank and undoubted influence in the army is deeply disturbing.

But we should step back for a moment and ask ourselves whether we are reacting to the simplistic language of uneducated men and whether perhaps there is nothing here to be concerned about. Like it or not, the majority religion in the Western armies is Christianity; like it or not, there will be many Christian chaplains ministering to these troops since, like it or not, many of these men and women are facing death on a daily basis, and it is only right that they should have professional colleagues whose role is to help them come to terms with death. This is a necessary part of any military organization in the field. So what is it that does not seem right about the statements of Boykin and Brandl? And others like them?

The first thing is that both of these men are, in fact, highly educated, albeit not in theology. As educated men, their language cannot be attributed to a simple life faith or ignorance of others' religious views. Instead, the use of these words and concepts reveals a particular approach to Christianity, one that sees the world in terms of the endless fight between good and evil; exploring the grey areas of compromise and tolerance is not a high priority for them.

Secondly, there is the suspicion that these men are the visible side of a more clandestine plan to infiltrate the armed forces with a theology that demonizes those who are not Christians of the fundamentalist type: a theology that teaches that Jesus will return, that the battle of Armageddon is to be fought in the Middle East, that the rapture will carry believers away from all trouble. This is a dangerous ideology disguising itself as religion, and we need to be certain that the men trained to kill in our name are not also trained to think that they are doing the work of Jesus. We have no passages in the Gospels stating that Jesus was a killer.

Adding to these suspicions is the fact that early in 2003, during the invasion of Iraq, Lieutenant General Boykin arranged to run a training session at Fort Bragg, North Carolina. This training session was not for special-forces troops but rather for church pastors, mostly Southern Baptists. It was an intensive two-day session, part of a scheme called the FAITH Force Multiplier: a "Force Multiplier" is defined by the Department of Defense as an addition to any combat force that significantly increases its fighting capability and so its chance of success. Military chaplain for the U.S. Army Corps of Engineers, Lieutenant Colonel Tim Carlson explained, "I suggest that the greatest force multiplier ever known to the world is faith."[17]

The pastors attending this session at Fort Bragg had been invited via a letter sent by a close friend of Lieutenant General Boykin, the Reverend Bobby Welch, who in 2004 was elected president of the Southern Baptist Convention. In his letter Welch wrote, "We must find a group of men who are warriors of FAITH, pastors who have the guts to lead this nation to Christ and revival."[18]

The military aspect of this program was toned down after complaints by Americans United for Separation of Church and State pointed out that Boykin was abusing his status by advancing the religious agenda of the Southern Baptist Convention.[19] The original scope of the project sounds sinister, but in fairness we must ask, is it really?

There are observers who certainly think so. While the U.S. armed forces have maintained a long tradition of chaplains' serving the various religious needs of all U.S. soldiers, Christian soldiers in particular have had access to a wide network of specialist chaplains, and there is at least one organization that is providing another level of religious support. The Force Ministries, headed by a San Diego pastor, the Reverend Dr. Gregory Wark, aims to bring "Christ-centered duty" to the military and to the police.[20] Among others, its members include U.S. Navy SEALs, a U.S. Navy captain based in Bahrain who coordinates its Middle East activities, and an ex-B-52 pilot with extensive combat experience in Vietnam who coordinates its missionaries. Though it is unclear just who these missionaries are seeking to convert, it's presumed that they are members of the U.S armed forces.

All of this raises several questions: since the army already has official Christian chaplains, why does it need another layer of Christian ministry? Especially one that is evangelical in its approach? The answer must be that Force Ministries has an agenda, which its missionaries propagate, an agenda that is not currently served by existing Christian military chaplains. And what exactly is that agenda?

The fear is that this plan by the FAITH Force Multipliers has two simultaneous aims: the first is the subtle introduction into the Christian fundamentalist and evangelical churches of this military technique called the Force Multiplier; the second is the introduction into the military of the extreme religious zealotry of fundamentalist Christianity.[21]

If this is right—and it is hard to argue against this analysis by the investigative journalist Katherine Yurica—then we are dealing with something very disquieting indeed: nothing less than the progressive ideological indoctrination of the armed forces in support of one narrow view of religion. For this to be spreading in an army fighting in the predominantly Islamic Middle East is bound to create great trouble. It would cause even more trouble if that indoctrination were to create a U.S. military more interested in its service to its religion than in its service to the U.S. Constitution. That this might possibly be the long-term plan of those who are behind this movement is cause for great concern. For, as we shall see in chapters to come, there are well-financed groups seeking to change the very constitutional basis of the United States.

There are other signs as well that such an indoctrination of the military is occurring, especially on the part of leading members in the Pentagon, not the least of which is the common use of language and acronyms with a decidedly biblical tinge. For example, the Iraqis were promised a war that would begin with "Shock and Awe." That this term was taken from the title of a report in 1996 submitted by a contractor to the Pentagon does not lessen the importance of the biblical nuances that exist when used by military war planners. To those familiar with the Bible, the words *shock* and *awe* are readily understood as the experience of those who before their death gazed upon the face of God. As the Bible states, "Thou canst not see my face: for there shall no man see me, and live" (Exodus 33:20).

Other examples of the Pentagon's overt use of biblical references can be seen in the naming of two powerful new weapons. At the beginning of the Iraq war there was talk of using a 21,000-pound bomb first tested in March 2003 at Eglin Air Force Base in Florida. The name of this weapon is the MOAB bomb. While MOAB is an acronym for Massive Ordnance Air Blast, it is also the name of the mountain range bordering the eastern shore of the Dead Sea. This connection does not seem coincidental, or innocent. Later, in 2005, information first began surfacing about a weapon under development called "The Rods from God." These are kinetic-energy weapons, essentially tungsten rods roughly twenty feet in length and one foot in diameter that could be dropped onto the earth by satellite and hit the earth like a meteorite so as to penetrate the deepest of buried bunkers. Rods from God, as the name suggests, carry with them not only the weight of destruction but also the weight of the Lord's name.

Despite all the Christian fundamentalists surrounding him, President George W. Bush managed to protect himself, as did his advisers, by making a constant effort to avoid any rhetoric that might directly link him with this perspective; but the mask did occasionally slip. Bush's technique was to use coded references that would mean little to nonbelievers but a great deal to those who were raised on a diet of fundamentalist thinking. To understand the implications of this, we first need to look at some statistics.

By the end of the nineteenth century in the United States, the Southern Baptists were a dominant force throughout the South. Membership in the churches affiliated with the Southern Baptist Convention increased from one million in 1870 to three million in 1920.[22] According to former Republican strategist and bestselling political writer Kevin Phillips, in his eye-opening book *American Theocracy*, the congregations linked to the Southern Baptist Convention during the early part of the twentieth century effectively served as "important nurseries of American fundamentalism."[23] He added that a literal interpretation of the Bible had been nurtured by the crisis in Scripture caused by the Civil War.

During the 1920s the Southern Baptists were at the forefront of prohibition and a leader in the efforts to prevent the teaching of Darwin's evolutionary theory in eight southern states. This culminated in 1925 with the Tennessee trial of a biology teacher, John Scopes, who had broken state law by teaching evolution, thereby directly challenging the literal interpretation of the biblical account. This trial became a circus that ended by comprehensively discrediting the fundamentalists and opening them to public ridicule. In consequence, during the 1930s and 1940s these fundamentalist religions withdrew from the public arena. But they did not go away. They built up their organizations in a move that we can now see enabled them to expand faster than the mainstream churches.

By the end of the twentieth century, the Southern Baptist Convention was the largest Protestant Christian group in the United States—and their stated mission was to teach the literal truth of the Bible. They and other similar denominations numbered forty million worshippers; by contrast, the mainstream Protestant churches held fifteen million.[24]

When a *Newsweek* poll conducted in December 2004 asked people whether they thought that the words of the Bible were to be taken literally, 55% said yes. Among those who were evangelical Protestants, 83% said yes. Earlier, in 2002, a poll conducted by *Time* magazine and CNN asked people whether they thought events in John of Patmos's Revelation would actually occur. Tallying the responses of all Christians together, a surprising 59% said yes; but when the poll was restricted to members of fundamentalist Christian groups, as many as 77% agreed with that statement.[25]

When asked whether the world might come to an end in the battle between Jesus and the Antichrist at Armageddon, 45% of all Christians said yes; 71% of fundamentalists did too, but only 28% of other Protestant groups thought so.

Furthermore, when people were asked whether they believed in Satan, a Gallup poll taken in 2004 revealed that 70% did. A Fox News poll taken during that same year found the same percentage.[26]

One can only conclude that with 70% of the U.S. Christian population stating a belief in Satan and 45% expecting Armageddon, the message that the Middle Eastern wars were necessary in the fight against evil had fallen upon very attuned ears; especially when it came to the southern fundamentalist Protestant groups.

Today the Southern Baptist Convention is by far the leading Protestant movement in the southern heartland: Texas, Oklahoma, Missouri, and across to Virginia, the Carolinas, Georgia and Florida. It is also one of the major religions in the West, from New Mexico, Colorado and Kansas to California.[27]

These southern states were traditionally Democrat, but this ended with President Carter who, despite being a Southern Baptist, failed to implement their fundamentalist aims and thus lost the church's approval. In the 1980 presidential election Republican Ronald Reagan took all the southern states except Carter's native Georgia.

In 1988 fundamentalist preacher Pat Robertson ran for president. But his opponent, George Bush Sr., had forged strong enough links with the Christian Right that the Southern Baptist Convention ignored Robertson and supported Bush, who subsequently won the election.

By 1992 the Republicans were split by internal disputes, and the Democrats chose Bill Clinton and Al Gore to run. Both were Southern Baptists but of a much more liberal perspective than the fundamentalists who were so influential. The elections that year drew a strong division between the secular voters and the religious: Clinton won three-quarters of the secular vote; Bush won two-thirds of the religious.[28]

At that time, the Southern Baptists were advocating a program that opposed abortion and gay rights, and they wanted Clinton to implement it. He did not, and by 1994 the frustration felt by the fundamentalists clearly aided the growing Republican domination in Congress and ultimately the election of George W. Bush as president in 2000. Bush had been forging links with political lobbying groups that had strong church ties. He was supported by 87% of the white religious right who were regular churchgoers. Shortly before, in 1999, he confided to a group of ministers in Texas that "he believed God had called him to run."[29]

It was this important constituency that Bush wished to keep on board at all costs, and it was to them that he was talking when he keyed certain important phrases into his speeches, phrases that would be missed or ignored by secular voters but which were immediately recognized by the religious, phrases that revealed he was "one of them."

In his inaugural address on January 20, 2001, Bush drew very obviously from Scripture, speaking of Americans as being "guided by a power larger than ourselves who creates us equal in His image."[30] Of course, he is referring to God here. But he confused and merged American "democracy and freedom" with Christianity itself: American faith in democracy and freedom, he said, was "a seed upon the wind, taking root in many nations." This is a direct allusion to the New Testament parable of the sower as we can see in the example of Mark 4:1–9.

We encounter here a theme that returns time and time again in Bush's speeches: in the New Testament parable, the "seed" represents the Christian message, how it flourishes or withers depending upon the community that receives it.

What Bush does here is substitute American democracy and freedom for Christianity, which has the effect of closely identifying the two: in other words, he suggests that American democracy is the work of Jesus and, by extension, that America is doing the work of Jesus in the world. All of this provides a context within which a dislike of non-Christians and non-American types of democracy are easily justified and maintained.

At the end of his inaugural speech Bush mentioned a statement that appears in a letter sent to Thomas Jefferson after the signing of the Declaration of Independence. Speaking of the storm that will be unleashed by this unilateral political action, the writer asked, "Do you not think an angel rides in the whirlwind and directs the storm?" The writer knew that there would be a bitter intensification of the conflict with England but felt that the Declaration of Independence and the drive for self-determination was the right thing to do.

Bush correctly explained that the story of American courage and dignity continues but, he added, "We are not this story's author." He explained that the author is he "who fills time and eternity with his purpose"—in other words, God. Here he would seem to be breaking down the separation maintained between the church and the state, and in a very direct manner.

Then, in his last sentence, Bush repeated, "And an angel still rides in the whirlwind and directs this storm." America, according to Bush, is divinely guided, implying that it can do no wrong.

Touching key points of fundamentalist faith, his repetition of this line undoubtedly invoked in his listeners images from Revelation where great battles were being waged by angels coming down from heaven, riding and fighting amongst the clouds—angels who, for example, can unleash the destructive power of the four winds upon an unsuspecting earth (Revelation 7:1–4). Shortly after the outrage of September 11, 2001, Bush ordered the U.S. armed forces to attack terrorist bases, training camps, and Taliban bases in Afghanistan. On October 7 he gave an address following the announcement of this military action. His words reveal even more that his belief in divine destiny guides his decisions. He spoke of the battles being fought, and of those yet to come, ending with, "We will not waiver, we will not tire, we will not falter, and we will not fail. Peace and freedom will prevail."[31]

These sound like the rallying words of any world leader under such extreme circumstances, but those knowledgeable in Scripture are reminded of Isiah:

Faithfully he brings true justice;
he will neither waver, nor be crushed
until true justice is established on earth.

—Isaiah 42:3–4

But who is "he" that Isaiah is speaking about? The beginning of the chapter makes it clear, it is, "my servant whom I uphold," says God, "my chosen one" (Isaiah 42:1). Bush, by invoking this Old Testament text, hints at himself as being the chosen servant of God and, at the same time, equates divine justice with "Peace and freedom." Again, this alludes to Revelation and to the new world, which he believes will appear after the return of Jesus. One could be forgiven for suspecting that the United States, in Bush's view, is working toward Jesus' plan for Armageddon and its dominant Christian aftermath. If only he had a copy of the Hindu sacred text, the *Bhagavad Gita*, which has all that is worth saying on the subject of warriors and battles.

Progressive Christian theologian Jim Wallis, who once enjoyed close access to Bush, has noted this apparent confusion between the divine mission of Jesus and the mission of the United States; he, too, is concerned over the blurring of the lines. He asks a blunt question, one with very significant and far-reaching implications: is the theology of George W. Bush truly Christian? "Does it take a global view of God's world," asks Wallis, "or does it just assert the newest incarnation of American nationalism in an update of 'manifest destiny'?"[32]

Wallis describes a particular example that worried him: in the 2003 State of the Union speech, when Bush, speaking of the problems faced by the United States, related, "The need is great. Yet there's power, wonder-working power, in the goodness and idealism and faith of the American people."

Wallis explains that this line comes from an old gospel hymn but points out that the meaning has been distorted. The hymn states that there is "power, wonder-working power in the blood of the lamb," meaning the power of Jesus. Wallis comments,

> The evangelical hymn is about the power of Christ in salvation, not the power of the American people, . . . It's a complete

misuse. . . . The resulting theology is more an American civil religion than Christian faith.[33]

And Wallis concludes,

To continue to confuse the roles of God and the church with those of the American nation, as George Bush seems to do repeatedly, is a serious theological error that some might say borders on idolatry or blasphemy.[34]

The implication that has emerged from all this is that Bush felt himself to be divinely guided in his role as president and commander in chief of the U.S. armed forces.

Further to this point, on October 11, 2001, the president gave a tribute to those who were killed when a hijacked aircraft hit the Pentagon.[35] The hijackers "were instruments of evil," Bush said, and backing them was a "cult of evil." The extent of its power and its plans for the future cannot be fully understood, he continued, but "It is enough to know that evil, like goodness, exists. And in the terrorists, evil has found a willing servant."

"I have called the Armed Forces into action" he explained, saying that the Taliban regime was given a choice, to give up the terrorists or face ruin. To applause, he then added, "They chose unwisely." These terrorists will be chased "until there is no place to run, or hide, or rest."

With these words, we see that Bush was not only firmly in support of the continuing reach of America's great economic and military power throughout the world, but he was adding a justifying moral and theological dimension to this.

Truly, the subsequent playing out of events in Iraq and Afghanistan seem to more closely resemble the ruthless fury of the Old Testament Yahweh and the blood-soaked Jesus of Revelation than the man who preached love, forgiveness, and tolerance in the Gospels. The terrible events of 9/11 brought this difference into focus, and Bush became evangelical about the divine military and economic mission of America. And yet, anyone who has ever looked at history knows that wars never end wars. Jim Wallis comments on Bush following 9/11, explaining that he became "a messianic Calvinist, promoting America's mission to 'rid the world of evil'."[36]

Many of Bush's associates and supporters felt that God had put him in the White House and that the mission of America is directed by God himself. Bush had no problem with that idea. Jim Wallis reports that a leading member of the Southern Baptist Convention, Richard Land, recalled Bush saying, "I believe God wants me to be president."[37]

Journalist Ron Suskind reports an occurrence that would chill all but the firmly fundamentalist: at an "Ask President Bush" event in a college gymnasium a retired dentist from Florida stood up before the president and spoke, "I also want to say this is the very first time that I have felt that God was in the White House."

Bush replied simply, "Thank you."[38]

What makes any of this relevant so long after Bush has left office, having been succeeded by a leader who does not share these views, is that Bush's messianic pretensions were readily accepted by his fundamentalist supporters. The context out of which he emerged and was sustained remains, albeit in retreat. Elections do not alter the beliefs of those who supported Bush's American empire and the identification of American economic and military power with divine purpose. All, of course, in the service of the end times when Jesus will return to make everything right—even global warming or the poisoning of our environment by companies that seek to dominate and exploit rather than protect. There are people who don't care what sort of crippled world is passed on to their children, since Jesus will heal it like he healed the blind man or the leper. There is nothing that precludes these people from ever running for public office, not even incompetence.

For the fundamentalists, the Southern Baptist Convention, and their associates, the introduction of their religion into politics was not just a cynical exercise; this was serious. There were many Southern Baptists in the administrations of Reagan and the two Bushes. The overall aim was to change the United States from a secular society to a religious one, to remove the separation between church and state.

Bush was backed by a theological and political machine, one raised on fundamentalism and evangelical faith; one focused upon the United States being an instrument of God, and its foreign policy helping the cause of Jesus up to, and beyond, the expected disaster of Armageddon. Interestingly, if one were to follow the logic of Revelation, the United States would no longer be ruled from Washington after Armageddon but from Jerusalem.

The machine that fueled Bush remains whether or not it manages to get another supporter into the White House in the future. So what does this great theological and political machine want? What vision of the future does it aspire to?

Perhaps the first thing we should be aware of is that for all its apparent monolithic and focused nature, the Christian Right is not unified over everything; neither, to date, has it been successful in all its endeavors. Certainly members of the Right have tried: political lobbyists who also had close contact with the fundamentalist and Pentecostal religious conservatives began planning a unified front embracing all these groups in order to create a powerful political force that could perhaps change America through influencing the administration in its laws, choice of Supreme Court justices, and policies followed by government agencies. It is here that their influence is strong and where success might come.

A prime figure in this aspiration was a veteran right-wing lobbyist and former John Birch Society member, Paul Weyrich, who died in December 2008. In 1973 Weyrich founded a Washington-based political lobby group called the Heritage Foundation, which opposed Democratic liberalism and supported a U.S. withdrawal from the United Nations amongst its program. It was partly funded by Joseph Coors, the famous brewer and long-time supporter of the political and religious right. In September 2005 after a large donation of funds from the Margaret Thatcher Foundation to the Heritage Foundation, a new division was created: The Margaret Thatcher Center for Freedom; Margaret Thatcher had long been a supporter of the Foundation. Its stated aims are to strengthen the connections between the United States and the United Kingdom and to "focus on how the United States and Great Britain can lead and change the world," and on the "dangers posed to U.S. interests by the European Constitution, the EU Common Foreign and Security Policy, and Franco-German efforts to create a federal European superstate."[39] There is something odd in a former prime minister of the United Kingdom setting up this center in the United States rather than in her home country. It is rather like a U.S. president basing his or her library in London.

The process of combining political groups with the religious in this way began in the latter years of the presidency of Jimmy Carter, whose pragmatic views had lost him the support of the religious right. A number of other organizations were created during this period, perhaps the best known being the Moral Majority, created in 1979 by Weyrich with the Reverend Jerry Falwell as president. The Coors family of Colorado committed considerable funds to this group too.

Events certainly seemed to be going their way at the time: by the elections of 1980 Carter had lost so much support that Ronald Reagan, a friend of Jerry Falwell and supporter of the Moral Majority, took ten of the eleven southern states. A few weeks after the election success Falwell reported to journalist Robert Scheer that Reagan agreed with his understanding of biblical prophecy. In fact, Falwell added that Reagan once admitted while campaigning in New Orleans, "I sometimes believe we're heading very fast for Armageddon right now."[40] Falwell elsewhere commented, "Reagan is a fine man. He believes what the Moral Majority believes, what God tells us."[41]

Ronald Reagan was the first president of the United States to be swept to power by means of the active support of the religious right, and he saw no reason to change what had become a very advantageous relationship.

In the elections of 1984 Reagan took all eleven southern states. The Christian Right seemed to have its foot well in the door to the room of power. Yet in 1989 the Moral Majority collapsed, lacking funds, and was disbanded. It had failed. And despite all the close contacts with Reagan, with George Bush Sr., and with George W. Bush, the Reverend Jerry Falwell also failed. He became increasingly sidelined, in part because of his intemperate and inflammatory statements, and because of outbursts that forced him into the humiliating position of having to make public apologies. Although Falwell is no longer alive, the legacy he and his colleagues nurtured continues to grow in strength through other groups formed to carry the plans forward.

A second, rather more discrete, group that was founded in 1981, early in President Reagan's first term, was the secretive Council for National Policy (CNP). The initial funds were provided by wealthy oil men, Nelson Bunker Hunt—a member of the John Birch Society and the Moral Majority—and his brother William Herbert Hunt. The president of this group was Tim LaHaye, who later went on to write the bestselling Left Behind series of rapture- and Armageddon-obsessed novels. His wife, Beverly, served on the board of governors in 1982 and 1996. The permanent secretary and treasurer of the CNP was the ubiquitous Paul Weyrich. The Coors family was well represented once again, with both Holly Coors and Jeffrey Coors serving on the council's board of governors.

The CNP was designed to be a conservative counter to the U.S. Council on Foreign Relations. It contains right-wing government and military figures, religious leaders, judges, members of Congress, as well as business executives. It has a plan for the future direction of America—involving both domestic and foreign policy. Weyrich, founder, in 1974, and chairman of the Free Congress Foundation (FCF), created a plan for ensuring that the Christian Right takes control of U.S. culture. This is detailed in an essay by Eric Heubeck published in 2001 by the FCF: supporters "must, as Mr. Weyrich has suggested, develop a network of parallel cultural institutions existing side-by-side with the dominant leftist cultural institutions."[42]

In 2004 one of the politically active organizations seeking basic changes to American culture, the Christian Coalition of America, produced a league table, which rated politicians according to their support of the Christian Right issues: 42 senators received a top rating as did 163 members of the House.[43] It is foolish not to take this political influence and allegiance seriously. To ignore it is irresponsible for anyone concerned about democracy.

These statistics reveal that there are powerful political, financial, and religious groups assiduously seeking legislative support. Unfortunately they are working to subvert the Western world's secular democratic countries, beginning with the United States. They shelter their agendas beneath a religious concern for freedom, whatever that might mean in their authoritarian context—the freedom only to agree?

As is evident, fundamentalist believers do not always see eye to eye, but their approach to the future tends to fall into one of two camps: There are those like Jerry Falwell who expect the rapture to herald the battle of Armageddon and the Second Coming. And then there is another, shadowy and even more insidious group, which teaches that the Messiah Jesus will not come until the world has been put right by armies fighting under the divine banner.

It is a familiar refrain. Yet it comes not from the Middle East, but rather from Middle America.

TEN

PLANET RUSHDOONY

*D*emocracy is heresy! The message of Christian Reconstruction is blunt. *The United States Constitution must be discarded! All law must come from God, not the state! Public schools are doing the work of Satan! All transgressors against Christian Values, notably adulterers, abortionists, homosexuals, blasphemers, prostitutes and heretics, should be publicly stoned to death!*

Christian Reconstructionists want to bring back biblical law—*theonomy* they call it. And while there is no doubt about their beliefs once you are exposed to them, Christian Reconstruction just about manages to be discrete. There is no official Web site, no central office where one can call or pick up literature or speak to members. In fact it is not so much an organization as a mode of thought, a focus of intention held in common. Yet, despite this apparent diffuseness, its supporters always know where to find its high priests. They flag their presence to others by means of self-descriptions that seem innocuous enough to the rest of us, but which are a type of code recognized by those who understand.

Insiders get the message when people such as disgraced former House of Representatives majority leader Tom DeLay, a member of CNP, speaks of his desire for a "God-centered" nation; when the Reconstructionist organization, American Vision, seeks to convert the United States into a "truly Christian nation"; when the Promise Keepers call for "godly men" to influence the world; when Reconstructionists prominent in the Coalition on Revival promote the "implementation of a biblical and Christian worldview"; when the Alliance Defense Fund, a national group opposing homosexual marriage, advocates an America-based upon "biblical law"; when the Traditional Values Coalition pushes its aim of "empowering people of faith," using "Bible-based traditional values"; when Faith2Action states its mission as "Turning people of faith into people of action to win the cultural war together for life, liberty, and the family"; when the Institute for Christian Economics supports those who seek "moral solutions to the economic crisis"; when a lobbying group called the Family Resource Council promotes "faith-based initiatives" in Congress; and when the National Reform Association forms a political lobby group to meet with representatives and senators to advocate for what they, too, call a "biblical worldview." The pattern is clear enough—as is the extent of the movement's reach.

To those whose lives have remained within a secular or conventional religious context, these descriptions may sound harmless, even worthy. But are they really? Or are we just deluding ourselves to think so? A look behind the smiles and the hyperventilated preaching of strutting fundamentalist performers reveals what has been concealed in plain view. In the spectacle of many fundamentalist events we can see the breath of some dark beast exhorting the crowds to ecstasy. But some forces simply should not be played with; some forces spin too easily out of control. Could this be happening with the Religious Right in the United States in the same way that it has already happened within fundamentalist Islam?

Rabid enthusiasm and blind obedience in many circles are commonly misread as spirituality. That a still and silent piety has always been a sure path to the center has been forgotten amidst the jangle of guitar strings, rhythmic words, and heaving breasts. On these heavily stage-managed occasions we are seeing nothing more than Christian voodoo, with the innocent manipulated by the greedy.

Reconstructionists simply don't "do" piety. As one of the move-ment's biggest proponents, the late Francis Schaeffer, argued in his influential work *A Christian Manifesto*, first published in 1981, piety gives a "defective" view of Christianity because it focuses upon the spiritual world and withdraws from direct action in the material world.[1]

For Schaeffer, Christianity must act *in* the world; it has a political role: he believed that Christianity imparts to citizens a moral obliga-tion to resist an unjust and tyrannical government.[2] Brave words, and certainly hard ones to argue with when we recall Nazi Germany and its excesses, except that it was the democratically elected U.S. govern-ment that Schaeffer had in mind when he made this statement.

William Martin, in his book *With God on Our Side*, makes the point that Schaeffer actually caused a permanent alteration in the attitude of Christian evangelists toward political action. As evidence, he points to "Schaeffer's increasing emphasis on the need for evangelicals to plunge into the public arena and try to redirect the course the nation was taking."[3]

But Christian Reconstructionists are not alone in their efforts. They rest in conjugal harmony with what is termed *Dominionism*. In fact, it is almost impossible to prize these two lovers apart. Dominionism arises from the literal interpretation of Genesis 1:26:

> God said, Let us make man in our image, after our likeness: and let them have dominion over the fish of the sea, and over the fowl of the air, and over the cattle, and over all the earth.

Christian Reconstruction theology further insists that Christians were given a "dominion covenant," that is, "a God-given assignment to conquer in His name."[4] This refers to another text in Genesis where, following Noah's survival of the flood, God makes a covenant with him and all of his descendants (Genesis 9:9). Speaking of the beasts, fowls, and fishes, God promises that "into your hand are they delivered" (9:2).

Taken literally, as Christian Reconstructionists and other support-ers of Dominionism are taught to do, these passages from Genesis seem sufficient justification for their political—and environmental—stance together with their autocratic aspirations.

Those who have allied themselves with Reconstructionist ideas share in the plan to create, firstly in the United States, a theocratic state where democracy and the rule of manmade law no longer functions. The only rule, and the only law, will be God's, the heart of which is expressed in the six hundred and thirteen laws of Moses written down in the Old Testament. They want these laws to replace those of the U.S. Constitution and its amendments as well as all state law or those determined by decisions of the Supreme Court. The plan is to turn the United States from a democracy into a theocracy governed by God through a priestly caste. There is no separation between church and state in this view. And they want a heavily armed theocracy, since they hold that a crucial task of the U.S. government is to maintain armed forces that are trained to conquer "in the name of Jesus."[5] U.S. foreign policy would become an aggressive shambles, for what other countries would want to ally themselves with a fundamentalist theoc-racy based in Washington, DC?

The belief is that once success has been achieved, Jesus can return to rule his kingdom. By this assertion the Christian Reconstructionists, like the vast majority of their fundamentalist fellows, have completely misunderstood the words attributed to Jesus both in the four Gospels and in the second-century texts holding similar memories. The "king-dom" to which the Gospels refer is not some physical secular kingdom but something rather more mystical and uninterested in physical politi-cal power.[6] Luke describes Jesus, responding succinctly to a query by some Pharisees about when his kingdom would come: "The kingdom of God cometh not with observation: Neither shall they say, Lo here! Or lo there! for, behold, the kingdom of God is within you" (Luke 17:20–21).

There is no sanction here for a theocratic kingdom in the United States even if Christian Reconstructionists replaced the White House with a great temple for Jesus to return to. There is, though, sanction for the piety that Schaeffer so dislikes.

The crucial point to note is that Christian Reconstructionists hold that Jesus will not return until the Christian church has completely taken over all governments and the world has been converted to Christianity. This view differs from that of Jerry Falwell and others who preach of the rapture and Armageddon. They consider that the return of Jesus and the rapture are events that come before the fight for world control rather than after it.

Lounging self-importantly in the background of this theocratic aspiration like some fat medieval cardinal is the Chalcedon Foundation, a group dedicated to the promotion of Christian Reconstruction and a U.S. theocracy. It does have a Web site, a vision, and, naturally, an online bookshop.

The Chalcedon Foundation, based in Vallecito, California, was a project of the Reverend Rousas John Rushdoony who founded it in 1965. Rushdoony, who died in 2001, was a theologian of Armenian descent whose parents had arrived in the United States in 1915, fleeing the Turkish destruction of the Armenian nation. He received an MA in education from the University of California, Berkeley, in 1940 and was ordained a Presbyterian minister in 1944. He later became a member of the politically right-wing John Birch Society, a board member of the Rutherford Institute, a group founded in 1982 to focus on conservative legal issues, as well as serving until his death as a member of Paul Weyrich's politically active Council for National Policy. Both the latter organizations received funding from the Coors family of Colorado whom we have already noted. We can see from this that Rushdoony was in the midst of the Christian Right; indeed he has helped develop its social and political aspirations although not all would openly acknowledge it.

Professor of sociology at Rice University William Martin, writing in the mid-1990s, commented on this queasiness amongst the Christian Right leaders,

> It is difficult to assess the influence of Reconstructionist thought with any accuracy. Because it is so genuinely radical, most leaders of the Religious Right are careful to distance themselves from it. At the same time it clearly holds some appeal for many of them. One undoubtedly spoke for others when he confessed, "Though we hide their books under the bed, we read them just the same."[7]

It goes a bit further than this, as Martin discovered. He noted that Jerry Falwell and James Kennedy of the influential megachurch Coral Ridge Ministries, in Florida, both supported books by Reconstructionists, both knew Rushdoony, and both had him as a guest on their media programs on a number of occasions. Kennedy was a signatory of the 1986 manifesto issued by the Coalition on Revival along with Rushdoony, Tim LaHaye, and others. Martin quotes the founder of the Coalition, Jay Grimstead, as saying,

> A lot of us are coming to realize that the Bible is God's standard of morality . . . in all points of history . . . and for all societies, Christian and non-Christian alike. . . . It so happens that Rushdoony, [Greg] Bahnsen, and [Gary] North understood that sooner.[8]

And Martin noted that Grimstead added,

> There are a lot of us floating around in Christian leadership—James Kennedy is one of them—who don't go all the way with the theonomy thing, but who want to rebuild America based on the Bible.[9]

Rushdoony's aim was to get the supporters and ideas of Christian Reconstruction into the programs of all the other Christian Right groups, "Christian crusaders," as he termed them, who will "conquer and convert the world, by the sword if necessary, before Jesus will return," the ultimate goal of Christian Reconstructionists.[10]

In 2005, award-winning journalist John Sugg wrote a devastating piece on the group for the investigative magazine *Mother Jones*. Sugg's report was ominous: Reconstructionists require that all Christians either remove the components of government or assume control over them. Sugg comments: this "twist offered hope to the pious that they could change things—as long as they got organised."[11] For the Reconstructionists it is war; one prominent spokesman explained it this way: "The battle for the mind is between the Christian reconstruction movement, which alone among Protestant groups takes seriously the law of God, and everyone else."[12]

This terminology infects others: Representative Tom DeLay described the presidential election of 2000 as a "battle for souls."[13] Sugg, in another look at the Reconstructionists in 2006, discovered that "A major task for the government key Reconstructionists envision is fielding armies for conquest in the name of Jesus." He makes the crucial point that "what has made the theology such an explosive addition to public life is not its dogma on individual issues so much as its trumpet call to action. This is a faith in which religion is not an influence on politics; it *is* politics."[14]

The Chalcedon Foundation seems to be rather sensitive to all the criticism it has received. It has placed on its Web site a long statement detailing what it believes and explaining how its aims are misunderstood by critics. It denies that it is engaged in a covert attempt to take political power in order to foist biblical law on Americans. Unfortunately, this denial is significantly undermined by assertions in their statement that "a Christian state should enforce the law of God" and that "Biblical civil legislation" is not for "modern, secular Western democracies at war with God. Our first objective is to work to Christianize them."[15]

In the end, Chalcedon's attempt at a benign spin is demolished by an arrogant statement that "Christians suckled on a pietistic view of the Faith and life simply cannot conceive of a world-conquering Christianity."[16]

John Sugg is correct; Christian Reconstruction *is* politics.

Rushdoony's theology is expounded in his 890-page volume *The Institutes of Biblical Law*. In his view democracy opposes Christian teaching. He explains that "The heresy of democracy has . . . worked havoc in church and state, and it has worked toward reducing society to anarchy."[17]

Rushdoony's book is structured upon the Ten Commandments and argues the case for biblical law being established as the basis of the legal system and explores the practical implications of basing a modern legal system upon these ancient laws. He argues that the very basis for any society, past or present, is the law that comes directly from God. He explains that there is a precedent in the very earliest settlements in seventeenth-century New England, especially that of New Haven, which adopted biblical law. Rushdoony sees this as the important formative moment in U.S. history and indicative of the true heritage of the nation: that of a nation governed not by secular laws but by divine laws.

Rushdoony stated as a basic principle that "there can be no tolerance in a law-system for another religion."[18] However, there was an exception allowed for Judaism, which is hardly surprising since the laws derived in the main from the Jewish scriptures. Equally radical is Rushdoony's argument that the freedom of religion granted by the First Amendment to the Constitution of the United States has been misread. According to Rushdoony, it simply restricted the power of the federal government to interfere in matters of religion; it did not mean to guarantee religious liberty.[19]

The colony of New Haven was first established in 1638 by a hard-line Puritan group from England that, from the beginning, planned to create a community governed as a theocracy. For them this represented a return to what they perceived as the original Christianity. This settlement was an independent colony until 1662 when a royal charter was granted to Connecticut by which it absorbed New Haven and its associated towns.

At first the colony of New Haven had no formal laws; its affairs were simply ordered by what was termed a "Plantation Agreement." This stated that the laws in New Haven were to be *"the judiciall lawes of God, as they were deliuered by Moses."*[20] In this way the founders sought to create a theocracy on the banks of Long Island Sound. As one historian concluded, "The community was not to be a state but a church."[21] And no one in the community could become a citizen unless he or she was also a member of that church.

Rushdoony expressed his complete agreement with this approach and revealed that the point of his book is to help revive this early strict observance: "It is intended as a beginning, as an instituting consideration of that law which must govern society, and which shall govern society under God."[22]

An important characteristic of this biblical law, Rushdoony continued, "is that it constitutes a plan for *dominion under God*."[23] Since God was the source of all law and "established the covenant [renewed first with Noah and finally by Jesus] as the principle of citizenship," there is no support for any kind of equality, "Only those within the covenant are citizens."[24] Thus there are irrevocable restrictions on citizenship negating the principle of democracy, which, naturally, has no place in this theocratic system.

Homosexuality is also condemned: "The homosexual is at war with God," explained Rushdoony, "his every practice is denying God's natural order and law."[25] Homosexuals will not be considered as citizens of Rushdoony's brave new world.

Lest we might think that in his obsession with the law he was drawing Christianity back to the Judaism it emerged from, he gives us the position bluntly: "It is blasphemy . . . to separate the law from Jesus Christ. The fact that this is being done is an evidence of religious decline and collapse."[26]

In fact many of the Christian Reconstructionists have a distinct animus against Judaism—they seem to have forgotten that Jesus was a Jew. Reconstructionist minister David Chilton wants us to believe that,

> The god of Judaism is the devil. The Jew will not be recognized by God as one of His chosen people until he abandons his demonic religion and returns to the faith of his fathers—the faith which embraces Jesus Christ and His Gospel.[27]

Rushdoony spends some time exploring the relationship of power and law, and it is from this starting point that a number of his most controversial conclusions derive; for example, "Law is not law if it lacks the power to bind, to compel, and to punish."[28]

For Rushdoony, the commanding power allotted to the husband in the Scriptures justified his position that "A woman's holiness and devotion is subject first of all to the authority of her husband. God's law disallows all vows of service which a woman vows without her husband's or father's consent."[29] She is, therefore, the legal possession of her husband.

The ruthlessness in his rule of law is evident elsewhere too. He called for adulterers to be stoned to death. He prescribed "death without mercy" for idolatry, which proscription leaves Hindus, and perhaps even Roman Catholics with their images of saints, in a difficult position. Pity was specifically forbidden; the law was the law, there was no escape from its demands. Whoever is a delinquent, "stubborn and rebellious," whoever disobeys his parents, and whoever is a "glutton and a drunkard" should, even today, in accordance with Old Testament law, be executed by stoning (Deuteronomy 21:18–21). Rushdoony commented, "The law is clear enough; if only the interpreters were as clear!"

Rushdoony's book is well referenced, and Rushdoony was well read, but it is noticeable that a number of the footnotes refer to articles in *Playboy* magazine, others to various writings of the Marquis de Sade! This strikes a discordant note. Still, we must remember that his reading was all for the purpose of research.

Since Rushdoony's death his family has maintained an influential presence: the Chalcedon Foundation is headed by his son, Mark, and Rushdoony's daughter, Sharon, married Dr. Gary North, a Christian Reconstructionist who, after an unfortunate and terminal row with Rushdoony, moved to Tyler, Texas, and started the Institute of Christian Economics. Despite the acrimony, it, too, promotes the theology of Rushdoony. North is not squeamish about what needs to be done.

He explained in his book *The Sinai Strategy* in 1986 that "The integrity of the family must be maintained by the threat of death." North argued further that cursing one's parents should also be punishable by death, as should blasphemy.[30] Along with many others, he would happily impose the death penalty on homosexuals as well. In fact, Gary North is rather keen on execution. He likes the idea of a transgressor being publicly stoned to death by members of the local community: it is cheap, he explains, since the necessary stones will be readily to hand, and with local people involved, it becomes a positive community project.[31] He seems to see it as something of a social occasion that brings the community closer together—well, all except one member, of course, who would be under a pile of stones.

It is easy to see why Gary North is nicknamed by both followers and opponents as "Scary Gary."[32]

It is striking how often there are ancient parallels to modern dilemmas; human technology has changed, but human thinking has remained consistent with its flaws and self-interest.

History can provide a sense of where current policies might lead—in the same way that a flood of water will surge its way down a wide valley however we might attempt to direct it. Only two things can be guaranteed: that the water will reach the lower ground and that it will forge its own route in doing so. Ideas tend to do the same thing through history. All movements, rivers, or ideas inevitably move out of human control and create a new reality with which we must contend.

Reading the theology—if it can really be dignified with that title—of Rushdoony, I was struck by a strong sense of déjà vu. I had been here before: when my colleague Richard Leigh and I wrote our book *The Inquisition*.

This cruel and venal institution, acting in the name of Jesus but doing the work of a far darker god, first arose in the early thirteenth century during the brutal crusade against the Cathar religion in the south of France. It was later taken up by the Spanish rulers and as a result dominated the life of the Roman Catholic Church from the late fifteenth into the nineteenth centuries. In a modified form it still exists, with an American, the former Archbishop of San Francisco, at its head.

Around 1468, two highly educated Dominican monks in southern Germany and Austria collaborated on a book that was to change the face of Europe. One of the authors, Heinrich Kramer, about six years later, was to be appointed the Inquisitor for Salzburg and the Tyrol. His Dominican colleague, Johann Sprenger, in 1480 was appointed dean of the Theology Faculty at the University of Cologne and the next year was made Inquisitor for the provinces of Cologne, Mainz, and Trèves. Seven years later he became the head of the Dominican

Order for the entire province of Germany. Evidently the book they wrote did no harm to their careers.

Their book was a manual for witch burners, the *Malleus Maleficarum*—the "Hammer of Witchcraft." It proved immensely popular and went through many editions; indeed, it was still being printed in the twentieth century.

In its own demented way this book was logical. It pointed out all the crimes the witches committed, the tricks they would employ to ensnare others, and the relevant punishment that should then be applied by the Inquisition. It rapidly became the ultimate authority on the subject.

But it is a book emanating from some utterly deranged parallel universe and written by men who, behind all their legalistic posturing, were completely terrified by women, especially pretty women. A woman, the writers assure us, is "beautiful to look upon, contaminating to the touch and deadly to keep."[33]

The origins of witchcraft, in their minds, come from this beautiful source: "All witchcraft comes from carnal lust which is in women insatiable."[34]

A number of practical procedures to avoid contamination or influence by these powerful and insatiable women had obviously been tried out in the field by Messrs. Kramer and Sprenger, and the poisonous fruit of their research was passed on to the reader in the *Malleus Maleficarum*.

To enable the efficient running of the Inquisitorial court, witches were brought in backward so that the judge would not become bewitched by their gaze. These women were carried high off the ground in baskets or on a wooden board so that they could not establish contact with the earth, which was reckoned to be the source of their influence, a conduit of sorts to the demonic realm they served. Judges were warned not to let themselves be physically touched by these women, and they were especially advised to avoid contact with the bare arms or hands of any of the accused.

And in what now is a deeply tragic record of the misery these poor women were subjected to by powerful, intellectual, and intolerant men, the accused were to be watched for any tendency toward suicide. After a session of torture and prior to the next, "the Judge should also take care that during that interval there should always be guards with her, so that she is never left alone, for fear lest the devil will cause her to kill herself."[35]

The book reveals that women had attempted to stab themselves with their own hatpins or to hang themselves with shoelaces or garments; naturally encouraged by the devil. One can only imagine their anguish and hopelessness.

The main intent of the *Malleus Maleficarum*, and the preceding papal bull of 1484, which for the first time recognized the "reality" of witchcraft, was to produce a logical view of the world in which the cruelty and ignorance of the Inquisitors could be made acceptable. Their world looked, felt, smelled, and tasted the same as ours, but to enter it was to enter one where all morality was placed in the service of those who wielded power. It was one where the forests and beaches were still beautiful, where the clear mountain water was still chilled and sweet, but where the burning to death of innocent women was quite normal.

Reading the work of Rushdoony, it struck me that a very similar process was at work. If his world should come into existence, the heavens might still be beautiful, but they would look down upon an earth grown much darker by virtue of the rules he would lay down. It would be a world that might look normal on the surface but is twisted askew from the real one.

The German poet Stefan George, the mentor of Claus von Stauffenberg, who precipitated the last attempt on the life of Adolf

Hitler, was sufficiently aware of this phenomenon to write a poem called *Der widerchrist*—the Antichrist. Even though it was written in 1907 it presaged the attraction and the methods of Hitler and, indeed, any other aspiring dictatorial demigod on this earth. George describes the world of the Antichrist as,

> A hairs-breadth impure, but you'll not note the fraud
> With your stunted and stultified senses.[36]

On Planet Rushdoony, the powers that be may not openly declare that they want to burn witches—though death is prescribed for witch-craft in the Bible—but one gets the feeling that a public burning would not be too far down the line if they ever succeeded in gaining power; Planet Rushdoony is a world that is "a hairs-breadth impure." And just like those ancient Inquisitors, Rushdoony's acolytes invoke God to justify their madness.

Yes. We can say it. Planet Rushdoony is a new Salem creeping out of intelligent but demented minds like an elderly mad turtle, awak-ened after three hundred years of slumber, poking its head out of an old shell most had long thought empty. And it is this world that the Christian Reconstructionists want to create in order to attract Jesus back to earth. It is no exaggeration to say that the Reconstructionists want to create hell and call it heaven.

It reminds us that we need to take care. Ideas have power, and we often underestimate that power until it is too late.

And lest we might think that this power that lurks like a silent barracuda in the depths of Planet Rushdoony will remain a theoreti-cal teaching, never to be actualized in our modern world, we must think again. The fear and hatred of witchcraft is indeed exercised today by certain fundamentalist Pentecostal Christian preachers. In particular we see it emerging in southern Nigeria where, unlike the Muslim north, Christianity is the dominant religion—a Christianity mixed with age-old African beliefs and fired by the rapid spread of extremist Pentecostal churches and preachers through Nigeria's sixty-million-strong Christian community over the last fifty years.

Late in 2008 a report was published in a major British newspaper, the *Daily Telegraph*, of the sadistic torture, maiming, or murder of young children who were accused of being witches. These children are condemned as witches, possessed by Satan, by extreme Pentecostal preachers. These preachers broadcast throughout their community the belief that these young witches can destroy families, bring about the death of relatives, and cause others to be touched by demonic forces. The priest's mode of exorcism can involve, as charity workers have discovered, being "beaten or slashed with knives, thrown onto fires, or had acid poured over them." One preacher claimed that he had killed over one hundred and ten individuals accused of witchcraft.[37]

These beliefs have traveled with tourists and immigrants abroad. In particular, London has seen some horrific crimes attributed to this belief in the living power of Satan. In the fall of 2001 the torso of a small African child was found floating in the river Thames. Tests on his body revealed sufficient evidence to indicate the killing occurred in a context of witchcraft. Police searching for missing children discovered that around three hundred other young African boys aged four to seven had gone missing in the three months prior to the discovery of the floating torso.[38] Also in London, in May 2005, a ten-year-old African girl, a refugee orphaned by fighting in Angola, was discovered stuffed into a laundry bag, about to be drowned in a river. She had been subject to extreme violent abuse, which could have killed her. This abuse was begun because the adults who held her claimed she was a witch.[39]

Just as Rushdoony never underestimated the power of ideas, neither do his followers. As we have seen, the mission of Christian Reconstruction is to spread its ideas throughout the Christian Right groups. Rushdoony's vision may only be openly advocated by a vocal few, but the basic underlying concept of Christian Reconstruction and Dominionism—that biblical law should serve as the law of the land— has certainly been broadcast widely throughout the Christian Right of the United States and beyond. It is fair to say that these ideas have insinuated themselves into the wider Christian Right agenda in the United States, an agenda that moves stealthily toward a goal of replacing the Constitution and democracy with a hard-line theocracy; this agenda can result in a North American Christian version of a Taliban state if not checked. The tragedy is that these ideas have, in a sinister manner, manipulated the beliefs of many simple Christians whose private devotion would harm no one.

The effects of Reconstruction theology are being felt, especially in the nation's courts and legislature, both federal and state, where followers or sympathizers have gained office and influence. One very visible example is in the widespread opposition to abortion. While it is important to keep note of the fact that while abortion is a messy and distasteful business of questionable morality, it is still necessary for it to remain an option however one might wish otherwise. One would not, for instance, ban the armed forces because war was messy, distasteful, and of questionable morality. But Rushdoony sees no possibility of compromise on the subject of abortion: it is murder, a contravention of the sixth commandment, and punishable by death. Furthermore, any other person who is involved in the killing of an unborn child should also be killed.[40] Surely, he must have realized what he had unleashed by this theological position.

In the United States arguments rage over the very availability of abortion; in Europe the arguments are more concerned with the age of the fetus at the time of termination. The moral arguments are clear, but the ground is shifting as new medical advances allow younger and younger fetuses to be nurtured to life. Yet, at the same time, medical advances allow us to more readily identify congenital disease or damage, either of which may cause the birth of someone devoid of the possibility of any quality of life.

The passions generated by this issue are strong, and strong passions can be focused and aimed. Participants in the anti-abortion violence are drawn into a worldview in which the anger they unleash is condoned and encouraged. Followers of the Christian Reconstructionists were quick to capitalize on this.

Previously, the main opposition to abortion came from Roman Catholic groups, but Rushdoony provided Protestants with a theology that justified their opposition to abortion too. In 1981 a Rushdoony supporter, Francis Schaeffer, added the call for direct action; he wrote of the need for a "crusade" to openly and relentlessly fight against abortion. His call for action was heard by hundreds of thousands of people. As a result, large numbers of activists became embedded in the cause while at the same time becoming familiar with Christian Reconstruction theology.

This cause turned increasingly violent: a follower of Christian Reconstructionism, Paul Hill, in 1994 murdered a doctor and an assistant outside their abortion clinic in Pensacola, Florida. He was executed in 2003. Operation Rescue, founded in 1987 by Randall Terry, was also much influenced by the Christian Reconstruction message. Terry was arrested on many occasions for his direct action against abortion and the clinics that performed them.

These campaigns have had a direct effect upon abortion in the United States: roughly two-thirds of all the clinics where abortions were performed have ceased operation over the last decade or so. Abortions can no longer be obtained in an estimated 87 percent of U.S. counties.[41] We can see clearly that Christian Reconstructionism may appear as a very small blip on most people's radar, but it has caused far-wider-reaching effects than its trace might suggest was possible. Due to its concern with political lobbying at a municipal, state, or federal level, it knows the buttons to push. And this knowledge is valuable in the task of encouraging politicians to make changes in the laws.

Christian Right legal and lobbying groups have sprung up: the Eagle Forum and Michael Farris's Home School Legal Defense Association are two nationwide organizations that lobby to change existing laws or prevent new ones from being passed by politicians and to defend Christians against state control. Christian Right constitutional lawyer Michael Farris, in an appendix to his 1992 book *Where Do I Draw the Line*, lists the details of eighteen legal and lobbying organizations that are supporting the Christian Right agenda across the United States together with twenty-eight state-based organizations.

Even now the Christian Reconstructionists are chipping away at the separation between church and state and are aiming directly at the First Amendment, added to the Constitution in 1791. The aim of this amendment was to preserve the freedom of religion, speech, and the press:

> Congress shall make no law respecting an establishment of religion or prohibiting the free exercise thereof; or abridging the freedom of speech, or of the press; or the right of the people peaceably to assemble, and to petition the Government for a redress of grievances.[42]

Because of the First Amendment, public-school students are able to hold any belief they choose, and the schools' administrations and teachers are not permitted to promote or preach any religious beliefs. For this reason prayer is forbidden in public schools: the U.S. Supreme Court has established that such prayer runs the risk of "indirect coercion."

Christian Reconstructionists and Dominionists, however, would like to see the First Amendment removed, because they find it anti-Christian.

The Rutherford Institute, for example, which has received funds from the Coors family and on whose board Rushdoony served, is a conservative Christian legal group that exists to defend civil rights and religious liberties with a particular focus upon First Amendment issues.

Its online bookstore offers some rather interesting works: a biography of Francis Schaeffer, and a book that questions the separation of church and state in the First Amendment. It is strictly pro-life in the abortion debate and sells a pamphlet detailing a strategy to influence the community the reader lives in. Another called "Christians Involved in the Political Process," as its blurb says, "will challenge you to examine your political convictions and inspire you to act on them. Stop watching from the sidelines and join the game—before it's too late."[43] Another pamphlet provides instructions on how the church might become involved in politics, help in campaigns, and support or criticize those running for political office. It also reveals how the church might avoid the risk of thereby losing its tax-exempt status. Naturally it sells many books by its founder, John Whitehead, who argues for the adoption of a "biblical world-view" in "the arts and sciences and our schools and courts." This all smells very familiar. Could it be smoke drifting in over the horizon?

There is another area where Rushdoony's Christian Reconstruction theology is having a profound effect: homeschooling. In time, it might prove to have the greatest effect of all.

As communities developed across the United States, education for children was vital, and in order to maintain a common standard, during the nineteenth century all of the education in the United States was brought under state regulation. Since then there have been certain sections of society that have not wanted to involve their children in the state system, nor have they wished to create another school; instead they've wanted to educate their children at home in the way that they felt best.

Many of the original advocates of homeschooling were concerned with the public-school system's child-centered, secular approach to education. They either sought to avoid the pitfalls of institutional learning or wished to educate children who had special needs more individually outside of the system. But it was only a matter of time before those who belonged to churches that were at odds with conventional religions, or with the state itself, realized that they could use the same principle to raise their children within their own particular worldview. Thus was born religious homeschooling, which aims to raise children in a "godly" life. This is now the most common form of homeschooling in the United States.

The hatred and fear of public schooling reaches such a pitch amongst some advocates that one wonders at the source of such spite; secular homeschool supporter Mary McCarthy quotes one Reconstructionist attorney as stating that "Sending our children to the public school violates nearly every Biblical principle. It is tantamount to sending our children to be trained by the enemy."[44]

The father of such religious homeschooling is said by many commentators to be Rousas John Rushdoony. It is hard to disagree with them. His attitude was simple: "Christian homes which have sent their children into public schools have denied their faith and asked for moral anarchism."[45] The Reconstructionist homeschooling raises children who will later support a theocracy in the United States. "Scary Gary" North reveals the plan:

> So let us be blunt about it: we must use the doctrine of religious liberty to gain independence for Christian schools until we train up a generation of people who know that there is no religious neutrality, no neutral law, no neutral education, and no neutral civil government. Then they will get busy in constructing a Bible-based social, political and religious order which finally denies the religious liberty of the enemies of God.[46]

The kind of curriculum taught is obviously up to the individual parents, but organizations exist that supply ready-made schooling programs, precooked and attractively packaged. One such supplier is the Christian Liberty Academy School System. They offer a fully formed curriculum for all school grades, which aims to deliver a "Godly education." Looking at it, one can easily spot the Dominionist religious orientation. For example, eighth graders study a course called "Exploring Creation with General Science"; tenth graders study "God and Government"; eleventh graders study "U.S. History in Christian Perspective." Of course the Academy also runs a bookstore, and among the books it supplies are those of "Scary Gary" North.

Regardless of what people say about the freedom of education or the independence from state control, what much of religious homeschooling is all about is the manipulation of children's belief structures. It's a kind of intellectual and spiritual pedophilia. They take the children early and indoctrinate them into a particular rigid worldview, which, in its black-and-white attitudes, allows for no gray, no flexibility. It is, of course, a tried and tested means of manipulation. As one anonymous commentator put it succinctly, homeschooling "is first and foremost about the ideological control of children." The Jesuits used to say "give us your boy till he is seven, and we have him for life." The Islamic madrassas, too, take children early and teach them very little other than their interpretation of the Koran. And we all know the problems this has caused.

Many religious homeschoolers want to train the leaders of tomorrow. They are happy to state this explicitly. "Scary Gary" North is quoted as saying, "All long-term social change comes from the successful efforts . . . to capture the minds of a hard core of future leaders."[47] Journalist John Sugg comments, "Card-carrying Reconstructionists are few, but their influence is magnified by their leadership in Christian right crusades, from abortion to homeschooling."[48]

And how are they doing? Rather well, it has to be said.

This blend of religion and politics we have been looking at has been incubating for a lot longer than we might think. One small example: in 1976 "Scary Gary" North, Rushdoony's son-in-law and member of the Chalcedon Foundation, served on the staff of Texas Republican congressman Ron Paul in Washington until Paul's defeat in 1977 (Paul was later reelected and, as of this writing, is still serving in the House). We would expect that this small but telling incident might reveal an accord between Ron Paul and the aims of Rushdoony's foundation. And we would be correct to do so.

The Chalcedon Foundation supports the reduction of big government, the removal of state control over finance, medical care, or education. It particularly, as we have seen, promotes homeschooling.

In 1992 Ron Paul supported and advised staunch social conservative and culture warrior Patrick Buchanan in his unsuccessful bid for the presidency. Ron Paul ran as a candidate himself in the presidential race of 2008. His platform stressed his support for homeschooling: "The federal government," he wrote, "does not own our children. Yet we act as if it does by letting it decide when, how, and what our children will learn."[49] And he added, "I will use my authority to prevent the Department of Education from regulating home school activities."[50] In fact, he would like to shut down the entire U.S. Department of Education.

Furthermore, if we look at the legislation proposed to Congress by Ron Paul, we see further parallels to those interests of Chalcedon: in 2002 Ron Paul proposed legislation to abolish the U.S. Federal Reserve system. While he does not state it explicitly, the implication of his proposal is the return to the gold standard.[51] He also wants to bring federal income tax to an end. He is strongly pro-life, and in 2005 he introduced a bill to Congress that affirmed that life begins at conception and in addition removed abortion from the Supreme Court's remit. This would render the *Roe v. Wade* decision, which allows abortion in the United States, irrelevant, thus ending the right to abortion. The bill failed to pass.

Ron Paul abandoned his bid for the presidency in early 2008, but he remained active in the campaigning circus. On the second day of the Republican Convention in Minneapolis, September 2, 2008, Paul held a large "Rally for the Republic" with speakers and country-and-western singers entertaining the crowd. The list of sponsors for this rally is interesting: one of them was the Chalcedon Foundation. Another was the John Birch Society.

We should not be too surprised; the Chalcedon Foundation likes Ron Paul. As one supporter of both Ron Paul and the Chalcedon Foundation stated, "every Chalcedon supporter I know is an ardent supporter of Dr. Ron Paul."[52] The official Chalcedon Web site also supports him. In May 2008 the site carried an article by Rushdoony arguing that the only true currencies were gold and silver; printing paper money was tantamount to counterfeiting. In September 2008 early in the worldwide banking crisis, Chris Ortiz, the director of communications for Chalcedon, bitterly criticized the financial sector and those who control it. He posted a clip from a CNN "Late Edition" interview with Ron Paul who was advocating reform of the financial system by means of a "return to sound money."[53] These two figures may not be saying exactly the same thing, but they are certainly happily locked into orbit around each other.

Congressman Ron Paul may never have expressed support for Chalcedon's Calvinistic theocratic aspirations, but, however decent and honest he might be as a man, he is helping to ease the way for those who do. And no amount of smiles, godly actions, and "down home" camaraderie can remove that stain.

Christian Right influence has reached Congress, the Senate, and further: five of the 2008 Republican presidential candidates—senators John McCain (Arizona) and Sam Brownback (Kansas), together with representatives Duncan Hunter (California), Ron Paul (Texas), and Tom Tancredo (Colorado)—all received high scores from the Christian Coalition for their support of Christian Right issues.[54] Candidate Tommy Thompson (Wisconsin) was not rated, but in 1998 he was listed as a member of the Council for National Policy along with Rushdoony, "Scary Gary" North, Tim LaHaye, Holland Coors, Lieutenant-Colonel Oliver North, and Major-General John K. Singlaub and others.[55] When the Council for National Policy began in 1981, two of the founders were Christian Reconstructionists, Rushdoony and North.

And just how much has this influence already soaked into the "givens" of U.S. foreign policy? How much did the ideas affect decisions in the war in Iraq for example? How many soldiers of all ranks serving in the Middle East and the Pentagon hold a "biblical worldview"? Do the answers to these questions explain, for example, the phenomenon we have already explored where U.S. weapons and military events often carry names with a biblical resonance—the "shock and awe" language, the MOAB bomb; the "Rods from God" weaponry? It seems very plausible.

In 1986 when the Coalition on Revival, which adhered to the principle of the inerrancy of the Bible, was founded as a "network of evangelical leaders," it produced "A Manifesto for the Christian Church" dated July 4 that year. Those who assigned their signatures to this document along with the Coalition director, Jay Grimstead, included R. J. Rushdoony (Chalcedon Foundation), "Scary Gary" North (Institute for Christian Economics), Peter Gemma (National ProLife Political Action Co.), Duane Gish (Institute for Creation Research), Michael Farris (Home School Legal Defense Association), D. James Kennedy (Coral Ridge Presbyterian Church), Tim LaHaye (American Coalition for Traditional Values), coauthor of the Left Behind book series.[56]

The late Paul Weyrich, founding president of the Heritage Foundation, which we have noted, also revealed a familiarity with

Rushdoony's theology. Weyrich stated that one of his targets for the manipulation of voters was the homeschooling fraternity.[57] The Coors family, large donors to the Heritage Foundation have, among many other bequests to the religious right, also given funds to the home-schooling movement.[58]

Above all, "godly" homeschooling is a danger to America and perhaps to Western society in general. Belief systems, grown into, are hard to subsequently change. Many Islamic terrorists were educated as young children in the madrassa system; all they know is the Koran and *sharia* law. Are we to have Christian terrorists in the future just as we have Islamic ones now? Terrorists raised in particularly ideological homeschool systems? Sadly, on current trends, it seems likely.

Especially so, if in the same way that young Muslims are taught to hate the *kaffirs*, or non-Muslims, young Christian students are taught that nongodly Christians are doing the work of Satan. The sanction for then executing them as enemies of the "godly" is established. It just takes one final step—a Supreme Court decision perhaps, or a president who uses the power of his or her office to overthrow or cripple the Constitution.

It could happen.

And that possibility was brought home to observers on September 3, 2008, at the Republican National Convention, in St. Paul, Minnesota, when Republican presidential candidate John McCain produced his vice-presidental candidate, Alaska governor Sarah Palin. It was not lost on those present that John McCain was seventy-two years old with health issues and Sarah Palin was a healthy, hunting and fishing, forty-four. She could have become president. So her competence and her beliefs came under intense scrutiny. And what the media found was very worrying.

Firstly she had made statements revealing a worldview firmly informed by fundamentalist religious tenets. During an address given to a class of graduating students in the Assembly of God church in her hometown of Wasilla, Alaska, in June 2008, she made the point that the fighting in Iraq needed to be divinely inspired:

> Pray for our military men and women who are striving to do what is right. Also for this country, that our leaders, our national leaders, are sending [U.S. Soldiers] out on a task that is from God. . . . That's what we have to make sure that we're praying for, that there is a plan and that that plan is God's plan.[59]

She had already asked the audience to pray for the successful negotiations to build a $30 billion gas pipeline through Alaska, which she also considered was "God's will."

However, she was very careful not to publicly reveal her religious beliefs; nevertheless, she has spent most of her adult life in a religious milieu, which gives cause for concern in a public servant. When she was twelve years old, she and her family were baptized at the Assembly of God church in Wasilla. As late as 2005 when she was beginning her successful campaign to become governor of Alaska, she was anointed by three pastors in a special ceremony held at the church. Two of those pastors have confirmed that "believing Christians, as they define those, can learn to raise from the dead." They also "believe that crime and social pathologies are caused when 'demons' possess geographic areas and that 'curses' can be transmitted from one human generation to the next."[60] One of these pastors, the Kenyan Thomas Muthee, reportedly "implored Jesus to protect Palin from 'the spirit of witchcraft.'"[61] It is, then, useful to look more closely at her church and the belief systems it advances since she will have absorbed at least some of them over the twenty-six years she attended it.

Officially, Palin left her Wasilla church in 2002 and attends another in the state capital of Juneau, but she remains classed as a "friend" of the Wasilla church. Both these churches are part of the Assemblies of God network and both adhere to a hard-line theology, one which we have noted before. They are part of a movement called the New Apostolic Reformation, a movement that was condemned in 1949 by the majority of the Assemblies of God, a condemnation that was repeated in 2000. As journalist Bruce Wilson explains, "They're working to bring about a Christian theocratic government." The danger is, he says, "If you are against them, you are working for the devil."

Wilson reveals that members of the New Apostolic Reformation "believe that God is anointing them with special powers in order for them to battle the ungodly themselves, and that Jesus can't actually return until they have finished conquering the world."[62] These churches, in other words, follow the Dominionist worldview. If Sarah Palin had become vice president, and if some tragedy should have occurred, propelling her into the White House, then we would have needed to know what she believes, for as president and commander in chief of the armed forces, her view of the world would have been helping create it—or destroy it.

We have then, in today's United States, a widely shared vision of an American empire run from a rigid religious center brooking no opposition to the rule of God's law universally and ruthlessly applied, a pitiless law governed by a book, every word of which is held to be absolutely true. Does this not seem just a little familiar?

How is such a program of a theocratic empire under biblical law different from the Islamic fundamentalist's demand for a worldwide caliphate and the introduction of sharia law? We need to shift our gaze to Islam.

We have two ideas before us, each claiming to serve a different god, each insisting on its divine right to rule the world.

I do indeed see smoke and flames. Welcome to the war.

ELEVEN

THE CALIPHATE

"**D**emocracy is *haram*! Forbidden in Islam. Don't you know that?" An English convert to Islam warmed to his theme, a heated denunciation of the corrupt and crumbling West.

"Democracy is a Greek concept . . . people's rule. In Islam, we don't rule; Allah rules. Human beings do not have legislative power. The world today suffers from the malignant cancers of freedom and democracy."[1]

For eighteen-year-old English Muslim Ed Husain, this kind of talk was fresh and new; dangerously, it stirred his blood; listening to it made him feel more of a Muslim, enabling him to reject the very basis of the Western society that had nurtured him. He felt strangely liberated and attracted to the group advocating these ideas. He did not realize it then, but it was going to take quite some time for him to see what a deceptive and dangerous illusion these exciting words were conveying.

Ed Husain was born in the East End of London to a family of moderate Muslims who had come to England from Bangladesh in 1961. His father in particular was insistent upon practicing his religion in a manner that was personal, nonpolitical, and nonconfrontational with the English. Even the part of London in which he chose to live reflected this commitment, as it was heavily populated by Jewish and Hindu society. To Ed, however, this tolerant accommodation seemed less a mark of spirituality than one of weakness and submission. By the age of sixteen, he had already become politically active in this new hard-line cause.

But it wasn't until his years of higher education that he came into contact with truly radical Islam, in particular, with a group called *Hizb ut-Tahrir*—the "Party of Liberation." This organization was founded in Palestine in 1952 with the primary aim of forming a huge Islamic state under a caliph, which would ultimately rival the power blocs of the United States and the European Union—a caliphate that would embrace every country that presently has a Muslim population together with those countries formerly ruled by Islam such as India and most of Spain—the medieval emirate of al-Andalus, the last residues of which fell to the Christian Spanish armies of the *reconquista* in 1492. The idea of such a caliphate was not a wholly new concept.

The formation of the original caliphate came very early in the history of Islamic expansion. When Mohammed died in A.D. 632, he did so without having made provisions for a successor—which, given the fact that he had no sons, left the burgeoning Islamic movement with something of a problem, one which has never been satisfactorily resolved since. At the time, however, Abu Bakr, Mohammed's father-in-law, took the title *Khalifat rasul-Allah*—"successor to the Apostle of God"—and it is from this that the title *caliph* is derived. The caliphate fell into the hands of dynasties based firstly in Medina, then Damascus and Baghdad.

The other candidate for the post of successor was Ali, the husband of Mohammed's daughter Fatima, and the man the Shiites have regarded as the true successor ever since. The Shiites' embrace of Ali and their outward rejection of the authority of the other caliphs based in Damascus and Baghdad naturally led to considerable friction.

The title eventually faded in prestige as the power of the sultans of Egypt increased. The whole institution was brought to an abrupt end in 1258 when the invading Mongol army swept down from the northeast and destroyed Baghdad together with whatever remained of the caliphate. In time, leadership in the Islamic world passed from Egypt to the Ottoman sultans of Turkey, but it was not until much later, in the nineteenth century, that the title of caliph was taken up by these sultans. This line, too, came to an end in 1924 when Atatürk, the great reforming leader of Turkey who created the modern secular state, abolished it. For members of Hizb ut-Tahrir this was a disaster, which they were determined to rectify.

Hizb ut-Tahrir had no qualms about advocating the assassination of any Muslim leaders who stood in the way of the arrival of the new caliph and the overthrow of their states. Naturally, this caused the Hizb ut-Tahrir to be banned throughout the Middle East as well as in certain European countries—but not in England, where, led by Omar Bakri Mohammed, the organization actively and openly recruited university students. During an outbreak of realism, the UK government finally recognized the organization's radical tenets for what they were and deported Omar Bakri to Lebanon.

There may not have been any formal connection between the Hizb ut-Tahrir in England and prime figures behind later terrorist events, but the total freedom the group had enjoyed under Omar Bakri's leadership in London surely must have made communication and coordination between the extremists in England and extremists in other countries much easier. It is certainly true that a number of terrorists, amongst them Osama bin Laden, his subordinate Ayman al-Zawahiri, and the shoe bomber Richard Reid, had been influenced by the uncompromising views of Hizb ut-Tahrir; other al-Qaeda officials such as Abu Musab al-Zarqawi and Khalid Sheikh Mohammed were actually noted members of the organization.[2] The teaching of Hizb ut-Tahrir, that a conspiracy by Zionists and Christians was intent upon oppressing the world's Muslims and that the sole defense was to fight for a worldwide caliphate, is today acknowledged "as the cornerstone of al-Qaeda's ideology."[3]

It is this message that caused a student at the London School of Economics, Ahmed Omar Saeed Sheikh, to move to Pakistan and embrace terrorism. He is now imprisoned there, having been convicted of the brutal killing of American journalist Daniel Pearl. The same message turned Omar Khan Sharif, a student at Kings College, London, into a suicide bomber who attempted to detonate his bomb in a Tel Aviv bar.[4]

But Ed Husain was different from these other young men. Over time, he began to harbor doubts about the group; he first lamented their lack of spirituality, for he had always understood the "essence of Islam" to be "spiritual surrender to serenity."[5] Pondering further upon these doubts, he asked himself, "If Islamic governance was of such importance, why did not one classical Muslim text have a chapter dedicated to this? The entire notion of the 'Islamic state' is a modern phenomenon."[6]

He then asked a more dangerous question: "If God was on the Muslim side then why had we failed to establish the Islamic state? Why were the 'enemies of God,' as we viewed the West, politically dominant?"[7]

Furthermore, Ed saw that socially the system that the group proposed and lived by did not seem to be working very well; he noted that women were treated as spoils of war or like cattle. Other oddities abounded too: pornography, for example, was permitted by the group since it was not expressly condemned in the Koran. In fact, Hizb ut-Tahrir officers went out of their way to find passages that appeared to sanction it. Leaders in the group held fantasies about concubines and blond eastern European women. They seriously planned for a change in lifestyle and an increase in status when the caliphate ruled the world.[8] It was as if this new state would emulate the corruption, decadence, and idle pursuit of pleasure that typified Ottoman rule over the Middle East—an empire where even the minor provincial governors acted as though the world owed them a living; where a constant supply of good food, young boys, and opium delivered to their palaces was all that was needed to keep the peace and permits for the endemic corruption flowing. Was this really what modern Muslims wanted? It seemed most unlikely.

While the founder of the Hizb ut-Tahrir advocated segregation between the male and female members of the organization, Ed noticed that few were actually adhering to this rule. In fact, many were in less than discreet relationships with each other. When he queried one of the local leaders on this point, the reply he received annoyed him intensely: "Women are like the plague," the leader exclaimed, "Avoid them at all costs."[9]

With such misogynistic attitudes so openly expressed, we should not be surprised to find that the rate of divorce is higher amongst members of radical Muslim groups than with other Muslims.[10]

As a result of his doubts, Ed turned away from this political group and moved toward that mystical stream within Islam that we call Sufi, one great exponent of which was the thirteenth-century Persian Islamic saint Jalaluddin Rumi, who was so revered that upon his death representatives of virtually every religion attended his funeral. One problem for the Sufi movement, however, is that they are regarded as heretical by the Wahhabi sect of Sunni Islam, the sect that dominates Saudi Arabia and is well funded by Saudi wealth funneled through numerous charitable organizations in order that it might maintain its influence internationally. Sufis were persecuted in Afghanistan under the rule of the Saudi-funded Taliban although most of the funds in this instance were privately donated, since the Taliban's friends, Osama bin Laden and his al-Qaeda organization, wished also to remove the Saudi leadership, which it regarded as corrupt. Al-Qaeda is as much an enemy of the Saudi Arabian government as it is of Western governments.

The Taliban, of course, felt justified, since they thought they were helping to establish the central part of the revived caliphate, beginning with a messianic Islamic state. The mindless destruction of huge statues of the Buddha in the Bamiyan Valley in 2001 was a further declaration of this intent.[11] In 1996 Taliban leader Mullah Omar went so far as to declare himself the expected messianic leader; most other Muslims simply laughed at him. They could see that the global caliphate was not going to come from Afghanistan on the point of a Kalashnikov assault rifle or in an intoxicating cloud of opium.

For most Muslims who awaited the caliphate, its appearance would be an apocalyptic event at the end of time ushered in by the Messiah—the Mahdi—the Caliph of God. At his side will stand Jesus.

Jesus standing shoulder to shoulder with the Mahdi?

Exactly what—we have good reason to ask—is going on here?

Before the Day of Judgment can begin, the Muslims must slaughter all the Jews without mercy—so explains one Muslim tradition dating from the ninth century A.D.:

> And the Jews seek refuge behind a rock or a tree, and the rock or tree calls out: "O Muslim, there is a Jew hiding behind me, come and kill him." But the thorny Gharkad tree will not call out because it is the tree of the Jews.[12]

This early *hadith* has found wide acceptance throughout the Muslim world, especially, and naturally, amongst those who wish to see Israel annihilated: the 1988 foundation charter of Hamas, article seven, states explicitly that the organization seeks "to implement Allah's promise" as communicated by Mohammed, that the Day of Judgment will not come until the Muslims have killed all the Jews.[13]

The aim is to ensure that not a single member of the Jewish race survives; to seize Jerusalem, which will then become the messianic capital of Islam; to take over all the technology developed by the West and put it in the hands of the true believers; and, finally, to convert the whole world to Islam, putting Allah's chosen people into their rightful position—in charge. That, in essence, is the Islamic apocalyptic vision of the end times.

If we leave aside the feral anti-Semitism, it is not so different from the vision of the Christian fundamentalists like Rousas Rushdoony and his Reconstructionists who want to convert the entire world to Christianity and rule from a new Jerusalem, which comes down from the clouds. And, with a few tweaks, its arrogant sectarianism is also compatible with the end-times visions of the Jewish fundamentalists who also want to rule from a Jerusalem with its mosques erased and a new Temple standing on the Mount. Jerusalem truly is the focus for the apocalyptic traditions of Judaism, Christianity, and Islam: they all claim it in the names of their religions.

On his way from Lebanon into Israel with his victorious army, heading for his destiny in the great battle of Armageddon, the Mahdi gives the following proclamation—at least as rendered by the best-selling and widely distributed Egyptian author Muhammad Isa Da'ud in 1997:

> Jerusalem is truly the city of peace, God is peace, and Islam is peace. The mobilisation of America and the West here is a war against the Lord of Peace, and they are the aggressors under the flag of the Jews. . . . Jerusalem is Arab Muslim, and Palestine—all of it, from the river to the sea—is Arab Muslim, and there is no place in it for any who depart from peace or from Islam."[14]

In Da'ud's work, all this talk of peace comes after the Mahdi and his army have conquered their way across the Middle East, beginning with Egypt and including Turkey, Iran, Afghanistan, Pakistan, the central Asian Islamic states as well as Malaysia and Indonesia. From there he will move to Africa, taking Libya, Sudan, and East Africa to Mozambique. Only then does he turn his attention to Lebanon and Israel.[15] In the midst of all this diplomacy, fighting, and capitulation, the Mahdi announces the formation of the caliphate. Other writers say that by this time all of Europe has either been conquered or has declared itself Muslim and joined the forces of the Mahdi.

With the Mahdi dominant in Lebanon, the United States decides to fight, and a fleet sails toward the eastern Mediterranean. But it is destroyed by a nuclear explosion. Another nuclear explosion destroys New York—apparently after a surprise attack by France—and a number of nuclear bombs destroy the Western and Jewish armies at Armageddon. Da'ud rather likes nuclear weaponry, but he doesn't really understand its power, since he depicts the Mahdi as moving into Jerusalem following all of these explosions. I suppose, however, that we are meant to suspend disbelief because these events occur under the control of God, so anything is possible. And, no doubt aiding matters, is the fact that Jesus returns from heaven once the Mahdi is in Jerusalem.

Reading this summary, the problem with Da'ud's story becomes quite clear, much like the problem with LaHaye's Christian fundamentalist vision: why would God need to use weaponry of any kind, let alone nuclear weaponry, when he already has a tried-and-tested arsenal for smiting sinners, including: thunderbolts, burning winds, plagues of frogs and floods or—as advertised in the Koran—boiling water to melt the skin, flames from the fires of hell to burn faces, crevices in the earth to swallow men, "lumps" to fall upon us from the heavens, and so forth. There seems to be plenty of choice and all without causing the land of Palestine to have a nuclear glow for the next fifty thousand years or so.

Further calling Da'ud's proclamation into question is the false prediction he made in 1997 that the battle of Armageddon would occur in 2001. He seems to have been especially quiet since that time.

Da'ud, of course, is not the only modern commentator attempting to tie the ancient traditions into current events. It is evident that earlier times have not seen the advent of the Mahdi, and the Islamic nations are still subjected to the domination of the hated West—a domination that, in the end, Muslims are promised, will be overturned by the Mahdi. The situation for Da'ud and these other writers is summarized by Dr. David Cook:

> Most of these authors subscribe to the idea of an international conspiracy against Islam . . . and to the idea that the best manner in which to counter such a conspiracy is to unite all Muslims into one state ruled by a caliph.[16]

These apocalyptic writings and their encouragement of a worldwide caliphate fit very well with the aims of politically radical Muslims such as the Hizb ut-Tahrir, which we have noted. The main difference, however, between these writers and these fundamentalist organizations is that the political radicals wish to fight to organize a caliphate now rather than wait for the advent of the Mahdi in a time frame none can yet determine.

We would be correct in thinking that there is something vaguely familiar in this perspective, as a similar split exists between the Christian fundamentalists, such as John Hagee and the late Jerry Falwell, who believe that Jesus is going to usher in the new Christian world and those such as Rousas Rushdoony and his Christian Reconstructionists who consider that this new world must be ushered in first through legislation, direct action, and, ultimately, force. Rushdoony's desire to have an American Christian empire run in accordance with Old Testament law, or theonomy, as he calls it, is by any sane standard indistinguishable from the Islamic radical's desire for a global caliphate to be run under the terms of traditional Islamic law or sharia.

This plan, which the fundamentalist factions of all three religions seem to have in common, took on a greater urgency in 1967: the crucial point for all came during the Six-Day War, when the Israeli forces finally took East Jerusalem and the Temple Mount was again in Jewish hands. As we have seen, this was the moment when fundamentalist Jewish groups began working on plans to rebuild the Temple in preparation for the coming of the Messiah and his theocratic rule over Israel. We have also seen that this was a crucial period for Christian fundamentalists, since following the formation of the state of Israel, it was the next important sign predicted to occur before the coming of Jesus—the Christian Messiah.

For Islam, there was the added urgency that we have already noted: the problem came to the fore with the humiliating and definitive defeats during the Six-Day War of the armies of the great Islamic states, especially those of Egypt and Syria, which had secular socialist governments. In particular it came from the loss of Jerusalem to the hated Israelis. A blend of Islamic political nationalism, fundamentalist theology, and a heady mix of anti-Semitism developed as a result. This, of course, is radical Islam with its major aims of the destruction of Israel and the formation of the worldwide caliphate.

It was out of the political aspiration of this movement that such militant organizations as Hamas developed. As we have seen, Hamas adopted elements of apocalyptic thought into their ideology, the founding covenant of Hamas incorporating as it does the hadith concerning the gharkad tree and the death of all Jews—a tradition that has been applied to justify permanent war and anti-Semitism in apocalyptic Islam. And it was out of the aspirations and speculation arising from such hadiths and their interpretation of this tradition that the modern apocalyptic literature concerning the Islamic Messiah, the Mahdi, has developed.

But before we explore this further, we must remember that there are two great streams in Islam—the Sunni and the Shiite—and there are two concepts of the coming Mahdi. When, for example, President Mahmoud Ahmadinejad of Iran speaks of the Mahdi, he is referring to an entirely different person than the Mahdi advanced by Da'ud and others coming from the Sunni world. It all—as always—goes back to the early days. Islam has a long memory.

Mohammed, as we have already noted, died without a successor, and the Sunni faction recognized caliphs who derived their ancestry from Mohammed's uncle Abu Bakr. The Shiites, on the other hand, held that the true line of successors came from Ali, the husband of Mohammed's daughter Fatima. The Sunnis hold that the Mahdi will be of Mohammed's family; the Shiites see him as the returning "hidden" or Twelfth Imam who disappeared in A.D. 874—the twelfth since the time of Mohammed. The two are not the same figure.

The Twelfth Imam already has an army dedicated to preparing the world for his arrival: the *al-Mahdi* army in Iraq. It was formed in June 2003 by a violently anti-American Shiite cleric, Hojatoleslam Moqtada al-Sadr, as a militia to protect the mosques and holy sites of the Shiites. This militia quickly grew in power, reaching an estimated sixty thousand members by summer 2006 and was based in strongholds such as Sadr City in Baghdad, Najaf, Al-Kut, and Basra. But it has proved a tempestuous force, rent by multiple loyalties, which al-Sadr has never seemed to fully control.

The traditional Sunni story of Jesus and the Mahdi depicts Jesus—in Islam tradition, *Isa ibn Maryam*—coming down from heaven to the mosque on the Temple Mount in Jerusalem. The imam, which in this case is the Mahdi, steps back so that Jesus can lead the dawn prayer. Instead, Jesus declines and, placing his hand between the Mahdi's shoulders, pushes him to the fore so, as their imam, the Mahdi rather than Jesus leads the worshippers in prayer. We find examples of this story dating back to early times—at least to the ninth century A.D.[17]

What this reveals is a little-known aspect of Islam's origin. It developed as an apocalyptic religion—perhaps it was even misunderstood as some type of Christian sect or heresy by many at the time. Its apocalyptic nature was one major driving force behind its expansion. In fact, it is considered possible by David Cook that the initial wave of Christians, at least, who left their own religion and joined Islam did so because of their strong belief in the end times.[18]

It undoubtedly helped that much of this end-times tradition came from already-existing Jewish and Christian texts, including Daniel and Revelation. There are early statements revealing that Muslim scholars consulted the holy books of the Jews and Christians, one of whom was a Western visitor to Constantinople in the mid-tenth century, Luitbrand of Cremona, who reported on the importance of the book of Daniel to both the Byzantine and Muslim scholars studying the end times. He relayed that they used them to determine the future and "to plan out battles."[19] This was hands-on apocalyptic speculation, and it cannot help but remind us that in many fundamentalist Christian minds, and perhaps in certain Islamic ones as well, the Iraq war and speculation over the battle of Armageddon yet to come are not so far apart.

Early Muslims believed that the world was going to end, perhaps the next day, and so there was nothing more important than instant conversion, an urgency that probably was mandated from the very top. Scholarship has revealed that Mohammed held a strong belief in the imminent appearance of the last day. In fact, early tradition has him saying that some of those with him will live to see it. Certainly many of his followers thought this would be so.[20] And this could quite possibly account for his failure to designate a successor. Perhaps he thought that there simply wouldn't be enough time for one to reign. To designate such a successor would be to undercut the powerful impulse derived from a belief in the imminent end of the world, a belief that he himself had unleashed.[21] This powerful impulse, according to David Cook, "provided one of the principal sources of the energy needed to conquer the enormous territory conquered by the Muslims during the first century of Islam, and to establish it as a vital religion."[22]

What Cook leaves unsaid is whether this belief in the end times and the urgency of preparing for it necessarily contains within itself the seeds of conquest and empire building. Perhaps inherent in end-times thought is a military adventurism and a justification of conquest in the name of the religion. If that is the case, we must seriously try to sideline any tendency toward end-times thought in our religions if we are truly to seek peace.

The feeling of urgency certainly is important amongst adherents to end-times beliefs; we have seen the same with Christian fundamentalists—from Ronald Reagan's declaring that it was possible for Armageddon to occur in his lifetime to the late Jerry Falwell's insistence that it was just around the corner. Perhaps, too, it is this urgency that leads believers toward cutting moral corners or taking a hard-line approach to biblical law. In the rush toward the end, some of the things normal human beings hold sacrosanct can easily get trampled underfoot.

But the Mahdi and his armies are not just fighting a coalition of disparate armies; there is a single directing force acting behind them—the force of the Antichrist, the Dajjal.

The Dajjal is a fearsome creature who appears out of the land like one of the beasts of John's apocalyptic vision on Patmos. According to at least one modern Islamic commentator, he lives in a castle in the middle of the Bermuda Triangle. And he is, naturally, Jewish. Indeed, an eclectic blend of paranoid fantasies have found their way into modern Islamic speculation on the end times. That, and a truckload of anti-Semitism.

These modern writers have gone far beyond traditional Islamic texts in the search for material to justify their end-times prophecies, and the Christian book of Revelation has proved a fertile mine to plunder. Material has been drawn from many sources, ranging from early Gnostic texts to the prophecies of Nostradamus to modern Western UFO literature.[23]

And it gets wild.

Bestselling Egyptian author Da'ud would have us believe in the existence of "the Antichrist army of Jinn [spirits] and demons, which kidnap unfortunates who wander into the area of the Bermuda Triangle. Those who are kidnapped are taken down into his fortress castle far beneath the waters."[24]

Perhaps the title of his 1992 book gives the game away a little; its Arabic title translates as, *Warning: the Antichrist is invading the world from the Bermuda Triangle.*

Da'ud is not alone in his marking of the Bermuda Triangle as the home base of the Antichrist. In fact, both Da'ud and writer Muhammad Izzat Arif explain that there is constant contact between this base and the Vatican.[25] In 1997 Arif, who considered rather more plausibly that this Bermuda Triangle base was above water, rather than below, explained to his readers that "The truth is that the Antichrist is a power chained on a remote island, sending his orders through demons subordinated to him, and working before him as servants,"[26] adding that "They inspire Jews, and their slaves the Masons."

Naturally the Jews and kidnappings feature in Da'ud's work too. It is not just the Bermuda Triangle that is a site for systematic abduction, but Muslim children, he says, are specifically targeted in a dastardly plan to build an army of believers for the Antichrist under the command of the Jewish military.

Da'ud exposes this demonic scheme, revealing that the Antichrist softens up these children to accept and believe his ideas by creating "an opening in the mind of each of them so that one of his demons can enter," and in this way a gigantic army is in the process of creation. The site of this military demon possession is in caverns or tunnels beneath the al-Aqsa Mosque on the Temple Mount in Jerusalem, which became accessible after the taking of Jerusalem and the West Bank in the Six-Day War in 1967. He further maintains that all building and excavating in the area is part of a plot to create the needed space.[27]

These demons under the control of the Antichrist have another specific role: they pilot the UFOs the Antichrist uses. In 1996 writer Hisham Kamal 'Abd al-Hamid explained that the flying saucers were not from extraterrestrial sources but rather from the earth, which he reminds us is inhabited by both humans and jinns. He concludes, as we noted earlier, that the "people of flying saucers are demons in human form."[28] And the cover of his book makes it clear how he sees this enemy's chain of command. It depicts

> A Jew, carrying a Star of David, being beamed down from a flying saucer and giving instructions to his black-robed and cowled Masonic acolytes before a golden temple marked "U.N." and decorated with Stars of David.[29]

Clearly, the Islamic apocalyptic writers don't like the Jews, or Israel; they want to see both wiped off the face of the earth.

It comes as something of a shock to confront the sheer viciousness of the anti-Semitism, which is mixed in with the Islamic predictions of apocalypse. It is hard to avoid the thought that if evil exists—like some mad snake running through human experience and aspiration—then this is surely a major sighting.

According to Da'ud, following the battle of Armageddon, the Mahdi will enter Jerusalem and all of Palestine will again be part of the Muslim lands. By this time most of the world's Jews will have been killed—Da'ud says 85 percent—and the "ground will be soaked with their blood."[30] All trace of any Jewish occupation in Jerusalem will then be erased, and the Mahdi will make this ethnically cleansed Jerusalem his capital from where he will rule over the worldwide Islamic caliphate.

Apocalyptic writers like Da'ud have absorbed just about all of the European anti-Semitic fantasies that exist, including the most insidious, the late-nineteenth-century forgeries known as *The Protocols of the Elders of Zion*. On one notorious occasion the late king Faisal of Saudi

Arabia spent time trying to convince President Richard Nixon and his advisor Henry Kissinger that they were true. The fact that the data presented in the *Protocols* is fraudulent does not seem to have been taken on board at all by the king.

The *Protocols* are testimony to a sad fact of human culture: a lie that serves a popular belief system will survive proof of its fraudulence. And, all too often, the bigger the lie, the easier it seems to believe it is true. All our masters of political spin know that. Their jobs depend upon it.

In the latter part of the nineteenth century anti-Semitism was flourishing in central Europe and Russia. Then in 1881 when the Russian czar was assassinated, Jewish involvement was assumed, and that year the first of many violent pogroms was unleashed against Jewish communities, killing or injuring the inhabitants and destroying their property. The next two czars, Alexander III and Nicholas II, proved to be dogmatic anti-Semites. Alexander introduced anti-Jewish laws and condoned the violence. Nicholas, the last of the czars, continued these policies even to the point of allowing the police and the army to instigate their own violent attacks on the Jewish population. This period, too, was when the idea of a worldwide Jewish conspiracy to destroy Christianity and to rule the world was actively, and officially, promulgated. Indeed, one czarist activist, oddly enough of Jewish ancestry, argued in print for the extermination of the entire Jewish race.[31]

Faced with this widespread and officially sanctioned opposition to their culture, Jews began emigrating: between 1881 and the outbreak of the First World War some 2,600,000 moved to the United States from Russia. Nevertheless, it was clear to many Jewish intellectuals that a permanent solution to this cultural enmity needed to be found to protect Jewish society. One such intellectual, Hungarian lawyer and journalist Theodor Herzl, concluded that the foundation of a Jewish state was the only possible solution to resolve the deteriorating situation. This aspiration became known as Zionism. The term was first used in 1890 to describe this movement dedicated to returning the Jewish people to Palestine.

In 1897 the Zionist movement held its first great congress in Basle, Switzerland, where Theodor Herzl was elected the movement's president. Beyond all expectations, this congress caught attention around the world and was to prove the seed from which the state of Israel would grow just over fifty years later.

That there was considerable international support for Zionism, and not just from Jews caught up in violence or discrimination, was clear. Indeed, from the first days of the Protestant Reformation in the early sixteenth century, messianic Protestant sects had supported the return of the Jewish people to Palestine as one of the preliminaries to the second coming of Jesus. In the nineteenth century in particular, the Plymouth Brethren, founded by John Nelson Darby, proclaimed that this return of the Jews was prophesied in the scriptures. We have already noted Darby as the early source for the concept of the rapture and acknowledged his subsequent influence on the writings and proclamations of fundamentalist groups today, virtually all of which hold strong Zionist convictions.

During the period of anti-Semitism and violent pogroms against the Jews in Russia, a curious document surfaced: in 1903, in St. Petersburg, Russia, a newspaper published a text that the editor stated was the translation of a French document titled *Minutes of the Meeting of the World Union of Freemasons and Elders of Zion*. A fuller version was published as a booklet in 1905 and proved so popular that it went through six further editions. This booklet was titled by the newspaper editor the *Program for World Conquest by Jews*.[32] We now know this text as *The Protocols of the Elders of Zion*. Such a publication suited the editor's personal beliefs very nicely; he hated the Jews and had personally initiated an anti-Jewish pogrom in his native Bessarabia.

During the same period, in 1901, Sergey Nilus, a mystical ecclesiastic who was popular in the czar's court, wrote a work called *The Great in the Small. Antichrist considered as an imminent political possibility.* In the third edition of this work, published in 1905, Nilus appended the text of the *Protocols.* The Moscow metropolitan, the leading ecclesiastic in the city, liked it so much that on October 16, 1905, he had it quoted in a sermon preached in all 368 Moscow churches.[33] Sergey Nilus wrote of them in his edition of 1917, the year of the Russian Revolution,

> These *Protocols* are nothing else than a strategic plan for the conquest of the world, putting it under the yoke of Israel, the struggle against God, a plan worked out by the leaders of the Jewish people during the many centuries of dispersion, and finally presented to the Council of Elders by . . . Theodor Herzl, at the time of the first Zionist congress, summoned by him at Basel in August 1897.[34]

There are twenty-four protocols detailed: in summary they propose that the "secret" Jewish rulers were preparing a king of the line of David to rule over the world and that Freemasonry was being used "as a screen for us and our objects."[35] Freemasonry, it is stated, was being used cynically in order to manipulate society toward the plan chosen by the secret Jewish controllers of the world.

At the end of the text it establishes its claim to Masonic power: "Signed by the representatives of Zion, of the 33rd degree."[36] Thus the document claims to have the imprimatur of members of the highest rank in that branch of Freemasonry, called in the United States the Ancient and Accepted Scottish Rite, an alternate but compatible form of Freemasonry to that practiced by the many U.S. Grand Lodges and around the world. Needless to say, the Ancient and Accepted Scottish Rite has no information on this at all. But in the fevered world of anti-Semitism fanned by the czarist secret police, it would seem a career-advancing gambit to concoct, from a range of earlier writings, a paranoid tract that condemned both the Jews and the Freemasons. For the czar opposed masons as well. Officially, Freemasonry had been banned in Russia since 1822.

The *Protocols* went through many editions; indeed it is still on sale in many languages, including English. Many people around the world took the *Protocols* seriously, some as wealthy and as influential as Henry Ford. And it is easy to see how they might continue to feed into Islamic paranoia and anti-Semitism. Yet in 1921 conclusive proof that the *Protocols* was a forgery appeared in the *Times* (London). It was discovered that the *Protocols* was primarily taken from a pamphlet attacking the French emperor Napoleon III published in 1864 and written by a French lawyer, Maurice Joly.[37]

So, the *Protocols* purports to outline a Jewish-Masonic plan to control the world. This suits the Islamic anti-Semites very well. And since, according to these Islamic apocalyptic writers, the Antichrist—the Dajjal—is a Jew, then this is further data that they can draw upon to support their case. And since the Antichrist is a Jew, the Islamic anti-Semites argue that the entire Jewish nation exists to do his bidding. And in much Islamic apocalyptic literature, Freemasonry is regularly condemned as one of the major organizations supporting world domination and the secret control of Muslim societies by the Antichrist and the Jews. To this extent they are true to the *Protocols*, which is readily obtainable in Arabic translation.

"The freemasons are the magicians of the twentieth century," writes Ahmad Thomson, a British lawyer who has specialized in works detailing what he sees as a Western conspiracy against Islam.[38] In 1986 he wrote a succinct summary giving a Western version of Islamic apocalyptic writing, *Dajjal the Antichrist*, which has been reprinted several times and was published in a revised edition in 1997.

Thomson supposes that two systems operate in the world: the *kafir* system—that which rejects the truth of Mohammed and is headed

by the Antichrist—and the true Muslim community under God. He
writes, "The ruling elite of the kafir system, that is the Dajjal system,
are the Freemasons."[39]

And the point of the Antichrist's system, according to Thomson,
is to destroy the Islamic world:

> One of the chief methods used by the *kafir* system, that is the
> *Dajjal* system, to erase living *Islam* is to introduce the *kafir* way
> of life into the Muslim countries. . . . Nearly all the traditional
> Muslim lands are today controlled and governed in accor-
> dance with the precepts of the *kafir* system, and not according
> to what is in the *Qur'an* and the *Sunnah*.[40]

And behind the Freemasons and controlling them, according to
these writers, are the Jews. Bashir Muhammad Abdallah explains to
his gullible audience,

> The Zionist control over this world is through the Masons. . . .
> The Zionists control by imposing famine and scientific and
> technical backwardness upon the Islamic world . . . most of
> the people of the world . . . have all become subservient to
> the evil powers. . . . And these evil powers, which are like
> mountains—the Jews sit upon their peaks in the form of the
> Hidden Government.[41]

Naturally this has allowed a useful justification for implacable
hatred of all Jews. In a book published in Cairo in 1996, Muhammad
Izzat Arif writes, "As for Zionistic Jewry, they are a bog of evil qualities and plagues," and due to their hatred of everything Islamic, they
fully deserve to be punished by "death and annihilation off the face of
the planet entirely."[42]

In 1998 Fahd Salim expressed the depths of belief in this international conspiracy:

There is a general purely Jewish conspiracy, which comprises the entire world for [the purpose of] control over it. Then there is the larger conspiracy . . . which is the Jewish-Christian conspiracy to subjugate the Arab world and the Muslim world and to enslave it.[43]

"The Jews are a poisoned dagger thrust into the heart of the Islamic [Nation]. An evil cancerous gland which spreads deep within the Islamic countries," stated a leaflet distributed in 2007 by the Islamic Shaksiyah Foundation, a registered Islamic charity in the United Kingdom, founded by female members of the radical Islamic Hizb ut-Tahrir. It runs two private schools for girls; the curriculum includes teachings from the Hizb ut-Tahrir, in particular that of the necessity for a worldwide caliphate. The author of the history curriculum has written of "her hatred of western society" and her "desire to see it destroyed."[44]

Many in England cannot understand why this radical Islamic party is allowed to operate since it is quite obvious that young minds are being encouraged to absorb poisonous and destructive ideas. It is clear evidence that Western governments are not taking the dangers seriously; they fail to appreciate that these beliefs are not just intellectual musings but rather calls for future action. It seems to be difficult for a politician raised in a secular political environment to comprehend that in Islam the state and the "church" are one and the same.

In the first centuries of Islam the Jews were not the enemy—at least apart from those holding out against Islam in their great fortified trading city of Khaybar, which straddled the major trade routes on the Arabian Peninsula. Rather, the enemy was the Byzantine Empire, called by the Muslims "the Romans," the beleaguered residue of the once-vast Roman Empire, based in its capital of Constantinople. It was the fall of Constantinople that the apocalyptic writers of early Islam were focused upon. Finally, in 1453, the invading Ottoman Turks broke through the formerly impregnable triple walls and conquered this great city. It became the capital of the Ottoman Empire.

The virulent anti-Semitism we now see is a more recent phenomenon. It began after the dismantling of the Ottoman Empire following their defeat in the First World War and the rule of Palestine by the British under a League of Nations mandate. The Zionist movement in particular began settling in Palestine Jewish volunteers who created communities and the distinctive collective farms. The Islamic leadership—and quite often the British leadership—opposed this settlement with varying degrees of bitterness. This ultimately culminated in the invasion and war that immediately followed Israel's declaration of statehood in 1948 and accelerated following the defeat of the Arab armies and the seizure of Palestinian East Jerusalem and the West Bank by Israeli forces in 1967.

Because most of the modern anti-Semitic apocalyptic literature was published in the 1990s, it is hard not to imagine the "crusading" First Gulf War of 1991 launched by George Bush Sr., who was then president of the United States, as having a significant effect on Islamic perceptions. We should also be aware of the possible effect the first intifada, which erupted in 1987 and continued until 1993, had on the Islamic psyche. It aimed to rebuild a sense of honor amongst Palestinians who felt daily humiliated by the obvious success of Israel and its free society and as frequently frustrated by their own inability to emulate it; young men with slings and stones dared to confront the Israeli army and, to their minds, gained in stature and dignity by doing so.[45] The current literature throws words rather than stones, but this means of fighting may very well have more effect in the long term as new generations are born into the hatred.

It is not surprising that this perception of a Western crusade driven by a sense of superiority combined with an Eastern sense of cultural inferiority can lead to absurd, even idiotic, events. One such involves a soccer game. In November 2007 the Turkish football team from Istanbul, Fenerbahçe, was in Milan, playing their team, Inter Milan. The symbol of the city of Milan is a red cross on a white background, similar to, but not identical with, the cross of the crusading Knights Templar of a thousand years ago, and this symbol was printed on the Milan players' shirts. Inter Milan won the game 3–0. A fervent Turkish fan, a lawyer, lodged a formal complaint in court. He demanded that the soccer authorities impose a heavy fine on Inter Milan "for displaying an offensive symbol." He explained, "That cross only brings one thing to mind: the symbol of the Templar Knights. It made me think immediately of the bloody days of the past." He added, to a Spanish newspaper, that the symbol was a reminder of "Western racist superiority over Islam."[46] He also wanted the result of the game annulled. Officials at the Italian club expressed astonishment.

By the end of the 1990s, and before the second intifada of late 2000 with its cynical use of suicide bombers, the end-times, anti-Semitism, the total destruction of Israel, and the death of all Jews were firmly conjoined in the minds of these writers and their readers. And now, this is the reality—however skewed it might be—that we have to deal with.

Perversely, as we have seen, much of the material comes from Christian sources, which seem well known to the Islamic writers. Da'ud claims that a book he wrote in 1997 on the Mahdi was a direct response to his anger at reading articles on the subject in the *New York Times*; Abd al-Jabbar cites both Hal Lindsey and Jerry Falwell in a complaint that the idea of Armageddon is being used against Islam.[47]

In fact, Jerry Falwell's writings, as David Cook explains, are "popular among Muslim apocalyptic writers," and he is "frequently cited as an authority who knows something about the end of the world." It all has the feel of an incestuous relationship. Others who receive a mention in the Islamic sources are Caspar Weinberger, Jimmy Swaggart, Jim Bakker, Pat Robertson, Oral Roberts, Kenneth Copeland, Richard

De Haan, Billy Graham, and, surprisingly, the Scofield Bible.[48] The battle against the Antichrist clearly straddles the religious divide.

David Cook explains how this Islamic literature is undergoing a process of development, bringing together the classical traditions, anti-Semitism, and an interpretation of the biblical texts drawn mostly from the Christian fundamentalist apocalyptic interpretations.[49] The idea is to provide some explanation of modern events to the readers.

The Muslim writers would also have been well informed on Christian fundamentalist plans to support the removal of the Islamic mosques from the Temple Mount and the rebuilding of the Temple. And as we have already seen, for Christian writers such as John Hagee the Antichrist is supported by the Jewish leadership in particular when he visits the rebuilt Temple.[50] This must have been read with great interest by those Islamic end-times writers for whom the Antichrist is Jewish. There is little mention of the Jews in early Islamic apocalyptic literature, so there is little to draw from for the modern writers. Only one tradition links the Antichrist with a large number of Jews: a hadith states that "the Antichrist will be followed by seventy thousand Jews from Isfahan."[51] It is not much on which to hang the weight of modern anti-Semitism.

This anti-Jewish backbone to modern Islamic end-times writing allows for a justification for the hatred of the United States. Sa'id Ayyub, reports Cook, explains such thinking this way:

> [The United States] is now the principal center for the Jews. History bears witness that the United States of America, which has been occupied in all areas by the beliefs of the Dajjal, is the chief enemy of Islam in every place.[52]

Bashir Muhammad Abdallah comments bitterly,

> The American people have become a colony and are humiliated by the Jews, despite their minority position. . . . The

American people are the most sunk, debased and slavish to the Jewish devil; they labor and toil to fill the storehouses of the Jews with gold—their life is for the sake of the Jews, and they make war and die to fulfil the Jews' strategic interests throughout the world.[53]

Da'ud claims that the very foundation of the United States was an attempt to suppress Islam and create an Israel beyond national boundaries. Speaking of America he explains that,

Its secret is greater, deeper and more dangerous—for it was founded with the purpose of being the basis for the debasement of the Muslims, and the establishment of Greater Israel which rules the world from its heart, while it is part of the lands of Islam.[54]

Da'ud also believes that "support for Israel is stated in the Constitution of the United States—despite the minor difficulty that the Constitution dates from 1787 and the State of Israel from 1948—and further, that "it is legally impossible for a president to be elected without swearing to abide by Israel's dictates."[55]

In short, the fate of the United States, according to the modern Islamic interpretation of biblical prophecy we have looked at here, is identical to that of Israel. When prophecy—according to their interpretation—reveals the destruction of Israel during the end times, it also means the destruction of the United States. The great battle of the end times, which Christians know as Armageddon, is, for the Muslims, to occur in the vicinity of the present-day Ben Gurion International Airport near Tel Aviv; the Jews and Christians opposing the Muslims will be annihilated. And along the way the United States will also meet its end, a prospect many Muslims who read this material find enticing.

We can see that the Islamic apocalyptic writers have much in common with the Christian apocalyptic writers, including the belief that the Temple will be rebuilt (by the Jewish supporters of the Antichrist according to the Islamic writers and by order of the renewed Sanhedrin according to the Jewish activists with the support of the Christian fundamentalists). They have much in common with the Jewish extremist writers too. Where things are different are as follows: the latter claim that the Islamic structures will be removed; the Muslims insist that this is rendered impossible by God's protection. They also suppose that the world will convert to Islam, while the Christians say the world will convert to Christianity, and the Jewish fundamentalists want no one but Jews to serve on the Temple Mount, though they don't seem to care about how the rest of the world shakes out. However, all three religions separately want exclusive rule over Jerusalem under the coming, or returning, Messiah. Each feels that it has God's sanction for this demand.

Confronted by this obsession with a Messiah and possession of Jerusalem, it is hard not to conclude that these apocalyptic writers from all three Abrahamic religions have more in common than with the moderate majority within their own traditions, a majority who have no great arguments with others. Indeed, Islam from the very beginning preached tolerance for the "peoples of the Book," while at the same time, as the many passages in the Koran attest, it preached intolerance for unbelievers. But the hardliners, in fact, need one another to maintain their own positions. They need an enemy to accuse, to act as the source of all ills, and to justify their own belligerent positions. It is a classic example of an age-old procedure: to maintain a tight and cohesive control over your own people, you need the threat of an external enemy. We see it operating in every war, where the enemy is always demonized. We see it in the war in Iraq, where the enemy—in many cases the Iraqi people—is seen as the servant of Satan by United States military figures. We see it in the writings of Christian fundamentalists such as John Hagee, where the Antichrist is behind the decay of the world as he sees it. And we see it in excess in the works of the

Muslim apocalyptic writers, where the enemy is also the Antichrist—
the Dajjal—which is working through the United States and Israel.
All writers from all three traditions are treading a well-worn path,
which can only lead to conflict. They all need to be stopped, right
now. For this kind of writing is the true pornography, twisting the
minds of the youth in the West and East. There really is no more
time for appeasement; the bombers have left the ground. They need
to be recalled, immediately.

The hardliners are methodically encouraging, even demanding, a
focus upon differences instead of seeking points of similarity, accord,
and mutual understanding. A separation is being created, which, in
time, will be so wide as to be all but impossible to bridge.

These divisive efforts are aided by well-meaning but ill-advised
public figures who seem to think that conflict can be avoided by dilut-
ing the strengths of each religion and by accommodating elements of
others in these weakened structures. But weakness is simply despised
and preyed upon in the real world. The strength of the middle needs
to be supported and maintained, since if one feels strong and confident in that strength, then tolerance for others is not seen as a threat
and can come that much easier.

But the move toward the rigid sectarian edges of the three religions
has probably now gone too far. Can we really believe that there is still
room for tolerance between the Islamic hardliners and the Jewish and
Christian fundamentalists?

We have found ourselves across the Rubicon, by default rather than
design. The question now is, what are we now going to do about it?

TWELVE

JERUSALEM

In a great many ways the Old City of Jerusalem is rather strange. There is no doubting its beauty: in the morning or evening light the soft buff-colored stones of its massive walls glow. Surmounted by the glinting, golden Dome of the Rock, Jerusalem never fails to move the heart.

And yet this city is also spring-loaded and tense, like a buried mine just waiting to be stepped on and detonated.

A quick walk through the Old City's narrow streets reveals a dynamic community of many religions and cultures all crammed together with a kind of gritted-teeth harmony brought about—it seems at first—by commercial self-interest.

Certainly discordant notes are quickly obvious: Israeli troops are very much in evidence, standing in groups, heavily armed but still adept at affecting an air of nonchalance, giving directions when needed and appearing casual and uninterested in the constant flow of residents and visitors most of the time. It's their searching eyes that give them away; for these soldiers the war may be low intensity, but it is very real: when vigilance falters, people die.

Closer observation and a few conversations with locals reveal even more: the increasing amount of souvenirs and mass-produced rubbish relentlessly taking over the stock of the shops is slowly converting the

tight, cobbled streets from a living, vibrant city to a themed shopping experience. The fundamentalist Jews who shoulder Palestinians and Bedouins
out of the way in their arrogant progress down these narrow lanes strikes
a sad and discordant note indeed. The practice by Islamic Palestinian
shopkeepers of arranging their crosses and other Christian mementos atop
insulting texts written in Arabic so that no tourists will notice they are
being mocked is simply pathetic. These retailers may quickly dismantle
their insulting displays when spotted, but there is no denying the subtle,
increasingly bitter separation of the different ethnic communities dwell-
ing in the city. Above all, there is a sullen antagonism among members of
the different Christian faiths protecting the religions' most sacred shrine,
the Holy Sepulchre, at a site "identified" in the fourth century A.D. by the
emperor Constantine's mother, Helena—an antagonism so strong it occasionally erupts into violence as monks of differing sects openly fight one
another over tiny patches of territory within the great stone edifice.

More than anything else, Jerusalem is a city where boundary disputes have run amok; separation and possession preoccupy the Holy
City. So *who* should own it? Shall it continue to succumb to claim and
counterclaim for the next two thousand years as well?

We can easily understand the Jewish claim over the city; it was,
after all, founded by the Jewish nation and was the site of the most
important events of that nation until the ruinous war of A.D. 66–73,
when the Romans took it and destroyed what was left of the Temple.

We can also understand the Christian claim over Jerusalem, given
that it was the site of the most important events of Christianity's
supreme figure, Jesus. According to the Scriptures, it was in, or nearby,
Jerusalem that his betrayal, trial, crucifixion, and burial occurred. But
to make such a separate claim is to forget that Jesus was Jewish; in
the end the Christian claim is self-evidently overtaken by that of the
Jewish nation. And then there is the claim by Muslims that Jerusalem
is one of *their* most holy sites, that of Mohammed's divine ascent.

But whatever the later Christian or Muslim claims are, we must face the fact that Jerusalem was founded by Jews and was not only the capital but the very symbol of the Jewish nation. If Jerusalem belongs to anyone then, it is to the Jewish people. To take this attitude is not to steal Palestinian history—as some would have it—but to restore it. Current disputes, however bitter, cannot change the past.

But *why* is Islam claiming Jerusalem?

Islam already has the holy city of Mecca, the site of the sacred black *Kaaba* stone and the focus of all Muslims who turn toward it at the time of prayer and who are encouraged, at some time in their lives, to make the pilgrimage to it—the *hajj*. Islam also has the important city of Medina, where Mohammed fled for refuge from his opponents in pagan Mecca and which was the site of the first Muslim community; his tomb now sits within the Mosque of the Prophet. Then there are the seats of the early caliphs: Damascus and Baghdad. The Shiites have the additional pilgrimage site of Karbala with its Mosque of Husayn, the end point of the important Ashoura festival; and Najaf with its gold-domed Mosque of Ali; then Mashad, the healing shrine of the imam Reza, the most visited site in Islam after Mecca and other holy sites dedicated to the memory of various early imams.

Why then do they need Jerusalem as well?

It seems a bit, well, greedy.

There are no imams buried there. There is no mention of it in the Koran. It played no part in the life of Mohammed or his family. It was never a seat of a caliph. There was not even a major battle there to be honored and remembered for the death of warriors or martyrs.

The only stated reason for the claim is an *assumed* mention in the Koran. According to "The Night Journey," a story relayed in the Koran, sura 17, Mohammed had traveled miraculously in the dark of night from Mecca to a mysterious location called the "Far Mosque." Tradition, based upon this brief mention in the Koran, has it that from this "Far Mosque" Mohammed was taken up by God and given a glimpse of heaven.

Tradition also has it that the "Far Mosque" of the Koran was located on the Temple Mount in Jerusalem—even though there could not possibly have been any Mosque there at the time. It was not until approximately A.D. 691, fifty-nine years after the death of Mohammed, that the caliph Abd al-Malik built the Dome of the Rock over the site; construction of the nearby al-Aqsa Mosque began around the same time. To call the site, in Mohammed's time, the "Far Mosque" flies in the face of well-known history.

There is no proof whatsoever that Jerusalem was the site of this "Far Mosque," but such has been the strength of tradition and passion that few now dare question its truth. Ironically, this golden-domed mosque is built over the rock where it's traditionally held by the Jewish people that God formed Adam, where Abraham almost sacrificed his son, Isaac, and where Jacob had his vision of the ladder reaching up to heaven. So in the same way that fundamentalist Jews regard Jerusalem and this sacred rock as the point where "God began the act of creation," fundamentalist Muslims regard Jerusalem and the Foundation Stone upon the Temple Mount to be crucial to the life of Mohammed and his gift of Islam to his people.

But this attitude did not always exist. It may not even have been what Mohammed had in mind when he wrote or dictated the suras of the Koran. To understand what was intended, we need to look at the inner tradition of Islam, at the mystical message behind the words rather than at the dogmatic approach with which we are most familiar due to media reporting and the hard-line statements made by those with more than axes to grind. These days, gentle peaceful Islam, a path for spiritual self-improvement and compassion for all the children of the Divine, which is preached in the vast majority of mosques, seems lost in the swirling dust of the warriors' horses.

The mystical in Islam has mostly—but not exclusively—been nurtured and passed down through the ages by an often-secretive group who call themselves *Sufis*. But this short name, which translated from Arabic means "purity," does not adequately describe them or their objective. Many Sufis would rather describe themselves, for example, as "a traveler on the path back to his maker."[1] They are all on a journey, a quest, a pilgrimage. The end of their journey is to return to the embrace of the Divine from which they emerged; that is, to achieve a "mystical union with God."[2] By this they reveal that the Sufi path is uncompromisingly spiritual.

In their daily lives Sufis wish to live in the world without being trapped by its countless distractions and temptations. While they are certainly Muslims—mostly Sunni—it is crucial to know that they read the Koran both exoterically and esoterically; certain verses, for example, might be considered symbolic and have a deeper mystical meaning only to be understood by those who, aware of the limitations of language, look well behind mere words.

In the thirteenth century, while the Crusaders were fighting their way toward their inevitable bloody conclusion, in western Turkey a Sufi, Jalal ad-Din Muhammad Din ar-Rumi, was famed for his teaching. Today he is more commonly remembered simply as Rumi. He was perhaps the greatest Sufi poet of all, and the journey back to the Divine formed the subject of many of his writings. His attitude toward the formal approach to Islam and the harmony between this and the Sufi journey is well summarized symbolically in his poem "The wave of that agreement." Rumi writes:

> *Muhammad leads our caravan.*
> *It is lucky to start out*
> *In such a fresh breeze.*[3]

Islam is the divine wind blowing the seeker onward and guiding the seeker on his or her path. There is no suggestion that Islam is the end of the path, for there is a dynamism in Rumi's symbolism, a movement onward, one which takes the seeker to new and unexpected vistas. Islam is the rudder and the sails of the ship together with the breeze that sets the ship on its way; it is not the destination.

The origin of the Sufis is something of a mystery, but it seems likely that its traditions are as old as all other Islamic traditions, the recording of which began in the early eighth century A.D.[4] But we cannot be certain; all we can say for sure is that the oldest surviving texts from Sufi sources date from the ninth century A.D., but it was not until the late tenth century A.D. that Sufism, as an organized practice with standard beliefs, was in place.

Yet, despite this organization, the Sufis have no canonical text or established form of teaching; both are dependent upon the approach of the individual Sufi master, or *Shaykh*, to whom individual Sufis are devoted. Over the centuries, the teachings of some early Shaykhs rose to prominence, and it is from these early teachers that the various Sufi orders or brotherhoods are derived, the first of the major orders beginning during the twelfth century A.D.

To the Western tourist, perhaps the best-known Sufis are those called the whirling dervishes, who perform a distinctive swirling dance. Unfortunately, these days this display has little to do with true Sufism and is treated as something akin to an entertaining folk dance. Nevertheless a rhythmic whirling dance certainly forms part of the practice of many varieties of Sufism. And it is this dance that transforms the participant into a state that is mindless yet devotional; it is a means of becoming closer to divinity. There are clear parallels with early shamanic practice here, and it is considered plausible that such influences could have moved down into the Middle East from central Asia.[5] The silk route from Asia running down through Persia would be an obvious conduit for such ideas, techniques, and rituals.

But whatever the techniques employed, the Sufi orders share a common approach toward spirituality: they seek for direct personal and experiential knowledge of Divinity. They want to know the truth, not just talk about it. Long ago the Sufis realized that in the search for God, divinity is to be found within, by experiencing it directly, not by following rules or slavishly repeating texts like some media promotional loop. That this attitude crosses cultures far removed from the Abrahamic religions can be shown, for example, by the Hindu *Bhagavad Gita,* which warns, "When thy mind leaves behind its dark forest of delusion, thou shalt go beyond the scriptures of times past and still to come."[6]

We are all aware of the alternative: book-obsessed zealots firmly locked into the rigid and the intellectual who have long forgotten the importance of the heart, which observation goes a long way toward explaining their arrogant attitude toward women. Those who have locked up their hearts find it difficult to bring love, compassion, and tolerance into their lives; so they also lock up their wives and daughters.

It is useful to remember that the author of the Sermon on the Mount had an easy and friendly relationship with the women among his following. None of the Marys, for example, in the Christian Gospels was ever shut away from men or an active involvement in the teaching of the Way to the kingdom of God. The Gospels themselves and the large range of other memoirs, which were common in the second century A.D., make this very clear. It is even recorded that some of the men, locked in more traditional practices, became upset about the equality women were experiencing.[7]

Sufism does not advocate a renunciation of the world but rather a disentanglement from it—an important difference—life's tasks being carried out in a spirit of sanctification. With this, its practice is very similar to the Hindu teaching of *Karma Yoga,* which is the spiritual "path of consecrated action" where all tasks are carried out for the Divine, not the self.[8]

In their lives and rituals, then, Sufis are directly opposed to the traditional Muslim approach to truth, which is based upon a literal reading of a holy book—the Koran—and pursued by means of study,

scholarship, and obedience. It is easy to see why such hard-line legalistic and scholastic Sunni groups such as the Saudi Wahhabis would
oppose the Sufis and denounce them as heretics. If there is one thing
that any tightly maintained authority dislikes, it is some alternative
that renders the authority's approach irrelevant.

With the story of Mohammed's journey to the "Far Mosque" we
have a good example of the difference between a literalist traditional
approach to understanding the Koran and that of the mystical Sufis.

Rumi approached this tradition head on: he saw the story of the
journey to the "Far Mosque" mentioned in Sura 17 of the Koran as a
mystical symbol. For Rumi did not take it literally. He explained, "The
place that Solomon made to worship in, called the Far Mosque, is not
built of earth, and water and stone, but of intention and wisdom and
mystical conversation and compassionate action."[9]

We can see here a dim echo of Jesus' words as reported in the gospel of John, where he likens his body to the Temple (John 2:21).

The Holy of Holies in Solomon's temple—the "Far Mosque,"
according to Rumi—can be seen as a symbol for the soul, where, symbolically, Divinity waits until it is discovered. Rumi explained that
this holy place and holy presence exists within every person and can
be found, and entered accordingly. It seems that the inner tradition of
Christianity spoken of by Jesus as a secret (Matthew 13:11) is expressing
the same teaching: Jesus is depicted in the Gospels as stating, "Behold,
the kingdom of God is within you" (Luke 17:21).

We can see that Rumi was following a long and well-established
tradition in stressing that the important shrine of pilgrimage for those
truly searching for God was not one of bricks and mortar but was
the holy place within each individual where, in stillness and silence,
divinity itself could be experienced, directly and personally.

Of course, the mystical path does not always sit comfortably with
the established religious pathways. It diminishes the importance of orga-

nized religion. It shifts the responsibility for divine knowledge from the organization to the individual. And to that extent, it causes religion to lose control over its people—which from the mystical perspective is a good thing. The common practice in religion is to maintain that control by threats and the instigation of fear coupled with a derision of the mystical as an irrelevant self-indulgence having nothing to do with the serious business of faith. How little they understand! One cannot help being reminded of the words attributed to Jesus in Matthew's gospel:

> *Alas for you, scribes and Pharisees, you hypocrites! You who shut up the kingdom of heaven in men's faces, neither going in yourselves nor allowing others to go in who want to.*
>
> —MATTHEW 23:13

One only has to read the agonizing that St. Teresa of Ávila went through in order to justify her own mystical experiences within the Catholicism of her day to understand how powerful such strictures and fears could be.

Organized religion is a helping hand onward rather than the Way itself, but few religious leaders will give up their power in order to recognize this. And this rigidity is especially so, as we have seen again and again, with the fundamentalist supporters within the three Abrahamic religions of Christianity, Judaism, and Islam.

So what are we to do?

On the face of it, Judaism, as the oldest of the three religions, would naturally be the original faith from which the other two derive. But what kind of fruit has it generated after all this time? Have we yet earned the right to freely eat of the fruit from the tree of knowledge of good and evil? And return to the garden?

Judaism's first Temple was built at least 2500 years ago according to many modern historians and archaeologists or perhaps 3000 years ago according to the biblical records. The death of Jesus was almost 2000 years ago—and we shouldn't forget the later interpretation of Paul. The much later "Messenger," Mohammed, died around 1600 years ago. Christianity holds that the teaching of Jesus subsumes and replaces that of Judaism; Islam holds that the teaching of Mohammed subsumes and replaces that of the previous two. We cannot escape the fact that these three religions are joined at the hip, so to speak. And speaking quite bluntly, no one can say that they have not had enough time to sort themselves out along with the baggage that they all carry.

So why are they still in dispute? Why are factions within each religion still arguing? What levels of egotism, selfishness, and craving for power still run bitterly through all three?

Islam puts forward an interesting approach in an attempt to resolve this problem: it claims that it was the original faith of the three, that Abraham himself, the father of the three religions, was, in fact, a Muslim: "Abraham in truth was not a Jew, neither a Christian; but he was a Muslim and one pure of faith."[10]

But one has to ignore history, redefine Islam, or suspend all critical faculties to accommodate that particular belief despite it having the support of the Koran.

While it is true that there is some magnificent poetry in the Koran, in general it seems to hold more in common with the Old Testament book of Deuteronomy; it is a collection of laws for living—in the seventh-century A.D. Arabian Desert. We have already noted that it is an approach to theology that was placed into a Christian context during the latter part of the twentieth century by Rousas Rushdoony in order to justify his planned brave new world for Christians. Routes to power are slow to fade.

Judaism, at first sight, seems to be trying to keep its people together rather than to take on the task of converting the world, for Judaism is the history and faith of a specific nation. But this is not quite the whole story. Fundamentalist Judaism, like that of Christianity and Islam, sees its success in terms of influencing the rest of the world. It makes much of the rabbinical statements in its tradition that "God first sends a blessing to Jerusalem, and from there it flows to the entire world."[11] It is to Jerusalem that the Messiah will come and

> redeem and perfect the Jewish people, creating of them a perfect society and bringing them back to an optimal spiritual status . . . the Jews will be able, in turn, to perfect the world around them, teaching all nations how to live in peace under the law of God. The society of mankind will thus be rectified and perfected for all time.[12]

According to Rabbi Aryeh Kaplan,

> In Jerusalem, the Jewish people will thus become established as the spiritual and moral teachers of all mankind. At that time, Jerusalem will become the spiritual capital of all mankind.[13]

This universal approach is seen with the other two faiths too: fundamentalist Islam, like fundamentalist Christianity, is evangelical; it is trying to convert the world with the added sense of urgency of the last days, which they believe are just around the next corner, shortly to begin, following a divine trumpet blast that heralds the great Day of Judgment.

It is just as it was with John on Patmos and with Islam in its very early days. Both religions have their expectation of Armageddon; but only Christianity has its concept of the rapture, which has since become a kind of joker in the pack.

There is one thing all fundamentalist supporters of Judaism and its two children, Christianity and Islam, share in common: they see this new "kingdom of heaven" as some theocratic political system where the church and state are identified, one which rules the earth like Rushdoony's new world with its theonomy as the basis for a legal system or the Islamist's global caliphate under the rule of sharia law or Judaism's Sanhedrin ruling over a universal application of the law of God as laid down in the books of Jewish scripture. None share Rumi's vision. For all of them truth comes from a book, not from the direct experience of Divinity. For all of them obedience is more important than wisdom.

For this reason, in my opinion, we have no alternative but to begin looking at the Abrahamic religions from a completely different angle. We need to have the courage to think far beyond our normal patterns. Events are moving so fast that I cannot see us having the luxury of time, indecision, or further procrastination. It is self-evident that we must come to grips with this new situation. It is yet another problem in our civilization that we are required, after all these years, to finally confront.

Just like global warming can be seen prizing apart the vast polar ice fields and splitting off huge glacial islands in a movement now impossible to stop, the religious fundamentalists are, slowly but relentlessly, moving the center of gravity of our religions toward the dogmatic edges and, by doing so, are prizing apart the three Abrahamic religions, splitting off all possibility of moderation and tolerance, leaving us with unbridgeable crevices and cold wild seas of mutual hostility.

In both cases our task has now become one of damage limitation. It may be a great technological and social challenge, but we can, with some focused effort, ride out whatever global warming brings; but can we survive what our religions bring in their mutually destructive race to the edge?

Or, could it be that after our brief sojourn on the face of our planet, we are all to soak back into the earth like a sudden tear falling from the eye of God?

THIRTEEN

WELCOME TO THE GODS

We are nearing the conclusion of our study, but before we arrive, I wish to look briefly at the beginning of the Bible, to make one final point. According to Genesis, God created the world in six days. Evidently there was a schedule. But a strange one, for on that first day God created light, and, we are told, the light was called day, and the darkness was called night. Later, on the fourth day, God created the sun, the moon, and stars (Genesis 1:16). This is all very beautiful, but something is clearly askew here: we are asked to believe that day and night were created before the sun and moon in a description of creation that appears to assume that the earth is fixed and does not rotate, but as we all know it is this rotation that is the cause of night and day. Surely God would have known that.

Here, at the very beginning of the Bible, in the first chapter of the first book, lies a strong clue that we should not be taking its stories literally. The stories contained therein seek to express a religious and moral perspective, one that was ideal for a group of warring hill tribes and city-states in the Palestinian highlands roughly three thousand years ago. But those of us reading it today need to be a little more flexible when we seek to apply its precepts to our lives. Not, of course, because we are any less needful of religious and moral guidance, but rather because a literal understanding of these stories has led some people into ludicrous positions in the past. As noted earlier, certain Christian fundamentalists believe that the world was created thousands, rather than billions, of years ago. Furthermore, since the fossil record clearly reveals the existence of dinosaurs, they, too, must have a relatively recent origin. Since they also believe that the Bible stories are true statements of history, they conclude that Adam and Eve must have lived among these prowling monsters. At least that's what a brochure from the Creation Museum in Petersburg, Kentucky, proclaims.[1] The fundamentalists who hold these beliefs reason that Noah must have had dinosaurs in his ark. All the fossilized dinosaurs discovered by paleontologists are those that had drowned in the great flood, they offer by way of explanation. It is not a very good one.

It is, of course, the finer details that reveal the more basic problems with their theory: just how did the dinosaurs fit into the ark? Some suggest that the ark had several decks allowing the largest of the species space to stretch up through them; others suppose that only baby dinosaurs were carried. But what of the dangers inherent in a boatload of dinosaurs? Wouldn't the two aggressive tyrannosauruses and the pair of hungry raptors and their lunch-time companions have attacked and eaten all of the other animals on the ark? Wouldn't Noah have been in a distinctly vulnerable position as well?

Naturally, the fundamentalists have a tidy answer to that question too: dinosaurs were originally vegetarian. Ah, you might reply skeptically, but what of the sharp teeth found in a tyrannosaurus' skull— dangerous-looking serrated teeth six inches long? Again, not a problem: they needed sharp teeth to eat hard-skinned fruits like watermelons, slicing easily right through them.[2] Apparently, all were friendly in the ark. But even if the creationists are correct and Noah did ensure that the dinosaurs survived the flood, where are they now? Hiding in Loch Ness?

Surely, none of the pat answers to these questions would seem remotely convincing, even to a young child, if they were offered without any emotional and social pressure. But these explanations, and more, are given to young people on a regular basis during their Christian home-schooling by their own parents or by their community leaders, teachers, and church pastors. It is estimated that more than a million children are taught these theories as truth. They hear it on their Christian television and radio stations. They read it in their Christian magazines and books, and they can even see reconstructions in special museums and traveling displays. Inevitably, they believe these explanations. We should worry about these children and the way their minds have been systematically indoctrinated; they are being failed by a social system that has capitulated to religious fanatics in a misguided interpretation of freedom and toler-ance, and which apparently no longer has the will to protect these chil-dren from the hatred, the prejudice, and the lies amongst which they are being raised.

Above all, these impressionable children grow to adulthood believ-ing that the battle of Armageddon will be fought and that Jesus will return to Jerusalem as ruler of the world. It is no wonder, as we have discovered, that there are U.S. troops in the Middle East, thinking they are fighting Satan in what would be the first skirmishes leading toward Armageddon. All of us in the Western world should worry when U.S. foreign policy, both in its strategic planning and at its tactical sharp end, begins falling into the hands of people who share even small parts of this fundamentalist belief.

One of the most pointed indictments of the cowardice of those who should be opposing this creeping Christian fascism comes from Pulitzer Prize–winning journalist Chris Hedges. In his book *American Fascists* he exposes the relentless fundamentalist infiltration of the United States administrative apparatus. It has taken over the Republican Party, he explains, and has the approval of 45 senators and 186 congressmen.[3] It has set up parallel institutions that will dominate society once power has been drained from the official organizations. Hedges reveals that these Christian fascists are on a roll. But he also directs his anger at the liberals who have misguidedly allowed it in the name of tolerance. One of his teachers at Harvard Divinity School, Dr. James Adams, who spent time in Nazi Germany from 1935 to 1936, saw the dangers early. Hedges explains:

> He despaired of liberals, who he said, as in Nazi Germany, mouthed empty platitudes about dialogue and inclusiveness that made them ineffectual and impotent. Liberals, he said, did not understand the power and allure of evil or the cold reality of how the world worked.[4]

Hedges is well aware of the Christian Reconstruction and Dominionist fanatics whom we have looked at. He explains how, as we have seen, they despise the liberal and enlightened society created by the U.S. Constitution and how these fanatics see this world as acting against their own best interests. After many years spent studying these Christian fundamentalists, Hedges concludes that their primary goal is the destruction of this liberal society.[5] He sees the United States facing a grave danger,

> Those arrayed against American democracy are waiting for a moment to strike, a national crisis that will allow them to shred the Constitution in the name of national security and strength.[6]

This scheme, and the acute dangers it poses for American—indeed Western—democracy, has not been appreciated by those whose lives are lived beyond the range of the fundamentalist preachers.

Journalist Joe Bageant in his *Deer Hunting with Jesus* explains sadly that one of the truly important events in American politics is,

> the conversion of millions of people from apolitical Christians into Christian political activists. Despite claims of independence, their churches have been deeply manipulated by

their own power-hungry leadership and by the Republican Party, beginning in the Reagan years.[7]

These religious political activists have become foot soldiers in a theocratic power dream, a cynical play for control, using religion as a cloak for far more selfish and venal motives. It is not just by chance that many large industrialists with unacceptable products or processes are funding this movement, those who wish to extract raw materials from the earth at minimum cost in the hope that Jesus will return and clean up the mess without shareholders incurring any expense. The world is going to end soon, so kick in its windows, break down its doors, and loot it to destruction. It won't matter.

Nor does it matter to those Christians who do not subscribe fully to the Reconstructionist end-times vision but who believe instead that Jesus and Armageddon will come first, before the worldwide theocracy, and that they will be raptured into the great coliseum in the sky. Who cares about the others left behind? After all, it's their fault for not submitting to the word of Jesus. But they are urged to make haste, the end of time is arriving soon. The world is going to crumble before the onslaught of Armageddon and from the power of the Messiah ruling from Jerusalem.

Jerusalem, I must emphasize, is the key. It is to its walls and stone-built streets that paranoia comes to play. We are promised that it will be the capital city of the world when the Messiah is in residence. But, as I've asked before, whose Messiah?

We have the fundamentalist rights of Judaism, Christianity, and Islam all feeding off one another. Islamic fundamentalist writers are producing apocalyptic works drawing upon Christian apocalyptic works—quoting not only from the Revelation of John of Patmos but also from the books of modern Christian fundamentalists. Muslim author Safar al-Hawali, for example, in his *The Day of Wrath*, shows at least a working knowledge of Revelation when he seeks to prove, by means of a twenty-eight point comparison, that the new Jerusalem that comes down from heaven in Revelation 21 is actually a description of Mecca with the Kaaba.[8]

As we have seen, in Jerusalem today we have the activity of a resurrected Sanhedrin that is seeking to rule by means of ancient Jewish law. Christian fundamentalists in the United States plan a government based on these same ancient laws, which they term "biblical" rather than "Jewish." We mustn't forget that despite the support of Israel, there is a distinct friction between many Christian fundamentalists and Judaism. They want Israel and Jerusalem to survive at all costs because that will enable the return of Jesus who will have been mysteriously converted from his native Judaism to Christianity. John Hagee, who founded the influential support group Christians United for Israel in early 2006, is clear about the problem for Christian supporters: "The Jewish people have yet to accept Jesus as their Messiah."[9]

Islamic fundamentalists are aspiring to a great worldwide state under the control of a caliph, a descendant of Mohammed, ruling by means of Koranic law, sharia. This caliphate will be a theocracy, as will be the new "biblical" United States under the domination of the Christian fundamentalists, as will Israel under the rule of the new Sanhedrin. All three groups want a state in which politics are subservient to religion. All three groups are awaiting the coming of a Messiah. All three groups want Jerusalem.

Everything about us eventually decays and crumbles; Shelley's poem "Ozymandius" well captures the effect of time's inexorable destruction, with its central image of a huge and ancient carved head toppled in the desert, discarded like a broken pot. It depicts an arrogant and ruthless despot, the ruler of some vast empire who long ago held the life and death of thousands in his hands. But the head now gazes forever over endless barren sands; the empire and the potentate having long vanished into the restless dust, his name but a dim and garbled memory, his great power exposed as an illusion.

Western culture, informed by its Judeo-Christian heritage, holds to a linear view of time, a movement from the past into the future. So ingrained is this that to even question it seems ridiculous. We are born and grow old and die. How could there be any other way of looking at time?

But of course there is another way to look at time, and it is a rather important way: the concept of time as a movement from past to future, now held by all of the Abrahamic religions, unfortunately leaves no room for eternity.

This view of time is as a relentless progression forward, whereas eternity lies outside this progression and has no connection with it. Eternity has always been and always will be. And just to make things a little more difficult to understand, we can say that it has nothing to do with time. We could say that eternity is a state of no time at all. It just is.

We have, then, two ideas of time: that which is linear, moving from the past to the future, and that which has no past or future but is an eternal present.

There are, and have been, cultures that have successfully operated using these two ideas of time simultaneously. The ancient Egyptian culture, for instance, happily accommodated the two into their lives. Linear time, that in which we live and die, in which monuments and buildings crumble, in which manuscripts fade and disintegrate, they called *neheh*.

Eternity, that which lies outside of time, they termed *djet*. But these two were not in separate places—in heaven and earth, for example. Rather, eternity was intertwined with linear time at every moment and at every point. To pass from neheh time into the eternity of djet was not so much a movement as a change of state, one which came at death but one which could also be induced during the hidden ceremonies of cultic initiation alluded to in fragments of texts.[10] These ceremonies were conducted in dark and silent crypts or chapels at night by priests who put themselves in a mysterious state of meditative trance called *qed*, the inner details of which we know very little.[11]

In the modern world we have the example of Hinduism, which is well aware of the distinction between daily life in the destructive progress of time and that eternal world beyond it. Furthermore, the yoga teachings of Hinduism regard the decaying and changeable world operating within time as an illusion; reality, they teach, is only to be found within the world that is eternal, the world that is outside of time.

The Hindu *Bhagavad Gita*, one of the world's great spiritual texts, explains that while a person's body comes to an end in its time, the inner essence of a person is eternal and cannot die.[12] Leaving aside the Hindu teaching that the spirit can return to a new body, this is not so far from Jewish, Christian, or Islamic teaching. There is, for example, good reason to consider that the concept of the kingdom of God voiced often by Jesus in the Gospels was a code to designate not a terrestrial political kingdom as most Christian fundamentalists understand it, but the eternal world beyond time.

How else should we understand the words attributed to Jesus when he explained to his disciples that the parables were for the masses but, "It is given unto you to know the mysteries of the kingdom of heaven" (Matthew 13:11; *see also* Mark 4:11 and Luke 8:9–10). Or, as we have already noted, Jesus' sarcastic description of the "scribes and Pharisees" whom, according to the Gospels, he accused of preventing access to this "kingdom" (Matthew 23:13). It is perfectly obvious that for Jesus the kingdom of heaven was a place to go into from this world: a place reached by a journey that was personal, experiential, and mystical. It is hardly the worldwide political empire dreamed of by the Christian Reconstructionists. But since the latter so dislike the pious and the mystical, it is not surprising that they simply don't get it.[13] The *Bhagavad Gita* has a response to these kinds of people:

There are men who have no vision, and yet they speak many words. They follow the letter of the *Vedas* [the sacred texts], and they say: "there is nothing but this.". . . When your mind leaves behind its dark forest of delusion, you will go beyond the scriptures of times past and still to come.[14]

John Gray, professor of European thought at the London School of Economics, has explored the influence of fundamentalist thought on politics in the West. He is direct: there are, he says, dangers implicit in Christianity and Islam. "Both," he points out, "are militant faiths that seek to convert all humankind."[15] While other religions have become involved in violence over the last century—he notes particularly the Shinto cult in Japan and the Hindu nationalism in India—only Islam and Christianity have given rise to mass movements committed to world domination. He concludes, "Interacting with the struggle for natural resources, the violence of faith looks set to shape the coming century."[16]

The definition of Western culture, he argues, is not what we might think. It is not our tradition of democracy or tolerance but "the belief that history has a built-in purpose or goal."[17] This has become entangled with the idea that the West will redeem the world, an old idea that we see in the nineteenth-century movement of Manifest Destiny in the United States and also in the British Israel movement. This latter maintained that the United States and the United Kingdom were the descendants of the lost tribes of the Jews and so heirs to the glories and wealth promised by God's covenant with Israel.

Much from both of these movements has fed into the fundamentalist ideas that the United States is a uniquely chosen nation that will lead the world to a glorious future, so long as it follows God's rules. Evangelical fundamentalist Herbert W. Armstrong, once associated with the Toronto branch of the British Israel World Federation and who founded the World Wide Church of God, has publicized the view that the Anglo-Saxon countries, with the United States foremost, are the modern representatives of God's "chosen race," destined to rule the world.

Religion can, on the one hand, lead a person to the discovery of meaning; on the other, it is a very effective tool of manipulation, something that is not lost on the politicians.

We need meaning in our lives just as we need air, water, and food; this grants enormous power to those who control the religions. The task of government does not involve a concern with meaning; rather it is to maintain a structure that allows divergent religions and philosophies to live together. A structure, Professor Gray explains, that will embody "a type of toleration whose goal is not truth but peace."[18] This view, he argues, is realistic. It is hard to disagree with him.

In the West—after paying in blood for hundreds of years—we have a society whose political system, in various different ways depending upon the country, maintains a distinction between church and state. Differences over personal belief systems cannot be allowed to affect the legally protected rights and dignity of the individual. But in Islam things are very different: there is no distinction between "church" and state; in fact, the whole concept is meaningless and incomprehensible to a fundamentalist Muslim.

A major difficulty with the three Abrahamic religions of Judaism, Christianity, and Islam is that they are "Book" dependent, and we should always be deeply suspicious of any man or woman who reads only one book, be it the Torah, the Gospels, or the Koran. The Jewish scriptures—the Old Testament—were, according to the most recent scholarship, created to support the formation of the monotheistic Yahweh Temple cult, which probably developed after the period of exile ended in 538 B.C., although it could have been a century or two earlier; no one knows for certain.[19]

Christianity's texts, of course, have some well-known problems: there are additions to the text such as the last part of Mark's gospel

(Mark 16:9–20), which describes the risen Jesus showing himself to Mary Magdalene and the disciples and supporting the speaking in tongues. This passage does not occur in many of the oldest manuscripts including the *Codex Sinaiticus* and the *Codex Vaticanus*. That this is a later addition to the text is well accepted, even by the Vatican itself.[20]

Then there is the actual choice of the books that finally made up the New Testament, not yet in existence during the early second century. Christians simply drew from a wide range of differing texts and Jesus memoirs they had access to. While lists of acceptable books began to be drawn up later that same century, the official canon of the New Testament was not finalized until the Council of Carthage in A.D. 396. In the Eastern churches the book of Revelation was not accepted until even later.

The Koran, too, has its textual problems. Despite the oft-repeated claim that nothing has been changed from the beginning, scholars estimate that there is roughly a 20 percent variation between the different traditions of the Koran. Scholars know of nine differing official versions of the Koran. A few years ago an ancient Koran—dating from the very earliest days of Islam—was excavated in Yemen and is now in the University of Heidelberg. There are considerable variations between this early text and the modern ones, a fact that shocked certain Islamic scholars. But little more is openly known about this particular text.

However, what is interesting about the Koran's approach is that it assumes the reader has knowledge of the earlier Jewish and Christian works, because many of its stories, like those of Noah, Joseph, and Moses, are presented in a précis form and can only really be understood against the background of the more detailed Old Testament stories. In many chapters of the Koran passages explain that,

> We sent down the Torah, wherein is guidance and light. . . .
> And We sent . . . Jesus son of Mary, confirming the Torah
> before him; and We gave to him the Gospel, wherein is

guidance and light, and confirming the Torah before it, as
a guidance. . . . And we have sent down to thee the Book
[the Koran] with the truth, confirming the Book that was
before it.[21]

But can Christianity, Judaism, and Islam agree that they are worshipping the same God?

The concept of a divine Jesus is a problem for Judaism and
Islam. For Muslims, the failure of the other two religions to recognize
Mohammed as the last prophet represents an additional departure
point. For the Jews, the failure by others to recognize the importance
of the Temple and its priesthood as a conduit between God and earth
is crucial. The three positions seem irreconcilable. So which of the
three versions is right? Or are we, in fact, dealing with three different gods? Fundamentalist Christian authors Tim LaHaye and Jerry
Jenkins are quite vocal on this point, writing,

> The idea that all religions point to the same god is blasphemy.
> So is the idea that there are many ways to God. Buddha,
> Mary, Gaia, Muhammad, and Christ are *not* in the same cat-
> egory. . . . Just one was God's "only begotten Son," and only
> He gives us access to God through prayer.[22]

In the end one must ask, is Jerusalem too volatile and dangerous to be dedicated to one religion? Could the Old City of Jerusalem
become, within its walls, a place of reconciliation and harmony for
the three Abrahamic religions? Could a Jewish temple and a Christian
cathedral be built upon the Temple Mount, and could their worshippers coexist with those attending the Islamic mosques, or could the
entire Temple Mount be a nonsectarian place of divine worship?

Unfortunately, it seems to me that the enmity and divisions among
the three are too deeply ingrained. It is very hard to imagine any solution to the problem of Jerusalem and who owns it that does not

involve violence. But why should a city—said to be so beloved by the Divine—be in such turmoil? And not just now but in 170–167 B.C. when the Syrians invaded, in 63 B.C. when Pompey captured Jerusalem for Rome, in 37 B.C. when Herod the Great attacked and besieged it, in A.D. 68–70 when the Romans attacked it, in 131–135 when Rome attacked again, in 1099 when the Crusaders attacked, in 1187 when the Muslims attacked under Saladin, in 1948 when seven Arab armies attacked, and in 1967 when the Jewish forces broke through the Lions' Gate and took it? What sort of God could create this?

Surely it is obvious that the concept of "God" has long been misunderstood: this idea of an elderly father god in the sky. And even stranger is the identification of this elderly father god with the youthful man Jesus as is defined by the Christian Trinity. Jesus never claimed to be God, specifically denying it in John 10:33–35. And in the words attributed to him, he expressly distinguished himself from "the Father."

If the fundamentalists are right and the Christian God is different from the Jewish Yahweh and the Islamic Allah, then there is a major problem that needs solving: why did God allow Islam to be founded in the seventh century A.D.? Wouldn't the Islamic Allah's very existence suggest that the Christian God was powerless, since despite the first commandment, "Thou shalt have no other Gods before me," (Exodus 20:3), God allowed that very situation to develop? Or perhaps the founding of Islam can be viewed as an example of God's allowing humans to exercise free will. Or maybe it suggests that Allah is the same as God and that all Christians should happily worship Allah and respect his prophet Mohammed. Certainly, Mohammed thought so: "our God and your God is One"[23]

So now, it appears as if we have two problems: the confusion and competition over the vision of God and the arrogant belligerence of the various supporters. Under such explosive conditions, it is hard to avoid the conclusion that we need a new vision of God.

We should remember that the vision of God common to Judaism, Christianity (as "God the Father" in the Trinity), and Islam is of an anthropomorphic God, an elderly male figure who is sometimes benevolent and sometimes enraged and that this vision derives from the Middle East—quite distinct from the Buddhist, Hindu, or Taoist mystical concept of the "One." While every other known society in the world believed in many divinities, it was in the Middle East that the monotheistic perspective as we know it today was developed. How and why this occurred is complex and impossible to fully resolve; certainly influences came from the Persian religion, Zoroastrianism, and from the latter days of the Babylonian Empire where the moon god, *Sin*, became dominant. All we can be sure of is that belief in a single god appears in the biblical texts dating as far back as the sixth century B.C.

Also confusing matters is the fact that the monotheism of the Old Testament emerged against a background of worship involving many gods and goddesses. According to a verse in Exodus, the Patriarchs—Abraham, Isaac, and Jacob—knew only El.[24] This god also seems to have been the earliest god of Israel; his name occurs in that of Israel itself, *yisra-el*.[25]

El is depicted in Middle Eastern iconography as an elderly bearded figure and is described variously as the "father of humanity" and the "creator of the earth."[26] At a number of different sites, however, archaeologists have found that the later warrior-god Yahweh absorbed the cult of El and took on many of the older god's traits. Eventually, in a late text of the Old Testament that dates from the exile period, an addition by an unknown author to the book of Isaiah, chapters 40–55, depicts Yahweh both as creator and warrior-king,

> *Yahweh advances like a hero,*
> *his fury is stirred like a warrior's.*
> *He gives the war shout, raises the hue and cry,*
> *marches valiantly against his foes.*

> ISAIAH 42:13

Yahweh is elevated to more than just a chief god: he is elevated to that of the *only* god. He is no longer simply the god of Israel but of the entire world.[27]

> *No god was formed before me,*
> *nor will be after me.*
> *I, I am Yahweh,*
> *there is no other saviour but me. . . .*
> *I am your God, I am he from eternity.*
>
> ISAIAH 43:10–13

But implicit in these words—in their expressed desire for domination, for Yahweh to be supreme, for him to be the chief of all gods—is an acknowledgement that there are indeed other gods around.

It was this insistence upon there being only one God that brought the Jewish nation into conflict with the Romans. This belief, and this conflict, reshaped our world two thousand years ago when it gave birth to Christianity, and today we are still living with the effects. Both Christianity and Islam have tried to replace or renew the ancient Judaic vision but have only succeeded in creating conflict.

Both historical and contemporary concerns force us to reconsider our position: we need a new approach to religion, a new vision for all the Abrahamic religions. Should we reject the authority of a vengeful and jealous warrior god who claims to be unique and return to the worship of many gods? People who have only one god are bound to argue against it.

We have edged close to a conclusion that seems unthinkable. Do we dare go further? Have we any other alternative if we are to survive? Has religion based upon a single God had its day?

We are partway there already. There is the matter of the Roman Catholic cult of the saints in which living people, after their deaths, become figures of worship. There may not be temples raised to these

Christian demigods, but within the great cathedrals there are chapels dedicated to them where one can often find the faithful praying for aid and intercession.

Saints were not a feature of the original Jerusalem community of Jesus, his brother James, and the others. It began later, spurred on by the number of Christians martyred for their faith, and by the mid-fifth century A.D. it had become widespread with sites of adoration ringing the entire Mediterranean. The cult was seen as connecting the two realms of heaven and earth, and so the living with the dead, the divine and the terrestrial.

As has often been noted, there are many parallels with the ancient Greek cult of heroes who were deified human beings, demigods who occupied a place midway between terrestrial life and the remote Olympian gods.[28] Graves of heroes with an associated cult can be found from the latter part of the eighth century B.C.

A hero is tied to a specific location, acting as a focus for the identity of the local community but with influence extending only around the general area of his grave. This grave would be set apart from others in a special place where sacrifices could be made and gifts brought. Sometimes at the grave site a monument was raised in his honor.

It is true that this local aspect is different from that of the saints whose influence can be wide, but it does have much in common with the associated practice of honoring relics of the saints—purported bones, skulls, and even blood—as powerful amulets, which themselves can become a focus of pilgrimage and adoration. The kissing of ancient bones is a common feature of religious ceremonies within this widespread cult of saints.

In the hero cult we find a practice identical to that of the saints': the major occasion in the year was the feast day in the hero's honor. This cultic practice is continued within Christianity, and we all know the feast days of at least some saints, many of whom are still celebrated as public holidays, even in the twenty-first century. Who can ever miss St. Patrick's Day on March 17?

But the greatest importance of the heroes is seen in times of battle, for they were believed to give direct aid to their communities, their cities, or their countries. We can see that this is precisely what occurs with saints as well. Ever since there have been Christian armies, they have marched forward bearing the banner of their patron saints before them. It is this martial aspect that the two cults hold in common, something completely absent from the Gospels, which reveals the heritage of the cult of the saints from the earlier cult of the heroes. The fact that saints, unlike the heroes, can act as intercessors with God, is but a theological spin that does not affect the structural pattern of the cult. Both heroes and saints are demigods.

There is another aspect to this cultic heritage that we also need to consider. In some way the modern cult of celebrity fits into the same pattern. Our celebrities are like the ancient Greek heroes who after death received a kind of popular canonization. Is not the continued devotion to Elvis Presley and his interestingly named home, Graceland, rather close to worship and popular sainthood? He has probably brought more joy to people than someone who has spent thirty years sitting at the top of a tall column as did St. Simeon Stylites. And what of the very curious business over Princess Diana?

Is it not time to accept that the Middle Eastern experiment with one God has failed, that it is leading us slowly but surely along a path to conflict and destruction? And that another path is needed? There is, of course, the path to the wisdom of the Far World, which the ancient Egyptians practiced—a path no longer printed on our sacred maps, a path that has long been forgotten by all save a hardy few who, despite popular derision, struggle to make the journey.

The ancient Greek mystery traditions described a netherworld they called Hades. It was a place where one could go during initiation and where one went after death. One was rowed across a river by a boatman, Charon, to the sunny Elysian Fields, which lay beyond. Crossing this river is, deep down, a universal aspiration and a universal experience, but most people, lacking any form of training for the journey, are fearful of it and avoid it until the day they die. But this was why many of the ancient cults existed—to allow people some knowledge of this journey. Because they were not permitted to speak of it afterward and because no one ever did, we are left with very few hints as to what typically occurs.

Sadly, these public mysteries no longer exist. The journey needs to be made almost clandestinely. Even the existence of the path is denied or derided. But this was not always so. And this denial need not be so today. The three religions all have their inner mystical traditions, which have survived despite many attempts to degrade or destroy the information and techniques they maintain. Islam has the Sufis, Judaism the Kabbalah, and Christianity both the tradition of St. Teresa of Ávila and St. John of the Cross as well as the more esoteric stream that goes by the name of Christian Cabala. Also in operation in the West, and perhaps the major bearer of inner traditions of initiation into the secrets of the Far World, is that teaching known as Hermetic Philosophy.

This philosophy was a major force in the eruption of the Italian Renaissance as it carried into fifteenth-century Europe secret material originating in the ancient Egyptian temples mingled with elements from the later Greek and Roman mystery traditions.[29] It is named after Hermes, the Greek name for the ancient Egyptian god *Djehuti*—transliterated as Theut or Thoth—the initiator, the guide into the Far World, the one who knew "the secrets of the night."[30]

There is an age-old conflict between those who simply wish to intellectually appreciate the religious journey and those who wish to actually tread the path. This is a journey of initiation, and those who wish to undertake it find that it matters little exactly how many gods the Divine might seek expression through. For always their attention is directed toward the one eternal source of all being. But despite the effort and the commitment, this was a journey that was always kept shrouded in secrecy.

Cicero (b. 102 B.C.), who was a member of the Roman College of Augurs (diviners), understood the need for a popular religion as well as a mystical tradition. His cynicism was pragmatic; his view was that practices such as those followed by the augurs were simple political expediency. He wrote in his book *On Divination,*

> Out of respect for the opinion of the masses and because of the great service to the State we maintain the augural [Divination] practices, discipline, religious rites and laws, as well as the authority of the augural college.[31]

Even the Koran, in some curious phraseology, hints at a knowledge of this distinction. While mostly the talk is of God as a kind of male being who must be obeyed at one's peril, occasionally the language shifts. It is subtle but revealing.

Sura 4 explains that, "God encompasses everything," and Sura 38, "There is not any god but God, the One, the Omnipotent."[32]

We can indeed say that the inner and the outer understanding of religion has been with us for millennia. For the outer popular understanding, a god or goddess is important as an authority figure, a source of morality, justice, and social harmony, one who can impose fearsome sanctions on those who transgress and promise gifts for those in favor. For the secretive inner understanding, such an authority figure is irrelevant, all the gods and goddesses are focusing and symbolizing different expressions of the one Divinity. Those who argue over a theocracy for the United States or the need for a Temple in Jerusalem to save humanity or the need for sharia law to save the world are misguided and mistaken, locked into the outer cultic aspect of religion.

All indications are that it is this superficial and shallow approach to spirituality that motivates those who are claiming Jerusalem as the center of the world. Furthermore, it seems fair to conclude that so long as we are dominated by this outer approach to religion, we will have no peace at all—neither in Jerusalem nor anywhere else.

To have a society that accepts different expressions of Divinity is one that allows a path for everyone. No one need fight over the name of the god—or goddess—one worships; if others do not like one, they can seek another. It doesn't matter. Ultimately, all these paths lead to the top of the sacred mountain, though some are perhaps rockier than others.

But all of us are under pressure from the relentless advance of fundamentalism. Emerging from the great religions, its current is slowly, but inexorably, drawing us toward the edges of our respective religious traditions. Here the clear water becomes muddied. Predators lie hidden in the undergrowth. Our river narrows and is stilled with weeds, its glittering fish harder to see. The light is fading. Soon, it will be difficult for us to find our way home.

But there is a solution: that we dive beneath the weeds; that we plunge deep into the waters still within our reach and head for the great ocean, where, once again, we can all swim freely.

All it takes is a shift of view and, naturally, some courage.

NOTES

Epigraph and Preface

1. Marvin W. Meyer, ed. and trans., *The Ancient Mysteries: A Sourcebook: Sacred Texts of the Mystery Religions of the Ancient Mediterranean World* (San Francisco: Harper & Row, 1987) 101. For texts and commentaries of all the plates, see Alberto Bernabé and Ana Isabel Jiménez San Cristóbal, *Instructions for the Netherworld. The Orphic Gold Tablets*, trans. Michael Chase (Boston: Brill, 2008).

2. Robert Lanham, "America's Religious Right: God's Own Country," *The Independent on Sunday* (London), December 16, 2006, 29–31.

3. John Hagee, *From Daniel to Doomsday* (Nashville: Nelson, 1999), 162.

4. *The Times* (London), January 4, 2007, 39.

5. Hagee, *Daniel to Doomsday*, 225.

6. Sa'id Ayyub, *Al-Masih al-Dajjal* (Cairo: al-Fath li-l-A`lam al-`Arabi, 1987), 286–88, quoted in David Cook, *Contemporary Muslim Apocalyptic Literature* (Syracuse: Syracuse University Press, 2008), 197.

7. Grace Halsall, *Prophecy and Politics* (Chicago: Lawrence Hill, 1986), 5, 45, quoted in Dan Cohn-Sherbok, *The Politics of Apocalypse: The History and Influence of Christian Zionism* (Oxford: Oneworld, 2006), 146.

8. Larry Jones and Gerald T. Sheppard, "Ronald Reagan's Theology of Armageddon," in Hassan Haddad and Donald Wagner, ed., *All in the Name of the Bible* (Brattleboro, VT: Amana, 1986), 32–33, quoted in Cohn-Sherbok, *Politics of Apocalypse*, 147.

9. Arnon Regular, "'Road Map Is a Life Saver for Us' PM Abbas Tells Hamas," *Ha'aretz*, June 26, 2003, quoted in Esther Kaplan, *With God on Their Side: How Christian Fundamentalists Trampeled Science, Policy, and Democracy in George W. Bush's White House* (New York: New Press, 2004), 9.

Chapter 1: Taking the Temple

1. Raymond of Aguilers as recorded in Steven Runciman, *A History of the Crusades* (Cambridge: Cambridge University Press, 1951), 1:287.

2. William, Archbishop of Tyre, *A History of Deeds Done Beyond the Sea*, trans. Emily Atwater Babcock and A. C. Krey (New York: Columbia University Press, 1943), 372–74.

3. William, Archbishop of Tyre, *A History of Deeds Done*, 372–74.

4. Koran 2:71.

5. Randolph S. Churchill and Winston S. Churchill, *The Six Day War* (Boston: Houghton Mifflin, 1967), 141.

6. For example, Ross Dunn, "Jews attack Orthodox school," *The Times* (London), January 1, 1998, 12.

7. Gershom Gorenberg, *End of Days:Fundamentalism and the Struggle for the Temple Mount* (New York, Free Press, 2000), 100.

8. Churchill and Churchill, *Six Day War*, 141.

9. Hal Lindsey, *The Late Great Planet Earth* (Grand Rapids: Zondervan, 1970), 50–51.

10. Lindsey, *Late Great Planet Earth*, 56.

11. Lindsey, *Late Great Planet Earth*, 44.

12. Gorenberg, *End of Days*, 121.

13. John Hagee, *Jerusalem Countdown* (Lake Mary, FL: FrontLine, 2006), 90.

14. Hagee, *Daniel to Doomsday*, 123.

15. David Cook, *Contemporary Muslim Apocalyptic Literature* (Syracuse, NY: Syracuse University Press, 2005), 215.

16. Cook, *Contemporary Muslim Apocalyptic Literature*, 145.

17. Cook, *Contemporary Muslim Apocalyptic Literature*, 13–21.

18. Cook, *Contemporary Muslim Apocalyptic Literature*, 22.

19. Quoted in Cook, *Contemporary Muslim Apocalyptic Literature*, 23.

20. Quoted in Cook, *Contemporary Muslim Apocalyptic Literature*, 23.

21. Cook, *Contemporary Muslim Apocalyptic Literature*, 85–86.

Chapter 2: The Red Heifer

1. Gorenberg, *End of Days*, 100.

2. Gorenberg, *End of Days*, 96.

3. Gorenberg, *End of Days*, 112–14.

4. Gorenberg, *End of Days*, 128.

5. Gorenberg, *End of Days*, 175.

6. Gorenberg, *End of Days*, 164, 175–76.

7. Gorenberg, *End of Days*, 176.

8. Gorenberg, *End of Days*, 176.

9. Chaim Richman, personal communication, January 1992.

10. Richman, personal communication, January, 1992.

11. Chaim Richman, *A House of Prayer for all Nations: The Holy Temple of Jerusalem* (Jerusalem: Temple Institute, 1997), 7.

12. Chaim Richman, "Rosh HaShana Blessings from the Temple Institute" September 21, 2006, www.templeinstitute.org/news.htm.

13. Chaim Richman, Letter of 1995, first printed in *The Restoration*, September 1995, http://members.aol.com/baryeh/richman.html.

14. Richman, Letter of 1995.

15. Lawrence Wright, "Letter from Jerusalem: Forcing the End," *New Yorker*, July 20, 1998, posted at www.lawrencewright.com/art-jerusalem.html.

16. Wright, "Letter from Jerusalem."

17. Gorenberg, *End of Days*, 9.

18. Lindsey, *Late Great Planet Earth*, 52.

19. Lindsey, *Late Great Planet Earth*, 167.

20. Hagee, *Daniel to Doomsday*, 153.

21. Hagee, *Daniel to Doomsday*, 237.

Chapter 3: Destroying the Mosques

1. Louis Sahagun, "Plotting the Exit Strategy," *Los Angeles Times*, June 22, 2006, http://articles.latimes.com/2006/jun/22/local/me-endtimes22.

2. "Long Term Objectives," Temple Mount and Land of Israel Faithful Movement, www.templemountfaithful.org/obj.htm.

3. "The Cornerstone for the Third Temple," Temple Mount and Land of Israel Faithful Movement, www.templemountfaithful.org/sukkot98.htm.

4. "The Cornerstone for the Third Temple."

5. Thomas McCall, "Gershon Salomon & the Temple Mount Faithful: An Interview," Levitt Letter, July 1997, www.levitt.com/newsletters/1997-07.html#SPECIAL.

6. Wright, "Letter from Jerusalem."

7. Peter Ephross, "American preacher devotes self to prophesied heifers for Israel," *J. the Jewish news weekly of Northern California*, September 10, 1999, www.jewishsf.com/content/2-0-/module/displaystory/story_id/12026/edition_id/231/format/html/displaystory.html.

8. Gorenberg, *End of Days*, 29.

9. Gorenberg, *End of Days*, 28.

10. The Temple Institute, "The Red Heifer: The Original Ashes," www.templeinstitute.org/red_heifer/original_ashes.htm.

11. Firas Al-Atraqchi, "Jewish groups: Raze mosques, rebuild temple," Aljazeera.net, July 28, 2004, http://english.aljazeera.net/archive/2004/07/20084915272229244.html.

12. Cook, *Contemporary Muslim Apocalyptic Literature*, 200.

13. Cook, *Contemporary Muslim Apocalyptic Literature*, 86.

14. Cook, *Contemporary Muslim Apocalyptic Literature*, 86.

15. Cook, *Contemporary Muslim Apocalyptic Literature*, 85n2.

16. Cook, *Contemporary Muslim Apocalyptic Literature*, 87–88.

17. *Encyclopedia Judaica* (Jerusalem: Keter, 1974), 14:837.

18. "Current members of the Sanhedrin," www.thesanhedrin.org/en/main/officers.html.

19. "New 'Sanhedrin' plans rebuilding of Temple," WorldNetDaily.com, June 8, 2005, www.worldnetdaily.com/news/article.asp?ARTICLE_ID=44672.

20. The Sanhedrin, March 7, 2005, posted at www.thesanhedrin.org/en/legal/
psak5765AdarI26.html

21. Yuval Yoaz, "Rabbis face criminal probe over death threat to IDF Officer,"
Haaretz.com, February 1, 2007, www.haaretz.com/hasen/spages/819950.html.

22. "Reestablished Sanhedrin Convenes to Discuss Temple," Arutz-7
IsraelNationalNews.com, February 9, 2005, www.israelnationalnews.com/
News/News.aspx/76624.

23. Arutz-7 IsraelNationalNews.com, February 28, 2007, www.templeinstitute.org/
news.htm.

24. www.templemountfaithful.org/policy.htm.

25. www.templemountfaithful.org/vision.htm.

26. Aryeh Kaplan, *Jerusalem, The Eye of the Universe* (New York: National Congress of
Synagogue Youth, 1976), 76.

27. Kaplan, *Jerusalem*, 78.

28. Kaplan, *Jerusalem*, 79.

29. Kaplan, *Jerusalem*, 82.

Chapter 4: Armageddon

1. For a general review and discussion see Steven Mithen, *After the Ice* (Cambridge,
MA: Harvard University Press, 2003), 20–39.

2. S. Belitzky, N. Goren-Inbar, and E. Werker, "A Middle Pleistocene wooden
plank with man-made polish," *Journal of Human Evolution* 20 (1991): 349.

3. Belitzky, Goren-Inbar, and Werker, "Middle Pleistocene," 351. A discussion of this
and a photograph can be found in Michael Baigent, *Ancient Traces* (London: Penguin,
1998), xi–xiii.

4. Communication from Professor Naama Goren-Inbar, October 8, 1996.

5. Belitzky, Goren-Inbar, and Werker, "Middle Pleistocene," 352.

6. Bob Holmes, "Take Me to Your Leader," *New Scientist*, April 22, 2000, 43.

7. For the story of the various scientific expeditions to find the *Mokele-mbembe*, see
Baigent, *Ancient Traces*, 57–70.

8. Lanham, "America's Religious Right."

9. John Ben-Daniel and Gloria Ben-Daniel, *The Apocalypse in the Light of the Temple*
(Jerusalem: Beit Jochanan, 2003), 4n4.

10. Eric H. Cline, *The Battles of Armageddon* (Ann Arbor: University of Michigan
Press, 2000), 3.

11. James B. Pritchard, ed., *The Ancient Near East*, 2 vols. (Princeton, NJ: Princeton
University Press, 1958), 1:176.

12. Pritchard, *Ancient Near East*, 1:180–81.

13. Cline, *Battles of Armageddon*, 98–100.

14. Flavius Josephus, *The Antiquities of the Jews*, trans. William Whiston, Book XV
(London: Willoughby, n.d.), 205.

15. Cook, *Contemporary Muslim Apocalyptic Literature*, 76.

16. Cook, *Contemporary Muslim Apocalyptic Literature*, 77.

17. Hagee, *Daniel to Doomsday*, 225.

18. G. B. Caird, *The Revelation of St. John the Divine*, 2nd ed. (London: A & C Black, 1985), 84.

19. Hagee, *Daniel to Doomsday*, 92–93.

20. Hagee, *Daniel to Doomsday*, 93.

Chapter 5: John of Patmos

1. Frank C. Whitmore et al., "Elephant Teeth from the Atlantic Continental Shelf." *Science* 156, no. 3781 (1967): 1477. *See also* Baigent, *Ancient Traces*, 117–27 for a discussion of the evidence for, and implications of, the melting ice cap and the rise in sea levels worldwide. For a good review of the discoveries on the eastern coasts of Canada and the United States, see Tom Koppel, *Lost World: Rewriting Prehistory—How New Science Is Tracing America's Ice Age Mariners* (New York: Atria, 2003).

2. Bede, *A History of the English Church and People*, trans. Leo Sherley-Price (Harmondsworth, UK: Penguin, 1968), chap. 16, 57–58.

3. Geoffrey Ashe, *King Arthur's Avalon* (London: Collins, 1957), 72–73.

4. Vali Nasr, *The Shia Revival* (New York: Norton, 2006), 43.

5. Nasr, *Shia Revival*, 227–28.

6. Nasr, *Shia Revival*, 236–37.

7. Nasr, *Shia Revival*, 20.

8. Nasr, *Shia Revival*, 20.

9. Nasr, *Shia Revival*, 22.

10. Cook, *Contemporary Muslim Apocalyptic Literature*, 140–41.

11. Cook, *Contemporary Muslim Apocalyptic Literature*, 145. *See also* 168, quoting `Abd al-Hamid, writing in 1998.

12. Cook, *Contemporary Muslim Apocalyptic Literature*, 71.

13. Anton La Guardia, "'Divine mission' driving Iran's new leader," *Daily Telegraph*, January 14, 2006, 10.

14. Nasr, *Shia Revival*, 133–34.

15. La Guardia, "'Divine mission'."

16. Caird, *Revelation of St. John the Divine*, 5.

17. Caird, *Revelation of St. John the Divine*, 21–23.

18. The year in which the crucifixion occurred is uncertain, but three particular years have emerged as the most likely. Arguments can be advanced for A.D. 30, 33, and 36, although the latter must be considered the most likely. The data is ambiguous: the New Testament states simply that the crucifixion occurred after the execution of John the Baptist at a Passover during which Pontius Pilate

was governor of Judaea and Caiaphas was high priest. Since both Pilate and Caiaphas were dismissed in A.D. 36, this provides a final date. The execution of John the Baptist cannot be dated with accuracy, but there is a strong suggestion in the New Testament that it was the result of his criticism of the marriage of Herod and his niece, Herodias (Matthew 14:3–5; Mark 1:14; 6:14–19). This marriage took place, it is generally agreed, in A.D. 35, the year when John was very likely executed. It therefore follows that the crucifixion of Jesus must have been on the Passover of A.D. 36 (see Hugh Schonfield, *The Pentecost Revolution* [Rockport, MA: Element, 1991], 45–55).

It is of relevance that among the messianic Jewish group that produced the Dead Sea Scrolls, a "marriage with a niece" was forbidden. This would be a good argument for John's adhering to the messianic Jewish camp (see Robert Eisenman, "James the Just in the Habakkuk Pesher," in *The Dead Sea Scrolls and the First Christians* (Rockport, MA: Element, 1996), 124. *See also The Temple Scroll*, col. 66, line 16–17 "A man is not to take his brother's daughter or his sister's daughter because it is an abomination," in F. García Martínez, ed., Wilfred Watson, trans., *The Dead Sea Scrolls Translated* (Grand Rapids: Eerdmans, 1996), 179). Such a marriage was also forbidden as incestuous in Rome until A.D. 49 when the senate passed a decree legalizing it so the emperor Claudius could marry his niece Agrippina (see Publius Cornelius Tacitus, *The Annals of Imperial Rome*, trans. Michael Grant [Harmondsworth, UK: 1979], 253–54. *Annales cap.* XII).

19. Irenaeus of Lyons, "Against Heresies," in *The Writings of Irenaeus*, trans. Alexander Roberts and W. H. Rambaut (Edinburgh: T & T Clark, 1868–1869), V, XXX, 3.

20. Tacitus, *Annals of Imperial Rome*, 352 (*Annales cap.* XV).

21. Gaius Suetonius Tranquillus, *The Twelve Caesars*, trans. Robert Graves (Harmondsworth, UK: Penguin, 1979), 302. (*Domitian*, iv). For a discussion see Caird, *Revelation of St. John the Divine*, 216.

22. Pliny, *The Letters of the Younger Pliny*, ed. Betty Radice (Harmondsworth, UK: Penguin, 1969), extract cited in "The Destruction of Pompeii, 79 A.D.," www.eyewitnesstohistory.com.

23. Lindsey, *Late Great Planet Earth*, 17–18.

24. Tim LaHaye and Jerry Jenkins, *Are We Living in the End Times?* (Wheaton, IL: Tyndale, 1999), 6.

25. LaHaye and Jenkins, *Living in the End Times?* 5.

26. Hagee, *Daniel to Doomsday*, 161–62.

27. Justin Martyr, *Dialogue of Justin, Philosopher and Martyr, with Trypho, a Jew* (Edinburgh: Kessinger, 2004), chap. 81, 201.

28. Justin Martyr, *Dialogue*, chap. 135, 270.

Chapter 6: Revelation

1. This important but difficult concept is perhaps best expressed by the ancient Egyptians as the *Duart*, the "Far World." This world was not seen as separate from normal existence; rather it was ever-present, existing with the physical world, intertwined with it but separated—the physical world exists in time; the Duart exists outside of time. For a discussion of the Duart, see Michael Baigent, *The Jesus Papers* (San Francisco: HarperOne, 2006), 160–63.

2. Philo of Alexandria, *De Vita Mosis*, II, XXI, 103 in *The Works of Philo*, trans. C. D. Yonge (Peabody, MA: Hendrickson, 1993), 491–517. *See also* Philo's *Quis Rerum Divinarum Heres*, XLV, 221, in *The Works of Philo*, 294. "The sacred candlestick and the seven lights upon it are an imitation of the wandering of the seven planets through the heaven."

3. Richard H. Wilkinson, *Symbol & Magic in Egyptian Art* (New York: Thames and Hudson, 1994), 136.

4. Jeremy Black and Anthony Green, *Gods, Demons and Symbols of Ancient Mesopotamia* (London: British Museum, 1992), 144.

5. Caird, *Revelation of St. John the Divine*, 106.

6. R. H. Charles, ed, "The Book of Jubilees," in *The Apocrypha and Pseudepigrapha of the Old Testament* (Oxford: Oxford University Press, 1979), 2:11–82.

7. Caird, *Revelation of St. John the Divine*, 245.

8. For a discussion of seven trumpeters in the Old Testament, see Caird, *Revelation of St. John the Divine*, 108–11.

9. For examples of its use see: Job 26:6, 28:22, 31:12; Psalm 88:11; Proverbs 15:11, 27:20. *See also* Caird, *Revelation of St John the Divine*, 120 and *The Jerusalem Bible*, Old Testament, 757, n.d. relating to Job 26: "In Hebr. 'Abaddon'. . . synonym for 'Sheol'."

10. Lindsey, *Late Great Planet Earth*, 81–82.

11. Herbert W. Armstrong, *The Book of Revelation Unveiled at last!* (Pasadena, CA: Worldwide Church of God, 1972), 38–39.

12. Hagee, *Daniel to Doomsday*, 233.

13. LaHaye and Jenkins, *Living in the End Times?*, 191.

14. LaHaye and Jenkins, *Living in the End Times?*, 191.

15. Hisham Kamal `Abd al-Hamid, *Iqtaraba khuruq al-masih al-Dajjal* (Cairo: al-Fath li-l-A`lam al-`Arabi, 1996), 136, quoted in Cook, *Contemporary Muslim Apocalyptic Literature*, 81.

16. *Jerusalem Bible*, *The New Testament*, 441, n.b referring to Revelation 12:1.

17. Caird, *Revelation of St. John the Divine*, 150.

18. Theodore J. Lewis, "Syro-Palestinian Iconography and Divine Images," in Neal Walls, ed., *Cult Image and Divine Representation in the Ancient Near East* (Boston: American Schools of Oriental Research, 2005), 80.

19. *Jerusalem Bible*, Old Testament, 1437, column 1, n.e.

Chapter 7: The Day of the Beast

1. For a discussion on this see Baigent, *From the Omens of Babylon* (London: Arkana, 1994), 81–82.

2. See, for example, Iamblichus, *On the Mysteries*, ed. Stephen Ronan, trans. Thomas Taylor and Alexander Wilder (London: Chthonios, 1989), 1:17; 7:3.

3. See Baigent, *Omens of Babylon*, 78–82 for a longer discussion of this topic.

4. "Asclepius," in *Hermetica*, trans. Brian P. Copenhaver (Cambridge: Cambridge Univesity Press, 1992), 38.

5. LaHaye and Jenkins, *Living in the End Times?*, 197.

6. Irenaeus, *Against Heresies*, V, xxx.1–3.

7. Caird, *Revelation of St. John the Divine*, 175.

8. Caird, *Revelation of St. John the Divine*, 163.

9. Suetonius, *Twelve Caesars*, 309.

10. Sixteen hundred furlongs in the text.

11. Tacitus, *Annals of Imperial Rome*, 366.

12. Hagee, *Daniel to Doomsday*, 176.

13. Hagee, *Daniel to Doomsday*, 221.

14. Hagee, *Daniel to Doomsday*, 178–79.

15. Hagee, *Daniel to Doomsday*, 180.

16. LaHaye and Jenkins, *Living in the End Times?*, 176.

17. Hagee, *Daniel to Doomsday*, 184.

18. *Jerusalem Bible, The Old Testament*, 1409, chapter 38, n.b.

19. Caird, *The Revelation of St. John the Divine*, 256.

20. For a full exploration of this see Baigent, "The Kingdom of Heaven" in *Jesus Papers*.

21. Cook, *Contemporary Muslim Apocalyptic Literature*, 205n3.

22. Eusebius, *The History of the Church*, trans. G. A. Williamson (Harmondsworth, UK: Penguin, 1965), 3.25, (134).

23. Recorded in a summary of the acts of the Council of Hippo, which was included in the acts of the Council of Carthage in 419. See F. W. Grosheide, ed., *Some Early Lists of the Books of the New Testament* (Leiden: Brill, 1948), 22.

24. Hagee, *Daniel to Doomsday*, 272.

Chapter 8: Carried Away by the Rapture

1. Tim LaHaye and Jerry Jenkins, *Left Behind* (Carol Stream, IL: Tyndale, 1996), 21.

2. Phillips, *American Theocracy: The Peril and Politics of Radical Religion, Oil, and Borrowed Money in the 21ˢᵗ Century* (New York: Viking, 2006), 88, 253.

3. Translations vary: the original Greek renders the phrase "of the way"; the Authorized Version loses the information regarding self-definition by saying, "of this way." The Jerusalem Bible gives the self definition in full "followers of the Way" and in a note explains that the "Way" is the characteristic way of life followed by the Christians who were—or perhaps more accurately, were becoming—a separate community. This concept is well known in the Dead Sea Scrolls, using *Derech*, "the Way."

4. Suetonius, *Twelve Caesars*, 202.

5. S. G. F. Brandon, *Jesus and the Zealots: A Study of the Political Factor in Primitive Christianity* (New York: Scribner, 1967), 328. *See also* Baigent, *Jesus Papers*, 24–25.

6. See, for instance, Paul's letter to the Romans 2:26–29; 3:28; and 7:4–6.

7. John Nelson Darby, *The Collected Writings*, ed. William Kelly (Kingston-on-Thames: Stow Hill, 1962), 11:153.

8. Darby, *Collected Writings*, 11:155.

9. C. I. Scofield, ed., *The Scofield Reference Bible* (New York: Oxford University Press, 1917), 1337n1.

10. Scofield, *Reference Bible*, 1228n1.

11. Scofield, *Reference Bible*, 1353n4.

12. Scofield, *Reference Bible*, 3.

13. Lindsey, *Late Great Planet Earth*, 138.

Chapter 9: Fighting for God

1. Ronnie Dugger, "Reagan's Apocalypse Now," *Guardian* (reprinted from *Washington Post*), April 21, 1984, 19.

2. Ron Suskind, "Faith, Certainty and the Presidency of George W. Bush," www.nytimes.com/2004/10/17/magazine/17BUSH.html.

3. Irwin Stelzer, "Lunch in the White House with George," *Sunday Times* (London), March 4, 2007, sec. 5, 2.

4. Michael Lind, "George W. Bush's Holy War," *Globalist*, March 23, 2003, www.theglobalist.com/StoryId.aspx?StoryId=3025.

5. Kaplan, *God on Their Side*, 21.

6. Kaplan, *God on Their Side*, 21.

7. Sidney Blumenthal, "Smiting the Infidels," *Salon*, May 20, 2004, http://dir.salon.com/story/opinion/blumenthal/2004/05/20/boykin/index.html.

8. Sam Felder, "Holy War, Anyone? Gen. Boykin Implicated in Abu Ghraib Scandal," Americans United for Separation of Church and State, May 20, 2004, http://blog.au.org/2004/05/20/general_big_god/.

9. With thanks to journalist Robert Fisk who reported in the *Independent* (UK), February 13, 1991, on a U.S. military briefing in Riyadh in February 1991, during the First Gulf War, saying "There was in fact no war at all, rather a husk of words from which all reality had been sucked."

10. With thanks to the syndicated comic strip "Doonesbury."

11. Seymour M. Hersh, "Moving Targets: Will the counter-insurgency plan in Iraq repeat the mistakes of Vietnam?" *New Yorker*, December 15, 2003, www.new yorker.com/archive/2003/12/15/031215fa_fact.

12. Katherine Yurica, "Infiltrating the U.S. Military. Gen. Boykin's 'Kingdom Warriors' on the Road to Abu Ghraib and Beyond," Yurica Report, October 12, 2004, www.yuricareport.com/Dominionism/InfiltratingTheUSMilitaryGenBoykinsWarriors.html.

13. Jeffrey Smith and Josh White, "General's Speeches Broke Rules," *Washington Post*, August 19, 2004, in Yurica, "Infiltrating the U.S. Military."

14. Smith and White, "General's Speeches," in Yurica, "Infiltrating the U.S. Military."

15. Mark Thompson, "The Boykin Affair," *Time*, October 26, 2003, www.time.com/time/printout/0,8816,526381,00.html.

16. Paul Wood, "Hunting 'Satan' in Falluja Hell," BBC News, November 23, 2004, quoted in John Gray, *Black Mass: Apocalyptic Religion and the Death of Utopia* (London: Penguin, 2007), 28.

17. Tim Carlson, "Faith Is a Powerful 'Force Multiplier,'" *Engineer Update* 23, no. 7 (1999): 2, www.hq.usace.army.mil/cepa/pubs/jul99/story3.htm.

18. Thompson, "Boykin Affair."

19. Yurica, "Gen. Boykin's 'Kingdom Warriors.'"

20. Force Ministries at www.forceministries.com/.

21. Yurica, "Gen. Boykin's 'Kingdom Warriors.'"

22. Paul Harvey, *Redeeming the South: Religious Cultures and Racial Identities among Southern Baptists, 1865–1925* (Chapel Hill: University of North Carolina Press, 1997), 30, quoted in Phillips, *American Theocracy*, 152.

23. Phillips, *American Theocracy*, 153.

24. Mark Noll, *Old Religion in a New World: The History of North American Christianity* (Grand Rapids: Eerdmans, 2002), 283–86, quoted in Phillips, *American Theocracy*, 107.

25. Phillips, *American Theocracy*, 102.

26. Phillips, *American Theocracy*, 102.

27. Phillips, *American Theocracy*, 169, provides a map showing this influence.

28. Louis Bolce and Gerald De Maio, "Party of Unbelievers," *Public Interest*, Fall 2002, 3, quoted in Phillips, *American Theocracy*, 189.

29. Phillips, *American Theocracy*, 192.

30. Inaugural address, posted on www.whitehouse.gov/news/inauguraladdress.html.

31. www.whitehouse.gov/news/releases/2001/10/20011007-8.html.

32. Jim Wallis, *God's Politics: Why the Right Gets It Wrong and the Left Doesn't Get It* (San Francisco: HarperSanFrancisco, 2005), 141.

33. Wallis, *God's Politics*, 142.

34. Wallis, *God's Politics*, 145.

35. Tribute posted on www.september11news.com/PresidentBushPentagon.htm.

36. Wallis, *God's Politics*, 139.

37. Wallis, *God's Politics*, 140–41.

38. Suskind, "Faith, Certainty and the Presidency of George W. Bush."

39. www.thatchercentre.org.

40. Dugger, "Reagan's Apocalypse Now."

41. *The Humanist*, July/August 1981, 15, quoted in Michael Baigent, Richard Leigh, and Henry Lincoln, *The Messianic Legacy* (London: Jonathan Cape, 1986), 189.

42. Eric Heubeck "The Integration of Theory and Practice: A Program for the New Traditionalist Movement, www.yuricareport.com/Dominionism/FreeCongressEssay.html.

43. Details posted on www.cc.org/2004scorecard.pdf.

Chapter 10: Planet Rushdoony

1. Francis Schaeffer, *A Christian Manifesto* (Wheaton, IL: Crossway, 1982), 18.

2. Schaeffer, *Christian Manifesto*, 101.

3. William Martin, *With God on Our Side: The Rise of the Religious Right in America* (New York: Broadway, 2005), 197.

4. Gary North, *Backward Christian Soldiers? An Action Manual For Christian Reconstruction* (Tyler, TX: Institute for Christian Economics, 1984), www.politicalamazon.com/cr-quotes.html#north.

5. John Sugg, "A Nation Under God," *Mother Jones*, December/January 2006, www.motherjones.com/news/feature/2005/12/a_nation_under_god.html.

6. See Baigent, "The Kingdom of Heaven," in *Jesus Papers*, 225–44.

7. Martin, *God on Our Side*, 354.

8. Martin, *God on Our Side*, 354.

9. Martin, *God on Our Side*, 354.

10. Sugg, "Nation Under God."

11. Sugg, "Nation Under God."

12. North, *Backward Christian Soldiers?* 65–66.

13. Glenn Scherer, "The Godly Must Be Crazy," *Grist*, October 27, 2004, www.grist.org/news/maindish/2004/10/27/scherer-christian/index.html.

14. Sugg, "Nation Under God."

15. "What Chalcedon Believes," The Chalcedon Foundation, www.chalcedon.edu/credo.php.

16. "What Chalcedon Believes."

17. Rousas John Rushdoony, *The Institutes of Biblical Law* (Nutley, NJ: Craig, 1973), 100.

18. Rushdoony, *Biblical Law*, 5.

19. Rushdoony, *Biblical Law*, 580–81.

20. Edward Chauncey Baldwin, "The Permanent Elements in the Hebrew Law," *International Journal of Ethics* 25 (1915): 365, www.dinsdoc.com/baldwin_e-1.htm.

21. Baldwin, "Permanent Elements in the Hebrew Law."

22. Rushdoony, *Biblical Law*, 2.

23. Rushdoony, *Biblical Law*, 8. Rushdoony's italics.

24. Rushdoony, *Biblical Law*, 99.

25. Rushdoony, *Biblical Law*, 423.

26. Rushdoony, *Biblical Law*, 713.

27. David Chilton, *The Days of Vengeance: An Exposition of the Book of Revelation* (Fort Worth: Dominion, 1984), 127, www.politicalamazon.com/cr-quotes.html.

28. Rushdoony, *Biblical Law*, 58.

29. Rushdoony, *Biblical Law*, 87.

30. Gary North, *The Sinai Strategy: Economics and the Ten Commandments* (Tyler, TX: Institute for Christian Economics, 1986), 59–60, www.politicalamazon.com/cr-quotes.html.

31. Jeremy Leaming, "Christian Reconstructionists Hope to Move Out of the Margins and Take Dominion in America—and They Have Some Powerful Friends," Americans United for Separation of Church and State, Fringe Festival, July/August 2007, www.au.org/site/News2?abbr=cs_&page=NewsArticle&id=9212.

32. John Sugg, "Christian Reconstructionists Believe Democracy Is Heresy," Americans United for Separation of Church and State, Warped Worldview, July/August 2006, www.au.org/site/News2?abbr=cs_&page=NewsArticle&id=8314&news_iv_ctrl=2081.

33. Jacobus Sprenger and Heinrich Kramer, *Malleus Maleficarum: The Hammer of Witchcraft* (London: Folio Society, 1968), 121.

34. Sprenger and Kramer, *Malleus Maleficarum*, 122.

35. Sprenger and Kramer, *Malleus Maleficarum*, 473.

36. Stefan George, *Werke*, trans. Richard Leigh, ed. Robert Boehringer (Stuttgart: Klett-Cotta, 1984), 256.

37. David Harrison, "'Child-witches' of Nigeria seek refuge," *Daily Telegraph*, November 9, 2008, www.telegraph.co.uk/news/worldnews/africaandindianocean/nigeria/3407882/Child-witches-of-Nigeria-seek-refuge.html.

38. Alan Cowell, "300 Missing Boys in Britain Fuel Child-Trafficking Fear," *New York Times*, May 15, 2005, www.nytimes.com/2005/05/15/international/europe/15missing.html.

39. Vikram Dodd, "Refugee Orphan 'Tortured as Witch,'" *Guardian*, May 10, 2005, www.guardian.co.uk/uk/2005/may/10/ukcrime.childprotection/.

40. Rushdoony, *Biblical Law*, 263.

41. James Oliphant, "Abortion Foes Take Battle beyond Roe," *Chicago Tribune*, June 10, 2008, available at http://pewforum.org/news/display.php?NewsID=15786.

42. The U.S. Constitution and Amendments are posted on www.usconstitution.net/const.html.

43. www.rutherford.org/shop/proddetail.asp?prod=221.

44. Mary McCarthy, "Reconstruction Theology and Home Education," quoting Christopher Klicka of the Home School Legal Defense Association, www.politicalamazon.com/fcf-homeschooling.html.

45. Rushdoony, *Biblical Law*, 621.

46. Gary North, "The Intellectual Schizophrenia of the New Christian Right," *Christianity and Civilisation* 1 (1982): 25, www.politicalamazon.com/cr-quotes.html.

47. McCarthy, "Reconstruction Theology."

48. Sugg, "Nation Under God."

49. www.ronpaul2008.com/issues/education/. Paul shut down his Web site after withdrawing from the presidential campaign, but see www.house.gov/paul/congrec/congrec2003/cr021103c.htm for his views.

50. www.ronpaul2008.com/issues/home-schooling/. This Web site is now shut down. He put forward his pro-homeschooling position in a speech to Congress on February 11, 2003, www.house.gov/paul/congrec/congrec2003/cr021103c.htm.

51. www.house.gov/paul/congrec/congrec2002/cr091002b.htm.

52. http://ronpaul.meetup.com/97/boards/thread/5483242/.

53. www.chalcedon.edu/blog/blog-php.

54. www.cc.org/2004scorecard.pdf.

55. The full list is posted on www.seekgod.ca/1998cnp.htm.

56. Posted on http://65.175.91.69/Reformation_net/default.htm.

57. "Christian Reconstruction in the Homeschooling Movement," www.politicalamazon.com/fcf-homeschooling.html.

58. Russ Bellant, *The Coors Connection: How Coors Family Philanthropy Undermines Democratic Pluralism* (Boston, MA: South End, 1991), 56.

59. Nico Pitney and Sam Stein, "Palin's Church May Have Shaped Controversial Worldview," September 2, 2008, www.huffingtonpost.com/2008/09/02/palins-church-may-have-sh_n_123205.html.

60. Bruce Wilson, "A Heartbeat Away, or Why Palin's Churches Matter," September 25, 2008, www.talk2action.org/story/2008/9/25/93553/3296/Front_page/A_Heartbeat_Away_or_Why_Palin_s_Churches_Matter.

61. Max Blumenthal, "The Witch Hunter Annoints Sarah Palin," www.huffington post.com/max-blumenthal/the-witch-hunter-annoints_b_128805.html.

62. Interview of Bruce Wilson posted at www.buzzflash.com/articles/ interviews/126.

Chapter 11: The Caliphate

1. Ed Husain, *The Islamist: Why I Joined Radical Islam in Britain, What I Saw Inside and Why I Left* (London: Penguin, 2007), 78.

2. Husain, *Islamist*, 86; David Davis, "The Wrong Voice for Muslim Britain," *Sunday Times* (London), August 5, 2007, Sec. 4, 3.

3. Sean O'Neill, "Extremists Who Prey on Impressionable Minds," *Times* (London), January 22, 2008, 4.

4. O'Neill, "Extremists Who Prey."

5. Husain, *Islamist*, 189.

6. Husain, *Islamist*, 188.

7. Husain, *Islamist*, 154.

8. Husain, *Islamist*, 101–3.

9. Husain, *Islamist*, 134.

10. Husain, *Islamist*, 70.

11. Cook, *Contemporary Muslim Apocalyptic Literature*, 174–75.

12. Abdullah ben Sadek, *Al Mahdi, Jesus and Dajjal (the Anti-Christ)*, trans. Shaykh Ahmad Darwish (London: Ta-Ha, n.d.), 33.

13. Noted in a submission by the World Union for Progressive Judaism to the fifty-ninth session of the United Nations Commission on Human Rights, February 18, 2003, 5. File No. E/CN.4/2003/NGO/226.

14. Muhammad Isa Da'ud, *Al-Mahdi al-muntazar 'ala al-abwab* (Cairo: al-'Arabiyya li-l-Tiba`a wa-l-Nashr, 1997), 179–80, quoted in Cook, *Contemporary Muslim Apocalyptic Literature*, 138–39.

15. Cook, *Contemporary Muslim Apocalyptic Literature*, 130–38.

16. Cook, *Contemporary Muslim Apocalyptic Literature*, 17.

17. Muhammad Arif ibn Izzat Muhammad, *Al Mahdi and the End of Time*, trans. Aisha Bewley (London: Dar Al Taqwa, 1997), 9, referencing, among others, al-Hakim (d. 1019) and Ibn Majah who, in the ninth century, was one of the scholars who produced a collection of texts considered canonical. The major collector of early Muslim apocalyptic literature was Nu'aym ibn Hammad al-Marwazi who worked in Syria and died in A.D. 844; his book *Kitab al-fitan* is of central importance to any study of this literature. See Cook, *Studies in Muslim Apocalyptic* (Princeton, NJ: Darwin, 2002), 21, 24.

18. Cook, *Studies in Muslim Apocalyptic*, 3.

19. Cook, *Studies in Muslim Apocalyptic*, 7–8.

20. Cook, *Studies in Muslim Apocalyptic*, 4.

21. Cook, *Studies in Muslim Apocalyptic*, 4n6.

22. Cook, *Studies in Muslim Apocalyptic*, 332.

23. Cook, *Contemporary Muslim Apocalyptic Literature*, 36 and notes.

24. Cook, *Contemporary Muslim Apocalyptic Literature*, 78.

25. Cook, *Contemporary Muslim Apocalyptic Literature*, 188.

26. Cook, *Contemporary Muslim Apocalyptic Literature*, 188.

27. Cook, *Contemporary Muslim Apocalyptic Literature*, 80.

28. Cook, *Contemporary Muslim Apocalyptic Literature*, 81.

29. Cook, *Contemporary Muslim Apocalyptic Literature*, 81n22.

30. Cook, *Contemporary Muslim Apocalyptic Literature*, 140, quoting Muhammad Isa Da'ud, (Text unspecified) 1995, 226.

31. Norman Cohn, *Warrant for Genocide: The Myth of the Jewish World-Conspiracy and the "Protocols of the Elders of Zion"* (London: Eyre & Spottiswoode, 1967), 59.

32. Cohn, *Warrant for Genocide*, 66.

33. Cohn, *Warrant for Genocide*, 67.

34. Cohn, *Warrant for Genocide*, 69.

35. *The Protocols of the Meetings of the Elders of Zion*, Protocol 4, 30.

36. *Protocols*, 89.

37. Cohn, *Warrant for Genocide*, 71–76.

38. Ahmad Thomson, *Dajjal the Antichrist* (London: Ta-Ha, 1997), 59.

39. Thomson, *Dajjal the Antichrist*, 59.

40. Thomson, *Dajjal the Antichrist*, 15.

41. Cook, *Contemporary Muslim Apocalyptic Literature*, 29.

42. Cook, *Contemporary Muslim Apocalyptic Literature*, 26.

43. Cook, *Contemporary Muslim Apocalyptic Literature*, 59.

44. Shiv Malik, "Schools are run by Islamic group Blair pledged to ban," *Sunday Times* (London), August 5, 2007, Sec. 1, 10.

45. Farhad Khosrokhavar, *Suicide Bombers: Allah's New Martyrs*, trans. David Macey (London: Pluto Press, 2005), 110.

46. Owen, Richard, "Muslim fan sues after his team is beaten by a crusader's cross," *Times* (London), December 12, 2007, 33.

47. Cook, *Contemporary Muslim Apocalyptic Literature*, 223n13.

48. Cook, *Contemporary Muslim Apocalyptic Literature*, 92nn9,10, 11.

49. David Cook, "America, the Second 'Ad: Prophecies about the Downfall of the United States," www.bu.edu/mille/scholarship/papers/A.D.A.M..html

50. Hagee, *Daniel to Doomsday*, 184.

51. Anas in Imam Nawawi, *Gardens of Righteousness*, trans. Muhammad Zafrulla Khan (New York: Routledge, 1975), 307, quoted in Sadek, *Al Mahdi, Jesus and Dajjal*, 31.

52. Cook, "America, the Second 'Ad: prophecies about the downfall of the United States," 3. Posted on www.bu.edu/mille/scholarship/papers/A.D.A.M..html

53. Cook, "America, the Second 'Ad.

54. Cook, "America, the Second 'Ad.

55. Cook, "America, the Second 'Ad.

Chapter 12: Jerusalem

1. Mark J. Sedgwick, *Sufism: The Essentials* (Cairo: American University in Cairo Press, 2003), 5.

2. Sedgwick, *Sufism*, 33.

3. *Rumi: Bridge to the Soul: Journeys into the Music and Silence of the Heart*, trans. Coleman Barks (New York: HarperOne, 2007), 66.

4. Julian Baldick, *Mystical Islam: An Introduction to Sufism* (New York: New York University Press, 1992), 27.

5. Baldick, *Mystical Islam*, 21.

6. *Bhagavad Gita*, 2:52.

7. For example in Karen L. King, *The Gospel of Mary of Magdala: Jesus and the First Woman Apostle* (Santa Rosa, CA: Polebridge, 2003), 10:3–4. See Baigent, *Jesus Papers*, 241–43 for a discussion of this.

8. *Bhagavad Gita*, 3:7.

9. Rumi, *The Essential Rumi*, trans. Coleman Barks (San Francisco: Harper, 1995) 191–92.

10. Koran, Sura 3, 67; Arberry translation, 55.

11. Kaplan, *Jerusalem*, 42.

12. Kaplan, *Jerusalem*, 75.

13. Kaplan, *Jerusalem*, 76

Chapter 13: Welcome to the Gods

1. Chris Hedges, *American Fascists: The Christian Right and the War on America* (London: Free Press, 2008), 121.

2. Hedges, *American Fascists*, 126.

3. Hedges, *American Fascists*, 22–23.

4. Hedges, *American Fascists*, 195.

5. Hedges, *American Fascists*, 202.

6. Hedges, *American Fascists*, 201–2.

7. Joe Bageant, *Deer Hunting with Jesus: Guns, Votes, Debt and Delusion in Redneck America* (London: Portobello, 2008), 188–89.

8. Safar ibn `Abd Al-Rahman Al-Hawali, *The Day of Wrath*, 26–27. Posted at www.islaam.com/books/intifadha.htm.

9. Hagee, *Daniel to Doomsday*, 153.

10. For a discussion of this, see Baigent, *Jesus Papers*, 159–63, 168–75.

11. Kasia Szpakowska, *Behind Closed Eyes: Dreams and Nightmares in Ancient Egypt* (Swansea, UK: Oxbow, 2003), 149–51.

12. *Bhagavad Gita*, 2:12–20.

13. For a discussion of this, see Baigent, *Jesus Papers*, 225–44.

14. *Bhagavad Gita* 2:42, 52 (author's modernization of the text).

15. Gray, *Black Mass*, 71.

16. Gray, *Black Mass*, 210.

17. Gray, *Black Mass*, 73.

18. Gray, *Black Mass*, 208.

19. Mark S. Smith, *The Origins of Biblical Monotheism: Israel's Polytheistic Background and the Ugaritic Texts* (New York: Oxford University Press, 2001), 150.

20. *Bible of Jerusalem, New Testament*, 89.n.c.

21. Koran, Sura 5, (Arberry trans. 107).

22. LaHaye and Jenkins, *Living in the End Times?*, 176.

23. Koran, Sura 29, 46 (Arberry trans. 408).

24. Exodus 6:2–3 "God spoke to Moses and said to him, 'I am Yahweh. To Abraham and Isaac and Jacob I appeared as El Shaddai; I did not make myself known to them by my name Yahweh.'" *See also* Smith, *Biblical Monotheism*, 141.

25. Smith, *Biblical Monotheism*, 142.

26. Smith, *Biblical Monotheism*, 136–37.

27. Smith, *Biblical Monotheism*, 179.

28. Professor Walter Burkert, undoubtedly the leading expert on ancient Greek religion, speaks plainly on the parallels between the cult of heroes and the cult of saints, "without doubt there is direct continuity as well as a structural parallel." Walter Burkert, *Greek Religion: Archaic and Classical*, trans. John Raffan (Cambridge, MA: Harvard University Press, 1985), 207.

29. Baigent and Leigh, *Elixir and the Stone*, 111–15. For the proof of the derivation of the Hermetic texts from the Egyptians see P. Kingsley, "Poimandres: The Etymology of the Name and the Origins of the Hermetica," in *Journal of the Warburg and Courtauld Institutes*, 57, 1994, 1–24.

30. Claas Jouco Bleeker, *Hathor and Thoth: Two Key Figures of the Ancient Egyptian Religion* (Leiden: Brill, 1973), 147.

31. Cicero, *De Divinatione*, trans. W. A. Falconer (Boston, MA: Harvard University Press, 1923), 2:33.

32. Koran, Sura 4, 126 (Arberry trans. 91); Sura, 38, 65 (Arberry trans. 469).

BIBLIOGRAPHY

Arif, Muhammad ibn Izzat Muhammad. *Al Mahdi and the End of Time*. Translated by Aisha Bewley. London: Dar Al Taqwa, 1997.

Armstrong, Herbert W. *The Book of Revelation: Unveiled at last!* Pasadena, CA: Worldwide Church of God, 1972.

"Asclepius." In *Hermetica*. Translated by Brian P. Copenhaver. Cambridge: Cambridge University Press, 1992.

Ashe, Geoffrey. *King Arthur's Avalon: The Story of Glastonbury*. London: Collins, 1957.

Avigad, Nahman. *Discovering Jerusalem*. Nashville: Nelson, 1983.

Bageant, Joe. *Deer Hunting with Jesus: Guns, Votes, Debt and Delusion in Redneck America*. London: Portobello, 2008.

Baigent, Michael. *Ancient Traces: Mysteries in Ancient and Early History*. London: Penguin, 1998.

———. *From the Omens of Babylon: Astrology and Ancient Mesopotamia*. London: Arkana, 1994.

———. *The Jesus Papers: Exposing the Greatest Cover-Up in History*. San Francisco: HarperOne, 2007.

Baigent, Michael, and Richard Leigh. *The Elixir and the Stone: The Tradition of Magic and Alchemy*. London: Penguin, 1997.

———. *The Inquisition*. London: Penguin, 1999.

Baigent, Michael, Richard Leigh, and Henry Lincoln. *The Messianic Legacy*. London: Jonathan Cape, 1986.

Baldick, Julian. *Mystical Islam: An Introduction to Sufism*. New York: New York University Press, 1992.

Bashir, Shahzad. *Messianic Hopes and Mystical Visions: The Nurbakhshiya Between Medieval and Modern Islam*. Columbia: University of South Carolina Press, 2003.

Bede. *A History of the English Church and People*. Translated by Leo Sherley-Price. Harmondsworth, UK: Penguin, 1968.

Bellant, Russ. *The Coors Connection: How Coors Family Philanthropy Undermines Democratic Pluralism*. Cambridge, MA: South End, 1991.

Ben-Daniel, John, and Gloria Ben-Daniel. *The Apocalypse in the Light of the Temple: A New Approach to the Book of Revelation*. Jerusalem: Beit Jochanan, 2003.

The Bhagavad gita. Translated by Juan Mascaro. Harmondsworth, UK: Penguin, 1962.

Black, Jeremy, and Anthony Green. *Gods, Demons and Symbols of Ancient Mesopotamia: An Illustrated Dictionary*. London: British Museum, 1992.

Bleeker, Claas Jouco. *Hathor and Thoth: Two Key Figures of the Ancient Egyptian Religion*. Leiden: Brill, 1973.

Brandon, S. G. F. *Jesus and the Zealots: A Study of the Political Factor in Primitive Christianity*. Manchester: Manchester University Press, 1967.

Brown, Peter. *The Cult of the Saints: Its Rise and Function in Latin Christianity*. Chicago: Chicago University Press, 1981.

Burkert, Walter. *Greek Religion: Archaic and Classical*. Translated by John Raffan. Cambridge, MA: Harvard University Press, 1985.

Caird, G. B. *The Revelation of St. John the Divine*. 2nd ed. London: A & C Black, 1985.

Charles, R. H. *The Apocrypha and Pseudepigrapha of the Old Testament*. 2 vols. Oxford: Clarendon, 1979.

Churchill, Randolph S., and Winston S. Churchill. *The Six Day War*. Boston: Houghton Mifflin, 1967.

Cicero. *De Divinatione*. Translated by W. A. Falconer. Boston, MA: Harvard University Press, 1923.

Cline, Eric H. *The Battles of Armageddon: Megiddo and the Jezreel Valley from the Bronze Age to the Nuclear Age*. Ann Arbor: University of Michigan Press, 2000.

Cohn, Norman. *Warrant for Genocide: The myth of the Jewish world conspiracy and the Protocols of the Elders of Zion*. London: Eyre & Spottiswoode, 1967.

Cohn-Sherbok, Dan. *The Politics of Apocalypse: The History and Influence of Christian Zionism*. Oxford: Oneworld, 2006.

Cook, David. *Contemporary Muslim Apocalyptic Literature*. Syracuse, NY: Syracuse University Press, 2005.

———. *Studies in Muslim Apocalyptic*. Princeton, NJ: Darwin, 2002.

Cross, F. L., and E. A. Livingstone, eds. *The Oxford Dictionary of the Christian Church*. 2nd ed. Oxford: Oxford University Press, 1983.

Davies, Philip R. *In Search of 'Ancient Israel.'* Sheffield, UK: Sheffield Academic Press, 1992.

Encyclopedia Judaica. 16 vols. Jerusalem: Keter, 1974.

Eusebius. *The History of the Church: From Christ to Constantine*. Translated by G. A. Williamson. Harmondsworth, UK: Penguin, 1965.

Farris, Michael P. *Where Do I Draw the Line?* Minneapolis: Bethany, 1992.

Fritz, Volkmar, and Philip R. Davies, eds. *The Origins of the Ancient Israelite States*. Sheffield, UK: Sheffield Academic Press, 1996.

García Martínez, Florentino. *The Dead Sea Scrolls Translated: The Qumran Texts in English*. Translated by G. E. Watson. Leiden: Brill, 1994.

Gorenberg, Gershom. *The End of Days: Fundamentalism and the Struggle for the Temple Mount*. New York: Free Press, 2000.

Gray, John. *Black Mass: Apocalyptic Religion and the Death of Utopia*. London: Penguin, 2007.

Grosheide, F. W., ed. *Some Early Lists of the Books of the New Testament.* Leiden: Brill, 1948.

Hafez, Mohammed M. *Manufacturing Human Bombs: The Making of Palestinian Suicide Bombers.* Washington, DC: United States Institute of Peace, 2006.

Hagee, John. *From Daniel to Doomsday: The Countdown Has Begun.* Nashville: Nelson, 1999.

———. *Jerusalem Countdown.* Lake Mary, FL: FrontLine, 2006.

Hedges, Chris. *American Fascists: The Christian Right and the War on America.* London: Free Press, 2008.

Husain, Ed. *The Islamist: Why I joined radical Islam in Britain, what I saw inside and why I left.* London: Penguin, 2007.

Iamblichus. *On the Mysteries.* Edited by Stephen Ronan. Translated by Thomas Taylor and Alexander Wilder. London: Chthonios Books, 1989.

Ice, Thomas, and Randall Price. *Ready to Rebuild: The Imminent Plan to Rebuild the Last Days Temple.* Eugene, OR: Harvest House, 1992.

Irenaeus of Lyons. "Against Heresies." In *The Writings of Irenaeus.* Translated by Alexander Roberts and W. H. Rambaut. 2 vols. Edinburgh: T & T Clark, 1869.

Jeffrey, Grant R. *The Signature of God: Astonishing Biblical Discoveries.* London: Pickering, 1998.

Jones, Alexander, ed. *The Jerusalem Bible.* London: Darton, Longman & Todd, 1966.

Josephus, Flavius. *The Antiquities of the Jews.* Translated by William Whiston. London: Willoughby, N.D.

Justin Martyr. "Dialogue of Justin, Philosopher and Martyr, with Trypho, a Jew." In *The Writings of Justin Martyr and Athenagoras.* Translated by Marcus Dods, George Reith, and B. P. Pratten. Edinburgh: T & T Clark, 1867.

Kabbani, Muhammad Hisham. *The Approach of Armageddon? An Islamic Perspective: A chronicle of scientific breakthroughs and world events that occur during the last days, as foretold by Prophet Muhammad.* Washington, DC: Islamic Supreme Council of America, 2003.

Kaplan, Aryeh. *Jerusalem, the Eye of the Universe.* New York: National Conference of Synagogue Youth/Union of Orthodox Jewish Congregations of America, 1976.

Kaplan, Esther. *With God on Their Side: George W. Bush and the Christian Right.* New York: New Press, 2005.

Kelly, William, ed. *The Collected Writings of J. N. Darby.* Kingston on Thames: Stow Hill Bible and Trust Depot, 1962.

Khosrokhavar, Farhad. *Suicide Bombers: Allah's New Martyrs.* Translated by David Macey. London: Pluto Press, 2005.

King, Karen L. *The Gospel of Mary of Magdala: Jesus and the First Woman Apostle.* Santa Rosa, CA: Polebridge, 2003.

Kleiman, Yaakov. *DNA & Tradition: The Genetic Link to the Ancient Hebrews.* New York: Devora, 2006.

LaHaye, Tim, and Jerry B. Jenkins. *Are We Living in the End Times?* Wheaton, IL: Tyndale, 1999.

Lewis, Bernard. *The Crisis of Islam: Holy War and Unholy Terror.* New York: Modern Library, 2003.

Lindsey, Hal. *The Late Great Planet Earth.* Grand Rapids, MI: Zondervan, 1970.

Malleus Maleficarum. Translated by Montague Summers. London: Arrow, 1986.

Martin, William. *With God on Our Side: The Rise of the Religious Right in America.* Rev. ed. New York: Broadway, 2005.

Mazar, Benjamin. *The Mountain of the Lord.* Garden City, NY: Doubleday, 1975.

Mithen, Steven. *After the Ice: A Global Human History, 20,000–l5,000 BC.* Cambridge, MA: Harvard University Press, 2003.

Na'aman, Nadav. "Sources and Composition in the History of David." In *The Origins of the Ancient Israelite States,* edited by Volkmar Fritz and Philip R. Davies, 170–186. Sheffield, UK: Sheffield Academic Press, 1996.

Nasr, Vali. *The Shia Revival: How Conflicts within Islam Will Shape the Future.* New York: Norton, 2006.

Newbolt, M. R. *The Book of Unveiling: A Study of the Revelation of St. John.* London: SPCK, 1952.

Newport, Kenneth G. C. *Apocalypse and Millennium: Studies in Biblical Eisegesis.* Cambridge, UK: Cambridge University Press, 2000.

Northcott, Michael. *An Angel Directs the Storm: Apocalyptic Religion and American Empire.* London: I. B. Tauris, 2004.

Pearson, Simon. *A Brief History of the End of the World: From Revelation to Eco-Disaster.* London: Constable & Robinson, 2006.

Philo of Alexandria. *The Works of Philo: Complete and Unabridged.* Translated by C. D. Yonge. Peabody, MA: Hendrickson, 2002.

Price, Randall. *The Temple and Bible Prophecy: A Definitive Look at Its Past, Present, and Future.* Eugene, OR: Harvest House, 2005.

Pritchard, James B., ed. *The Ancient Near East: An Anthology of Texts and Pictures.* 2 vols. Princeton, NJ: Princeton University Press, 1958.

The Protocols of the Meetings of the Learned Elders of Zion. Translated by Victor E. Marsden. Rev. ed. Chulmleigh, Devon: Augustine, 1968.

Richman, Chaim. *A House of Prayer for All Nations: The Holy Temple of Jerusalem.* Jerusalem: The Temple Institute, 1997.

Rumi: Bridge to the Soul: Journeys into the Music and Silence of the Heart. Translations by Coleman Barks. New York: HarperOne, 2007.

Runciman, Steven. *A History of the Crusades.* 3 vols. Cambridge, UK: Cambridge University Press, 1978.

Rushdoony, Rousas John. *The Institutes of Biblical Law: A Chalcedon Study.* Nutley, NJ: Craig, 1973.

Sadek, Abdullah ben. *Al Mahdi, Jesus and Dajjal (the Antichrist).* Translated by Shaykh Ahmad Darwish. London: Ta-Ha, N.D.

Schaeffer, Francis A. *A Christian Manifesto.* Wheaton, IL: Crossway, 1982.

Scofield, C. I., ed. *The Scofield Reference Bible.* New York: Oxford University Press, 1917.

Sedgwick, Mark J. *Sufism: The Essentials.* Cairo: American University in Cairo Press, 2003.

Smith, Mark S. *The Origins of Biblical Monotheism: Israel's Polytheistic Background and the Ugaritic Texts.* New York: Oxford University Press, 2001.

Suetonius. *The Twelve Caesars.* Translated by Robert Graves. Harmondsworth, UK: Penguin, 1979.

Szpakowska, Kasia. *Behind Closed Eyes: Dreams and Nightmares in Ancient Egypt.* Swansea, UK: Oxbow, 2003.

Tacitus, Cornelius. *The Annales of Imperial Rome.* Translated by Michael Grant, Harmondsworth, UK: Penguin, 1979.

Thompson, Damian. *The End of Time: Faith and Fear in the Shadow of the Millennium.* London: Sinclair-Stevenson, 1996.

Thompson, Thomas L. *The Bible in History: How Writers Create a Past.* London: Jonathan Cape, 1999.

———. *Early History of the Israelite People.* Leiden: Brill, 1994.

Thomson, Ahmad. *Dajjal the AntiChrist.* London: Ta-Ha, 1997.

Wallis, Jim. *God's Politics: Why the Right Gets It Wrong and the Left Doesn't Get It.* San Francisco: Harper, 2005.

Walls, Neal H., ed. *Cult Image and Divine Representation in the Ancient Near East.* Boston: American Schools of Oriental Research, 2005.

Wilkinson, Richard H. *Symbol & Magic in Egyptian Art.* New York: Thames and Hudson, 1994.

William, Archbishop of Tyre. *A History of Deeds Done Beyond the Sea.* Translated by Emily Atwater Babcock and A. C. Krey. New York: Columbia University Press, 1943.

Wykes, A. *Himmler.* New York: Ballantine, 1972.

INDEX